JUL 3 0 1990

D0712532

# South-Watching

The Fred W. Morrison

Series in Southern Studies

# South-Watching

Selected Essays by Gerald W. Johnson

Edited with an Introduction by Fred Hobson

The University of North Carolina Press

Chapel Hill and London

© 1983 The University of North Carolina Press

All rights reserved

Manufactured in the United States of America

Library of Congress Cataloging in Publication Data

Johnson, Gerald White, 1890–
South-watching.

(The Fred W. Morrison series in Southern studies)
1. Southern States—Civilization—Addresses, essays,
lectures. I. Hobson, Fred C., 1943–    . II. Title.
III. Series.
F215.J68    975    82–2620
ISBN 0-8078-1531-4    AACR2
ISBN 0-8078-4094-7 pbk

Illustration by Ed Lindlof

# Contents

# Acknowledgments

My greatest debt in this work is to Gerald W. Johnson who, in the two or three years preceding his death in March 1980, put up with my questions about his life and work and gave his support to my idea of collecting his Southern essays. I also wish to thank Mrs. Gerald W. Johnson for her encouragement and permission to reprint the essays included herein.

I am indebted, as well, to Gerald W. Johnson's sister, Miss Lois Johnson of Wagram, North Carolina, who provided valuable information about Mr. Johnson's early life; his close friends, Mr. and Mrs. R. P. Harriss of Baltimore, who shared with me their recollections of Mr. Johnson; Staige D. Blackford, editor of the *Virginia Quarterly Review*, for his permission to include in my introduction parts of an essay that appeared earlier in the *Quarterly*; Catherine Jones of the University of Alabama and Jane Hobson of Georgia State University for their help in obtaining books and essays by Mr. Johnson; the staffs of the Enoch Pratt Free Library of Baltimore, the Vanderbilt University Library, the Wake Forest University Library, and the Southern Historical Collection of the University of North Carolina at Chapel Hill for help with Johnson materials; the Research Grants Committee of the University of Alabama for providing research funds; the College of Arts and Sciences of the University of Alabama for providing typing funds; Antoinette Sullivan, who typed the manuscript; and, finally, the University of North Carolina Press, who proved, once again, a pleasure to work with. To Matthew Hodgson, Lewis Bateman, Gwen Duffey, and Malcolm L. Call, I am particularly grateful.

Finally, I acknowledge some personal debts: to my father, Fred Colby Hobson, who taught me to respect the human and political values for which Gerald W. Johnson stood; my mother, Miriam Tuttle Hobson, whose father, long ago, was a friend and admirer of Gerald Johnson's father, Mr. Archibald Johnson, and who told me early that Gerald W. Johnson was a writer well worth reading; and Cynthia Graff Hobson, who read the entire manuscript, made valuable suggestions for its improvement, and in the process came, despite her mid-western heritage, to understand and appreciate an earlier South.

F. H.

# Introduction

Gerald W. Johnson of North Carolina and Baltimore was the author of some three dozen books of history, biography, and commentary on American politics and culture. He was an editorial writer for the Baltimore Sunpapers from 1926 to 1943, a contributing editor of the *New Republic* from 1954 until his death in March 1980, and an advocate of American liberal causes for half a century. He was a fervent New Dealer in the 1930s, an adamant foe of Richard Nixon in the 1950s and 1960s, an early opponent of American intervention in Southeast Asia and of "American imperialism" in general. Adlai Stevenson called him "the conscience of America," and Harry Golden once referred to him as one of the most brilliant prose stylists America has produced. He ranks with H. L. Mencken and Walter Lippmann as a great American journalist of the twentieth century, and he was one of the outstanding essayists of any age. Yet, in evaluating Johnson's career as writer, a career stretching from 1910 to 1980, one might make the same claim for Johnson that Johnson himself, looking back in 1974 at the career of his friend Mencken, made for that other Sage of Baltimore: that, despite his prominence as man of letters and observer of American life, perhaps his single most important role was the one he played in the Southern critical and literary renascence of the 1920s and in the ensuing debate between the Southern Agrarians and Southern progressives in the 1930s.

Before Johnson examined the health of America, he examined the health of the South—and generally, in the 1920s, found it poor. The revival of the Ku Klux Klan, the Scopes evolution trial of 1925, the anti-Catholicism sparked by Al Smith's presidential candidacy in 1928, the labor violence of 1929—all these made the South of the 1920s America's number one news item, indeed reinforced a national image of a Savage South. Johnson was without question the South's leading native interpreter during this decade, a crucial one in the development of a Southern critical consciousness and in the making of a modern Southern mind. He was the loudest and clearest voice in the rising chorus of Southern self-criticism, the boldest of writers for the *Reviewer* of Richmond and *Social Forces* of Chapel Hill, journals that led in the new Southern expression, and the most perceptive of analysts for numerous national magazines that wanted the Southern story. He and sociologist Howard W. Odum of the University of North Carolina represented—in some ways, shaped—nothing less than a new Southern point of view.

Many were the Southern journalists in the 1920s writing about the
South, but Johnson was the only one among them who wrote as well as
the notorious outsider Mencken, and he understood the South much
better than Mencken ever could. His picture, though often harsh, was
always accurate. If the analysis of Southern civilization became a literary subgenre in the 1920s, he was its most artful practitioner.
To the Fugitive-Agrarians of Nashville, particularly Donald Davidson, he was the Southern bête noire. Davidson saw Johnson as a "fire-
eating Southern liberal" who found "nothing good . . . in the traditional
South." He was a "loud and persistent voice" in Southern self-criticism,
the most militant member of "the 'enlightened' North Carolina school,"
and he led a "Fifth Column of Southern journalists" during the "gay,
emancipated 1920s" when he was one of "the wonders of our stage."[1]
Other South-watchers of the time also acknowledged Johnson's significance if not his notoriety. Mencken saw him as the leading Southern-
born iconoclast of his generation as well as the "best editorial writer in
the South," and DuBose Heyward of Charleston described him as a
"suicidal, but ecstatic, spirit," a "fellow rebel."[2] But as much as rebel,
iconoclast, or bête noire, Johnson in the 1920s was precisely what he
always had been and would be: a realist. Then, as always, he declared
war on romantic illusion, fraud, sham, and hypocrisy; he expressed an
outright fury toward those who proclaimed Southern civilization as it
existed in 1920 a worthy successor to Greece and Rome. His message in
the early 1920s was that the South needed "hardminded men, who [see]
clearly, [think] straight, and [speak] the truth." The Southerner had to
"burst all bonds of conservative tradition, break with the past and defy
the present with the bald, unequivocal and conclusive assertion that
lying is wrong." After reading Edwin Mim's *The Advancing South*
(1926), a greatly publicized and generally optimistic assessment of
Southern life, he wrote in the *Virginia Quarterly Review*: "One
cannot avoid the feeling that the shattering battle axe might do more real
good to the South than the trumpet and cymbals, seductively as they are
used."[3]

When Donald Davidson placed Johnson in the "North Carolina
school" of Southern commentators, he meant that Johnson shared the
view associated with Howard W. Odum of Chapel Hill that the South
was in serious social and cultural condition and needed drastic reform.
But Davidson was also historically accurate. For the particular Southern
tradition to which Johnson belongs is the tradition of those Carolinians
who have long been called progressive or national—as opposed to
strictly Southern—in spirit. "The two great diagnosticians of the South-

ern condition," Johnson wrote in 1958, were "the ancient Hinton Rowan Helper and the modern W. J. Cash,[4] and his choices were not without significance. The "Hated Helper," author of that notorious antislavery tract *The Impending Crisis* (1857), grew up not thirty miles from Johnson's boyhood home. Abolitionist Daniel R. Goodloe also came from the Carolina Piedmont, as did the leading nineteenth-century progressive Walter Hines Page and Johnson's fellow iconoclastic journalist Cash. Other North Carolinians of Johnson's generation—Jonathan Daniels, Paul Green, Thomas Wolfe, Frank Porter Graham—shared, to varying extents, in this same tradition. Johnson included in this "progressive" tradition not only such Carolinians as Andrew Jackson and progressive governor Charles B. Aycock but also other Southerners as contemporary as Edgar Gardner Murphy of Alabama (whom Johnson hailed for his stand against child labor) and Woodrow Wilson, and as remote in time as Jefferson. Johnson, in short, can be placed squarely in what Virginius Dabney in 1932 called the tradition of Southern liberalism.[5] But his liberalism did not seem to be motivated so totally by racial concerns as that of liberals from the deeper South—Ralph McGill, Lillian Smith, James McBride Dabbs—often seemed to be. Slavery and its legacy he detested but as much for economic as moral reasons. "The great crime of the Old South," he once wrote, "was its neglect to exercise a larger measure of intelligence in its economic organization."[6] It was the Carolina point of view: Hinton Rowan Helper had said the same thing seventy years before.

Although Johnson grew up in the Piedmont, his roots were in the Cape Fear region of eastern North Carolina. His great-grandfather had come from Scotland in the early nineteenth century; another Scottish forebear had come about the same time as a Baptist preacher to the Scots in North Carolina. Notwithstanding Gerald Johnson's later indictment of slavery and the late Confederacy, both of his grandfathers were slaveowners whose homes lay squarely in the line of Sherman's march, and three of his uncles had fought for the Confederacy, one dying in a federal prison. He grew up, he later wrote, listening to Civil War tales that "convinced" him that Sherman was "a fiend in human form."[7]

But the Johnsons of Scotland County were hardly devotees of the Lost Cause. Even Gerald Johnson's favorite uncle, a good soldier who had ridden with Wheeler's cavalry, told him as a boy, "We lost that war because God Almighty had decreed that slavery had to go."[8] The Cape Fear Scots looked ahead, not backward. Gerald Johnson's father first established a newspaper at Red Springs, near Fayetteville, and then in 1895, when Gerald was five, moved upland to Thomasville to edit a Baptist publication, *Charity and Children*. The Johnson children grew up in a Baptist compound in Thomasville, but the religion they encountered was hardly the Baptist barbarian of Mencken's imagination. Archibald Johnson was orthodox but not fundamentalist, and in his church newspaper he discussed politics and public affairs as well as church business. The area around Thomasville was progressive for its day; Gerald was six years old when Walter Hines Page came to nearby Greensboro and made the famous "Forgotten Man" speech in which he appealed for education for the Southern masses—a speech from which journalist Johnson later drew in his own writing. And when it was time for Johnson to choose a college he chose Wake Forest, which two of his uncles and numerous cousins had attended. It was a Southern Baptist school that noted among its alumni the reactionary Thomas Dixon, author of *The Clansman*, but it was not so strictly religious and conservative a choice as it might have seemed. Its president, William Louis Poteat, was a German-educated Ph.D. in biology who annually placated those North Carolina Baptists who came to the state convention with the express purpose of denouncing his belief in evolution and throwing him out. Of Wake Forest, Johnson later wrote, "Light streamed from its windows over a darkling land." Professors such as classicist John Bethune Carlyle and English scholar Benjamin Sledd possessed a dedication "of a kind completely new to me then, and which I have seldom encountered since."[9] They de-educated as well as educated—disabused students of old notions and prejudices—and the former function was at least as important as the latter.

Even before he completed his degree at Wake Forest, Johnson was a newspaperman: he had established the Thomasville *Davidsonian* in 1910. A year later he went to work for the Lexington (N.C.) *Dispatch*, and in 1913 joined the Greensboro *News*. After serving with the American Expeditionary Force in Europe in World War I, he returned to North Carolina and, like many other young Southern writers of his day, fell under the powerful influence of Mencken. Johnson was an editorial writer in Greensboro in November 1920 when Mencken's *Prejudices, Second Series* appeared with its provocative third essay, "The Sahara of the Bozart." He agreed completely with Mencken's declaration that the South was "almost as sterile, artistically, intellectually, culturally, as the Sahara Desert," and he voiced his agreement when, in 1922, he was asked by the *Carolina Magazine*, a student publication at Chapel Hill, to give his opinion concerning a prospective poetry society for North Carolina. The "first business" of such a society, he responded, had to be "the extermination of the maundering imbecility, the sniffling puerility, the sloppy sentimentality, and bunk, bosh and tommyrot that pass for poetry in North Carolina." Such a society would be valuable only if it were "sufficiently vicious," only if it used a "butcher's cleaver and a club" on traditional Southern poetry. Mencken, who had a voracious appetite for Southern reading matter good and bad, read the article and recognized a voice similar to his own. Immediately he praised Johnson in the Baltimore *Evening Sun* for issuing "an admirable manifesto of the South": if other Southerners followed his lead, "a Confederate Renaissance" would dawn. When he saw Mencken's column, Johnson wrote a grateful letter to Baltimore praising Mencken for his own attack on Southern inadequacies, for the "superb accomplishment of a task that needed doing but which nobody else could have done so well, and which most of us were afraid to try." In "The Sahara of the Bozart," Mencken had said "so many things that I felt, but had not the wits to think out nor the guts to utter." But since the "Sahara," Johnson added, he had delivered "recitatives extracted from it" and thus was considered by "certain of the orthodox as a backslider from grace . . . hardened in sin."[10]

Mencken immediately championed Johnson as he had other young Southerners who had flocked to his banner. First he tried to bring the North Carolinian to Baltimore to write for the Sunpapers. When Johnson declined, Mencken urged the editors of the *Reviewer*, just begun by a colony of Menckenites in Richmond, to secure his services. What the *Reviewer* got in Johnson's first essay was a performance worthy of the master—and on Mencken's favorite subject. The South was not a "Sahara," Johnson now insisted in the July 1923 *Reviewer*. To the contrary:

> The South resembles more Sierra Leone, where, according to
> Sir Harry Johnston, "the mammalian fauna of chimpanzis [sic],
> monkeys, bats, cats, lions, leopards, hyenas, civets, scaly
> manises, and large-eared earth-pigs, little-known duiker bush-
> buck, hartebeeste, and elephant, is rich and curious." So is
> the literary flora; and if Mr. Mencken presumes to doubt it, I invite
> him to plunge into the trackless waste of the Library of Southern
> Literature, where a man might wander for years, encountering
> daily such a profusion of strange and incredible growths as could
> proceed from none other but an enormously rich soil.

The South was "not sterile," not the "treeless waste" of the Sahara. "On the contrary, it is altogether too luxuriant. . . . Its pulses beat to the rhythm of the tom-tom, and it likes any color if it's red." The South was "not the Sahara, but the Congo of the Bozart."[11]

Johnson's figure was more apt than Mencken's. The sixteen-volume *Library of Southern Literature* (a seventeenth volume would appear that same year) included some three hundred Southern contributors from

Adams to Young. Its biographical dictionary went from Abbey to Zog-baum. It was nothing but lush and luxuriant, nothing if not a jungle. Johnson was right, and what is more, he was just as dazzling as Mencken. Southern literature indeed had "the pulse of the tom-toms in its veins, the scents of the jungle . . . in its nostrils and the flaming colors of the jungle in its eyes." Such attributes had been injurious in the past: they had led to formlessness, sentimentalizing, great flights of rhetoric, a "Sir Thomas Browne complex" among Southern writers. But that very love of words and excess of imagination could be chan-neled into a new Southern literature that would be immeasurably better: "It will be colorful beyond belief; instead of a discreet maquillage it will come wearing smears of paint like a witch-doctor. It may be out-landish, but it will not be monotonous. It may be gorgeously barbaric, but it will not be monotonous. For all I know, it may be in some manifestations tremendously evil—it may wallow in filth, but it will not dabble in dirt."[12]

Johnson wrote this in 1923 during the brief, touted reign of Southern realism. It was a time in which Mencken was urging Southern writers to follow the example of Sinclair Lewis and to write Southern *Main Streets*. Many leading Southern writers, such as T. S. Stribling of Ten-nessee, were taking his advice. But Johnson, his own penchant for realism notwithstanding, knew the way of the future for Southern litera-ture was not in realism but romance, albeit in a new key—what others would later call Southern Gothic. Southern writing of the next two decades would indeed be "gorgeously barbaric," it would seem to some "tremendously evil," and it would put Southern rhetoric to a nobler use. What were reviewers in 1935 saying about the Savage South of Caldwell and Wolfe—and Faulkner—that Gerald Johnson had not prophesied in 1923? The South was indeed a Congo.

Mencken delighted in the essay. Johnson in fact had discussed it with him long before it appeared, although he had not revealed his figure of the Congo in advance. More Johnson essays followed in the *Reviewer*, some as elaborate and outrageous as the first. In "Fourteen Equestrian Statues of Colonel Simmons" he insisted that the South should erect monuments to William Joseph Simmons, founder of the modern Ku Klux Klan, for awakening the Southern consciousness and revealing to the enlightened Southern minority the twisted state of mind of many Southerners. "Greensboro, or What You Will" was a study of George F. Babbitt, Southern style. The city under investigation was Johnson's own Greensboro, or any other progressive Southern city that lived by the creed: "There is no God but Advertising, and Atlanta is his prophet." In "Onion Salt" Johnson declared what South-watchers half a century later would believe themselves original in saying: that while the South might appear to become part of a standardized America, it would in fact—like onion salt—flavor the whole. "It is folly to talk of the danger of any loss of [the South's] distinctive individuality, by its absorption into an amorphous mass. The danger lies all the other way. Ku Kluxism, Fundamentalism, White Supremacy, to mention only three ideas once distinctively Southern which are now national, prove that the South, so far from being beleaguered and at the point of surrender, has developed a sort of von Hutier attack, is apparently conquering by infiltration."[13]

Johnson was early acclaimed the most original contributor to the *Reviewer*, the magazine that led the way in the first phase of the Southern literary renascence. But once Mencken brought him to public attention, other journals sought his services. *Social Forces*, begun in 1922 by Howard Odum in Chapel Hill, served in the Southern critical renascence the same role that was performed by the *Reviewer* in the literary renascence. Although nominally a sociological journal, Mencken called it nothing less than the most important periodical ever published in the South because it took a hard look at social and cultural problems and specialized in frank, forthright criticism of the region.[14] Its mode was realism, and it was no accident that Gerald W. Johnson soon became its boldest spokesman. In its third issue he charged that the South dwelled in a "morass of ignorance" that produced "bigotry, cowardice and cruelty." In another essay he declared that the South needed criticism that was "ruthless" toward "bigotry, intolerance, superstition and prejudice . . . bitter towards them, furiously against them." "Such criticism will not be popular," he added, "but it will be respected . . . and it will be effective." Johnson knew well that he was describing his own brand of writing. "There is neither pleasure nor profit in being the official hard guy," he wrote Odum in 1923. But "it might as well be my job."[15]

There was, in some measure, both pleasure and profit. Johnson delighted in his role as exposer of the benighted South and to some extent in the notoriety it brought him. In 1924 he came to Chapel Hill as professor of journalism and immediately liked the atmosphere. The University of North Carolina, he wrote Mencken, had "neither conscience nor patriotism. It will hire a damyankee any time for any sort of job. A good third of the faculty, including the president, come from the wrong side of the Potomac, to the scandal of all 100% Tar Heels."[16] In Chapel Hill he continued his investigation of Southern life, and by the mid-1920s he was writing about the South for nearly every journal, regional or national, that was interested in the subject. Between 1923

and 1929 he contributed some two dozen essays on Southern life to the
*Reviewer, Social Forces,* the *Virginia Quarterly Review,* the *North
American Review, Harper's, Survey, Scribner's,* the *Current History
Magazine* of the *New York Times,* and the *American Mercury*—not to
mention hundreds of newspaper articles and editorials. The essays in
the *American Mercury,* in particular, brought him the national recognition he had earlier lacked. Mencken's *Mercury,* begun in 1923, was the
marvel of the age; it was read everywhere, particularly on college
campuses, even at Vanderbilt where Allen Tate went around with the
green-covered *Mercury* under his arm. Mencken ran what amounted to
a farm system for potential *Mercury* contributors, suggesting writers to
editors of lesser known journals across the country and bringing them to
the *Mercury* when they were ready. Since Johnson had proved himself
in the *Reviewer* and *Social Forces,* in July 1923 Mencken asked him to
contribute to the *Mercury.* Johnson responded with a series of essays on
the South. "The Ku Kluxer" was a study of the psychology of the Ku
Klux Klan ("the spiritual descendants of the Knights of the Round
Table," he had earlier written Mencken). "The South Takes the Offensive" purported to be a defense of the South against its Yankee critics,
although Johnson's irony fooled no one. The essay, he wrote Mencken,
raised "a moderate amount of hell in North Carolina." "Saving Souls"
was equally offensive to orthodox Southerners. Johnson claimed that
evangelical religion flourished in the South for the same reason that
Mencken had found for lynching: Southerners were starved for enter-
tainment. "If the poverty and spareness of the population makes it
impossible to support theatres and concert halls, and if the communal
*mores* prohibit horseracing, cockfighting, and dancing, the range of
emotional outlets is sharply restricted."[17]

Johnson sent the *Mercury* other essays on the psychology of the
Southern mill owner, the cowardice of most Southern journalists, and
Harry Woodburn Chase, the Massachusetts-born president of the University of North Carolina whose defiance of the fundamentalists and
courageous leadership had brought prominence to Chapel Hill.[18] In his
writing Johnson was reinforcing the image of a benighted South, but he
was not *creating* that image, as Donald Davidson later charged. The
Klan and the Scopes trial had done that, if indeed it had not been done
before. Moreover, as in the Chase essay, Johnson was sometimes guilty
of what Mencken called uplift, and he refused to write some essays
Mencken suggested—one, for example, on William Louis Poteat of
Wake Forest. To write of Poteat and his methods for outwitting his
detractors among North Carolina Baptists, Johnson wrote, "would put
the brethren on to themselves, and at the next convention they would

take the simple precaution of not letting Poteat speak. Then they would remain sober enough to fire him, and North Carolina's plunge back into the Dark Ages would be started.'' The essay on Poteat would not appear until 1943, after his death, and then in the *Virginia Quarterly*, not the *American Mercury*.[19]

Johnson was regarded in some quarters as Mencken's lieutenant. He had read Mencken so often and quoted him so frequently—had *absorbed* him so totally—that the same words, the same phrases, the same cadences filled his prose. "The Late Confederacy," "below the Potomac," "superior men," "right-thinkers," "the sacred cause of Service"—all were Mencken's terms. But if the style was nearly Mencken's, it was not identical. The Johnson style both drew on and parodied the tradition of Southern rhetoric, as Mencken's did not. And his allusions were more erudite. Johnson drew on an astounding variety of sources—classical literature, mythology, history ancient and modern, and principally the Bible. His metaphors, if anything, were more elaborate than Mencken's, and with metaphysical ingenuity he often sustained a figure through the better part of an essay. The jungle along the Congo, the hothouse literary climate of the South, was conducive to orchids: "Edgar Allan Poe grew them long ago, and Sidney Lanier too and James Branch Cabell grows them today."[20] He could even dress up an essay for so somber a journal as Odum's *Social Forces*. A contribution on the waste of North Carolina's human resources bore the title, "Issachar Is a Strong Ass." North Carolina, like Issachar in the forty-ninth chapter of Genesis, was a "servant unto tribute": it produced great men but could not keep them at home. An essay on social legislation in North Carolina was entitled "Mr. Babbitt Arrives at Erzerum." Mr. Babbitt was the solid citizen, the representative Tar Heel businessman, Erzerum the fortress stormed by the Russians in World War I, the capture of which Grand Duke Nicholas had called a gift of God. So was the ease, Johnson insisted, by which North Carolina had passed early social legislation. But now, "The gifts of God are about all present or accounted for. Erzerum has fallen. The campaign enters a new phase." Mr. Babbitt had to be persuaded that more expensive legislation was necessary.[21]

If Johnson was a writer with a keener sense of metaphor than Mencken—the "Congo" being more accurate than the "Sahara"—he was also, in his Southern essays, a more versatile writer. Mencken's tone in essays about the South was usually incredulity: he could not believe that such a place existed. Johnson was sometimes incredulous, often ironic, but also sometimes instructive, even hortatory. Most of his essays had a clearly defined persona, and that persona was often the solid, conservative, patriotic Southerner. In his *American Mercury* essay, "Journalism below the Potomac" (1926), he praised those "right-thinking" Southern newspaper publishers who were first and foremost sound businessmen, and he pretended to decry the presence of those few Southern iconoclasts. In another *Mercury* essay, "The South Takes the Offensive" (1924), he denounced the hordes of Yankee critics who descended into the South and pronounced its civilization inferior. In the early *Reviewer* essay, "Greensboro, or What You Will," he assumed the role of George F. Babbitt with a Southern accent, proud of his city's progress and growth. "Fourteen Equestrian Statues of Colonel Simmons" (1923) was written in praise of the founder of the modern Ku Klux Klan. And so on. But he was not always ironic; the stern voice of his Baptist fathers sometimes emerged. "Critical Attitudes North and South" (1924) exhorted Southerners to speak loudly and fearlessly against fraud and prejudice.

But the way in which Johnson most surpassed Mencken as a critic of the South was in his understanding of his subject. There existed in his essays, as there did not in Mencken's, a remarkable quality to empathize with those people with whom he disagreed radically—people whom Mencken put down summarily. His first lengthy essay for a national magazine, "Behind the Monster's Mask," was a study of the Southern cotton-mill owner in which he attempted to see that owner in relation to his society. The mill was in many respects the successor to the plantation, and the owner was the benevolent despot. He ruled his mills with an iron hand, but he was also paternalistic. He built schools, churches, and gymnasiums for his workers, partly to keep them happy, but partly because he saw himself in the tradition of noblesse oblige. He was motivated in part by greed, certainly, but also, at least in the late nineteenth century, by a sense of civic obligation. Most of all, he was genuinely puzzled as to why his workers were not satisfied. "The opinions of Mr. [Samuel] Gompers and Mr. Mencken to the contrary notwithstanding," Johnson concluded, "the Southern cotton mill man is not a monster. On the contrary, he is generally a kind man, honest according to his lights, astonishingly liberal in certain directions and sincerely anxious to improve the conditions of his employees."[22] Not only the mill owners but the workers were brought to life by Johnson. In one lengthy section of his Greensboro essay he captured all the pathos and futility of their lives: they pour into town from the mill villages on Saturday afternoon, they stand in front of shop windows judiciously inspecting the silks and fine things, not suspecting "the irony that might have set Olympus a-roaring," and then move on. To Mencken they were lintheads, but Johnson had seen the gleam in their eyes.

Johnson humanized his Southern subjects. Those who were abstractions to Mencken were all too real to him. His *Mercury* essay "The Ku Kluxer" portrayed the Klansman—one Chill Burton in this case—as, after all, a kind, decent, church-going fellow, just one who had been preyed upon by the rantings of preachers and politicians, who genuinely feared for the future of Anglo-Saxon civilization, and who, most of all, was "incurably romantic." Even the preachers Johnson portrayed more sympathetically than one writing for Mencken might have been expected to. "Saving Souls" declared that the Southern evangelist might be ludicrous, even crass, but he was no hypocrite; he was not even always a complete fraud. Johnson knew his South concretely as Mencken never had. To Mencken it was spectacle, a faraway mock kingdom-gone-mad whose darkness he did not penetrate until 1925. But Johnson had grown up in a Southern mill town, had attended Baptist revivals, had known kindly men who also happened to be Klansmen. The beat of the tom-tom, more aptly the thump of the pulpit, was in his blood too.

Johnson wrote his last essay for the *American Mercury* in June of 1929. By this time he was in Baltimore—he had crossed the Potomac in 1926 to work with Mencken on the Sunpapers—and the South had become only one of several interests. As it happened, the very month he ceased to write for the *Mercury* another North Carolina newspaperman began—another Wake Forest alumnus of iconoclastic spirit and Menckenesque style. It must have seemed to *Mercury* readers when W. J. Cash published "Jehovah of the Tar Heels" in July 1929 that Gerald W. Johnson had for the moment adopted a pseudonym. Indeed, the parallels between the two are remarkable: both had been born into strong Baptist families and had grown up in mill towns in the Carolina piedmont, both attended Wake Forest and, once there, were influenced greatly by William Louis Poteat and Benjamin Sledd, both became editorial writers for North Carolina dailies—Johnson in Greensboro, Cash in Charlotte—both taught briefly, were inspired by Mencken's "Sahara," began to contribute to the *American Mercury*, and became Mencken's two leading Southern apostles. Johnson wrote eight essays for the *Mercury* between 1923 and 1929; Cash, beginning the month Johnson stopped, wrote eight between 1929 and 1935. Their vocabularies were similar and so were their subjects: Southern politics, religion, racial conflict, and the psychology of the plain white Southerner. Johnson got there first, but Cash later received most of the credit. The reason, of course, is that W. J. Cash put all the insights and well-turned phrases of fifteen years into a single book, *The Mind of the South* (1941), which almost immediately became a Southern classic. Johnson went on to write some three dozen books, but no single book was as penetrating as Cash's. Johnson himself valued Cash enormously. He corresponded with him, wrote a letter on behalf of his Guggenheim application, and praised him in print. He must also have realized that Cash had been inspired not only by Mencken but by himself, for it was Johnson even more than Mencken who wrote about the South in the early *American Mercurys* to which Cash was addicted. He was ten years Johnson's junior, just as Johnson was ten years younger than Mencken, and Donald Davidson was not far off when he wrote in his review of *The Mind of the South* that Cash's interpretation of Southern history was "deeply colored" by the reading he had done in the 1920s "when Gerald Johnson and [economist] Broadus Mitchell" were leading intellectual influences.[23]

So Johnson, we see, got there first. To get there first is not always enough. T. S. Stribling, among novelists of the Southern Renascence, got there first—was the first to appropriate Southern violence, racial prejudice, and religious fundamentalism for fictional use—but what William Faulkner did ten years later with the same material makes Stribling, as Robert Penn Warren later described him, a paragraph in the history of critical realism.[24] Johnson is at least an entire chapter in the story of the rise of the Southern critical spirit. Nearly all of the subjects—religious frenzy, the Klan, the poor white and the subculture of the Southern cotton mill—that Cash treated in *The Mind of the South* Johnson had treated before. Not only that, but many of Cash's most penetrating insights Johnson had anticipated in his essays of the 1920s. In his book Cash called the South of postwar ruin "the frontier the Yankees made." Twelve years before Johnson had written, "The South after the Civil War was to all intents and purposes a frontier."[25] In his book Cash emphasized the extent to which the rise of the cotton mills in the post-Reconstruction South was an economic equivalent of war, a way finally to defeat the Yankees, and also the extent to which the mill was an extension of the plantation, with paternalism and noblesse oblige intact. Johnson, as we have seen, said the same things twenty years before. (Indeed, both he and Cash relied heavily on Broadus Mitchell's *The Rise of the Cotton Mills in the South*, published in 1921.) Johnson also anticipated Cash's insistence upon the essential romanticism of the Ku Klux Klansman, the role of chivalry in his conduct. In his early essays on Southern sensitivity to criticism, he identified Cash's "savage ideal" (though not by the same name), and in early discussions of the Klan he came very close to describing what Cash later called the "proto-Dorian" bond—that assurance that white men, whatever their rank or station, are superior to Negroes. He and Cash did not always speak with the same voice. Cash, in his *Mercury* days, could be nothing but irreverent. Johnson could be that too, but he was much more versatile. Cash also lacked Johnson's essential fairness, the willingness to present as clearly as possible even those points of view with which he did not agree. These were the traits that enabled Johnson to be far more than an iconoclast, a mere copy of Mencken.

It might have appeared, when he published his last essay in the *American Mercury* in the summer of 1929, that Gerald W. Johnson had left the South behind. After six years of furious composition, he issued no essays on Dixie in 1930. But if he had sworn off Southern topics, he soon was jolted back into action by a remarkable book that appeared in November 1930. *I'll Take My Stand* aroused Johnson just as the "Sahara of the Bozart" had ten years before. But it aroused him in a different way. Written by twelve Southerners, most of whom had attended or taught at Vanderbilt University, *I'll Take My Stand* bore as its subtitle "The South and the Agrarian Tradition." It was written to affirm the traditional South and to combat the assumption that the South should gracefully accept an industrial invasion. It was an indictment of liberalism, many varieties of progress, and what one of its contributors, Donald Davidson, called "the 'enlightened' North Carolina school." As a leader of that school, Gerald Johnson was compelled to respond. Now, geographically removed from the South, sitting at his editorial desk at the Sunpapers, he must have felt somewhat like Mencken as he surveyed the situation from afar.

Johnson had known well in advance of the plans for an agrarian manifesto. He knew because he had actually been asked to contribute.[26] Such an invitation would not have been surprising five years earlier. The Nashville Fugitives—those who became Agrarians—at that time had regarded him highly. Allen Tate in 1925 had found some merit even in Mencken because Mencken had "roused a person like Gerald W. Johnson, and that is an important business of satire." Even Davidson, early in 1925, had written that nothing was more necessary to the South "at this stage of its development than the kind of criticism which men like Gerald Johnson, Addison Hibbard, and Paul Green are beginning in the pages of 'The Reviewer.' " But that was before the Scopes trial of July 1925. After the embarrassment brought upon Tennessee, Davidson, Tate, and John Crowe Ransom grew resentful of Southerners who seemed to join the Yankee forces. By 1926 Davidson was attacking the "tart essays" of Johnson, whom he included among those Southern writers who were out of harmony with their environment.[27] Obviously, it was not Davidson who asked Johnson to contribute to *I'll Take My Stand*.

Johnson jumped on the manifesto as soon as it left the press. The reactions of Mencken and Odum were mild by comparison. Johnson did not at first defend industrialism; he himself was on record against its abuses, and also against mindless progress, advertising, and Babbittry. But the fact that the twelve Southerners "should turn to agrarianism as a remedy would seem to indicate that their sole knowledge of the South had been gleaned from the pages of Joel Chandler Harris and Thomas Nelson Page." He continued, in his January 1931 review in the *Virginia Quarterly*: "Have they never been in the modern South, especially in the sections completely ruled by agrarianism? Have they been completely oblivious to the Vardamans, the Bleases, the Heflins, the Tom Watsons, who are the delight of Southern agrarianism? Have they never been told that the obscenities and depravities of the most degenerate hole of a cotton-mill town are but pale reflections of the lurid obscenities and depravities of Southern backwoods communities?"[28] Apparently not, Johnson concluded. Thomas Nelson Page was still the problem. Realism was the solution.

Johnson had only begun. The next month, February 1931, he came out with a longer essay, "No More Excuses," in *Harper's*. He spoke as "a Southerner to Southerners," and again he cast the Agrarians as blind romantics: "At first blush it seems incredible that twelve men, all born and raised in the South, all literate, and all of legal age, could preach such a doctrine without once thrusting the tongue in the cheek or winking the other eye. . . . Of such a philosophy one can only say that it smells horribly of the lamp, that it was library-born and library-bred, and will perish miserably if it is ever exposed for ten minutes to the direct rays of the sun out in the daylight of reality."

Agrarianism had brought the South only a "hookworm-infested, pellagra-smitten, poverty-stricken, demagogue-ridden" civilization. The idea that the antebellum South, grounded in agrarianism, was "one of the ornaments of the world" Johnson described as "sentimental tommy-rot." Industrialism by contrast—despite the cotton-mill strikes and violence of 1929, despite "the evils which the growth of manufacturing" had brought into the South—offered hope. Johnson turned to his native North Carolina as an example. It was the most industrialized Southern state; it was also the most progressive in education and social legislation. "If industrialism created Gastonia and Marion, it also created Chapel Hill and that neighboring hill on which Duke University is now rising." The money had "come from industrialism." And industrialism, despite its flaws, was the way of the future. Indeed, it had already arrived, and "the job of the South" was "to take industrialism and with it fashion a civilization" in which Jefferson and Lee could live.

As for "sniveling and excuse-hunting on the part of intelligent South-erners," these were a "worse betrayal of their ancestors than are Gas-tonia, lynching, demagoguery, and religious fanaticism combined."[29]

Johnson came closer to anger in his *Harper's* discussion than he had ever come in the essays of the 1920s. The wit, the dazzling meta-phors—even, to some extent, the essential fairness—of his earlier pieces were missing. What angered him was that *intelligent* Southerners could defend agrarianism, even fundamentalism. It had been his as-sumption, along with Odum and Paul Green in Chapel Hill and James Branch Cabell in Richmond, not to mention Mencken, that all civilized Southerners were on their side, and indeed, before 1925, almost all—even the Fugitives of Nashville—had been. It is easy to see today why Johnson, Odum, and Mencken read *I'll Take My Stand* as they did: as a prescription for Southern ills and a very poor prescription at that, guar-anteed only to make the patient sicker. For Johnson, as Odum, had been accustomed to dealing only with a problem South, a South that required reforming and reshaping. He had treated the South as it *was* in a literal sense: it badly needed treatment. Some of his earliest essays had been written on social problems and written for sociological journals. He himself, in some respects, possessed the sociological vision although he certainly did not write like a sociologist. However, the Agrarians, at least the greatest of them, were poets, and as poets they were given to the image. *I'll Take My Stand* and its vision of the agrarian South, as Louis D. Rubin, Jr., has written, "can best be considered as an ex-tended metaphor,"[30] not a literal prescription for Southern ills. Exactly, but it was impossible for Johnson to see it as such. It was improbable that any Southerner—particularly any Southern realist distressed by the labor violence of Gastonia and Marion, concerned for the social and economic future of the South—would see it as such in 1931.

With his two responses to *I'll Take My Stand* Johnson jumped back into the Southern fray. As the debate raged in the early 1930s between the Agrarians and their adversaries—and two schools of thought devel-oped, one centered in Nashville, the other in Chapel Hill—it was clear that he stood with the Chapel Hill Regionalists. Some of the Agrarians, in letters to each other, sniped at him. Frank Owsley wrote Davidson that Johnson had "little ground . . . to stand on" (although he did agree that *I'll Take My Stand* "smells of the cloister"). Davidson viewed him as even more of a threat. Johnson was "carrying on the W. H. Page line of thinking, mixed with a bit of 'American Mercury' vocabulary," he wrote John Gould Fletcher. "He needs badly to be exposed, and it is up to one of us to hit him good and hard." Davidson hit often, once in the essay "Dilemma of the Southern Liberals," which he sent, strangely,

to the despised Mencken at the *American Mercury*. The article, Davidson wrote Edwin Mims, was an attack on "younger liberals—Gerald
Johnson & Co." because "they have had an opportunity that [Walter
Hines] Page did not have for making a frank estimate of the social and
political history of the South."[31] This is precisely what Johnson had
done and what he felt Davidson and Company had not.

If Johnson had not appreciated *I'll Take My Stand* as fully as he might
have, the Agrarians for their part never really understood him. If they
had read carefully those very 1920s essays that they attacked, they
would have realized he was far from uncritical in his acceptance of that
newest of New Souths. Who else but Johnson had sneered at advertisers
and industrial boosters, Babbitts and Rotarians. Not only Ransom, Tate,
and Davidson but also Johnson valued the Old South, although his Old
South, unlike theirs, no longer existed after 1830 and never quite
crossed the Appalachians. More than once he had praised the Virginia
of the eighteenth and early nineteenth centuries, and in 1925 he had
written that if the civilization of Jefferson became extinct "smoke stacks
and Rotarians can never replace it. If that civilization is extinct, the
South is dead, and its material activity is not a genuine revival, but a
species of galvanism, the horrible twitching of a cadaver stimulated by
electricity."[32]

Numerous other times he lamented the suffering of the South during
Reconstruction and hailed its attempt in the late nineteenth century to
rise from its ashes. "Did you see the Cadets of Newmarket [sic] in the
December Harpers?" William Alexander Percy wrote Davidson early in
1930 of one such essay. "Very fine, it left a lump in my throat."[33] In
addition Johnson published in November 1930—the same month *I'll
Take My Stand* appeared—a novel that, if Davidson had considered it,
he might have embraced. *By Reason of Strength*[34] was precisely the
kind of novel Davidson had urged Southerners to write—not a critical
novel, not a sociological one, not even a particularly realistic one, but
rather one that drew its strength from Southern tradition, not the tradition of Washington and Jefferson but that of the plain antebellum Southerner whom Davidson had championed. *By Reason of Strength* was the
story of early Scottish settlers, based on Johnson's own forebears, in the
Cape Fear region of North Carolina. Its heroine was Catharine Camp-
bell Whyte, a woman of enduring strength and courage. Horace Gregory
found the book a "first-rate romantic novel," and Jonathan Daniels—
who a year earlier had charged that Thomas Wolfe in *Look Homeward,
Angel* hated North Carolina and "spat upon" the South—had nothing
but praise for Gerald Johnson. He had "written about" what "he
loved."[35] But Davidson, if he read the novel, made no comment. He

never gave Johnson his due. He never even forgave him as he forgave
W. J. Cash. "Let's turn him loose," Davidson declared of Cash at the
end of his damning review of *The Mind of the South*. After all, "Mr.
Cash" was a Carolina boy who "went to Wake Forest College" (p. 20).
So was Johnson, but Davidson never extended him the same absolution.
He never let him go. As late as 1958 he was still attacking him,[36] long
after Johnson had left behind the battles of the 1920s and 1930s.

Gerald W. Johnson never actually stopped writing about the South.
He published in 1933 a second novel, *Number Thirty-Six*, set in the
North Carolina of his youth. The story of a newspaper editor's son who
grows up dreaming of the faraway North, then attends Wake Forest,
fights in France, and becomes a journalist, it obviously draws upon the
author's own life. It is also a story, similar to Sherwood Anderson's
*Poor White*, of the growth of a village into a troubled mill town. Johnson's final novel is significant for two reasons. First, it should again
have shown his Agrarian critics that he could be as severe a critic of
industrialism as they themselves: Rogersville as a village is much more
humane and pleasant than Rogersville as a boom town. Also, the novel
bears a curious resemblance to little-known novels of other Southern
expatriates, George W. Cable's *John March, Southerner* (1894) and
Walter Hines Page's *The Southerner* (1909), also semiautobiographical
works written after their authors were firmly established in the Northeast. Johnson's protagonist, as Cable's and Page's, tries to come to
terms with his own tradition; he is at the same time both attracted to and
repelled by the Northeast. Like Page's Nicholas Worth and Cable's
John March, he finally vows to remain at home. "I can do more in the
South," young Donald Watson says, "than any one man can do in New
York."[37]

But by this time Johnson, as Page and Cable when they wrote their
novels, knew he would never return South to live. All he could do was
write about it, adopting a role at least superficially like that of Menck-
en, the South-watcher of Baltimore. But just about the time he left the
South he also immersed himself in Southern history, as the Agrarians
currently were doing. Shortly after arriving in Baltimore he had written
biographies of Andrew Jackson and John Randolph of Roanoke. During
the next few years he wrote books on John C. Calhoun and Henry Clay,
Woodrow Wilson, and Southern industrialist Simpson Bobo Tanner. He
explored the origins of the Civil War and published, in 1933, *The
Secession of the Southern States*, a well-received study that saw the war
as essentially a burlesque and a farce brought about by crazed Northern
prophets (John Brown and William Lloyd Garrison) and Southern ora-

tors (Calhoun, Robert Barnwell Rhett, and William Lowndes Yancey). Four years later he produced *The Wasted Land*, a book drawing heavily on Odum's *Southern Regions of the United States* (1936) and concluding that the South, blessed with abundant human and natural resources, had misused them tragically.[38] He continued to contribute to Southern journals, particularly the *Virginia Quarterly Review*. Certain essays he wrote for the *Quarterly*—on his old mentors Poteat ("Billy with the Red Necktie") and Sledd ("Old Slick") of Wake Forest—were nostalgic, almost elegiac, in tone. Others retained the fire of the 1920s. "The Horrible South" (1935) contended that, in predicting in the "Congo" a "gorgeously barbaric" Southern literature, he had been nothing short of prophetic: Southern fiction of the 1930s was indeed savage, although for a purpose. Faulkner and Thomas Wolfe, T. S. Stribling and Erskine Caldwell, were "the real equerries of Raw-Head-and-Bloody-Bones," "the merchants of death, hell, and the grave . . . the horror-mongers-in-chief." "I am one who yawned over 'Dracula' and was never able to finish it," Johnson remarked. "I have read books about the interesting rites of the South Sea cannibals and eaten hog jowls and cabbage right heartily immediately thereafter; I have even dipped into 'Untrodden Paths of Anthropology' with only a few mild shudders. But 'Sanctuary' put me under the weather for thirty-six hours."[39]

Such had become Johnson's role as Southern critic by the late 1930s: he viewed the South from afar, with great interest, even fascination, but not as the preoccupation it had been before. It had ceased being that when Franklin D. Roosevelt entered the White House and Johnson turned his energies to a defense of the New Deal. The last forty years of his life would be given to reflections on American politics and culture in a larger sense. He would cover American life as journalist and commentator as closely as any man and in numerous books would try to find meaning and direction in it. He would write books or long essays on Americans as diverse as Thomas Paine, John Paul Jones, Alexander Hamilton, Pierre Samuel Du Pont de Nemours, Martin Van Buren, Daniel Webster, Horace Greeley, Henry George, William Jennings Bryan, Adolph S. Ochs of the *New York Times*, both Roosevelts, Mencken, philanthropist Edward A. Filene, and sculptor Gutzon Borglum. He would deal with nearly every phase of American life, and when he was through writing about it for adults he would undertake to explain it to children—in a highly acclaimed series of books on American history and institutions.

Basically Johnson remained a patriot and optimist, although some of his later works became increasingly apprehensive about the outcome of the American experiment. In several of the late, retrospective books he was less gleeful polemicist and more philosopher, less Henry Mencken than Henry Adams. *The Man Who Feels Left Behind* (1961) concerned the American of the 1960s who felt that events, science, knowledge in general had passed him by. Here Johnson questioned the idea of progress, lamented the disappearance of a sense of place among Americans, detected a loss of confidence in American society, but, despite all, insisted that the sixties were a good time to be alive. *Hod-Carrier: Notes of a Laborer on an Unfinished Cathedral* (1964) was an even more personal book and one touched with a sadness uncharacteristic of the earlier Johnson. In discussions of education, liberalism, racial prejudice, the decline of inner-city Baltimore, the population explosion, the United Nations, and the assassination of President Kennedy, Johnson surveyed the era to which seventy-four years had brought him. He was the hod-carrier, and the unfinished cathedral was not the Chartres of Henry Adams but the American nation. The lowest hod-carrier at Chartres built for the glory of God, yet the cathedral took two centuries to complete and those who began it did not live to see it finished. It was time, Johnson suggested, to hand over the tools to the next generation. He was a man who would not "be expected to hang around much longer."[40]

He was wrong. He would hang around another decade and a half, long enough to write six more books. He would also, in his last two decades, see the South return to center stage—precisely where he had left it when he had gone north thirty-five years before. For the South of the 1960s, Johnson surely realized, was in many respects like the South of the 1920s in which he had first flourished, a region both sinned against and sinning in an outrageous manner. The places were now Selma and Oxford and Birmingham, not Dayton and Gastonia and Marion, but the parallels were numerous. Reporters again flocked south in search of a story, reformers came with evangelical zeal, a new image of the Savage South emerged, and Johnson himself, after leaving Dixie alone for the better part of two decades, began to write of it once more—and now in more personal terms. At times he was furious at the inhumanity of his fellow white Southerners; after the 1964 murders of Schwerner, Goodman, and Chaney, he lashed out at that "Mississippi hell-hole ironically named Philadelphia."[41] But in other essays he manifested a deep Southern sentiment not always seen in the writings of the 1920s. One essay, "To Live and Die in Dixie" (1960), illustrates perhaps better than any other his continuing identity as a Southerner. A critical Southerner, to be sure: he had not changed his belief that the Civil War had been a ludicrous enterprise and Southern civilization from the 1830s to the early twentieth century largely fraudulent. Further, "acceptance of a fraud inevitably involves some deterioration of character." Yet, had not the South of 1960 "paid in full"? Had not the war, "ten years of military occupation, thirty years of poverty and grinding debt, ninety years of harassment, anxiety, frustration, and moral deterioration" been enough? "What then is the reason . . . for a Southerner's pride in his birthplace?" Johnson asked. "Why, its difficulties, of course." He himself shared that pride: "Men whom ambition or economic or professional necessity drove out of the South decades ago still tend to proclaim, rather than to conceal their origin." "I am a Southerner," he concluded, "and I want the fact to be known; for the land of my birth is right now enduring the discipline that makes a nation great."[42]

When Donald Davidson charged that Johnson approached the South with his head not his heart, he was only partially correct. Johnson did not deny the heart; he only distrusted its excesses. He understood well his own relationship to the South. "Even those who fled from the intellectual sterility of their early environment," he wrote at age seventy, "realize that its emotional wealth is prodigious; they may be able to think better almost anywhere else, but nowhere else can they feel as intensely, so they are aware that their voluntary exile is not all gain." But to "feel . . . intensely" was not what Johnson believed the South needed; rather, he said repeatedly, it needed a good dose of realism. As a son of Dixie, he was filled with pride *and* shame, a combination hardly unique for the sensitive Southerner. He was also, he wrote, "a little arrogant" in his demands on the South: "A civilization which I might regard as admirable in Kansas or in Ohio would seem for me woefully inadequate to Dixie. . . . We have built one civilization and seen it collapse; but the standards we created while building it still exist, and they are very high."[43]

Johnson's role as he saw it was to help recapture the spirit of that earlier civilization—the spirit of free inquiry of the age of Jefferson which he believed had been absent for a hundred years. To do so, he would have to smash old idols, challenge old truths, declare war on what passed as the Southern tradition. The Southern Renascence of the 1920s was more than the literary renascence. It was rather what Odum called the "critical-creative" renascence, and the social critics played a vital role in its inception. The "Southern-image breakers," Johnson wrote in 1928, were "part of the renaissance": the "same forces" that were responsible for the literary artists were responsible for the critics. He could have gone further: the critical function in fact preceded the creative. It freed the artist as it freed anyone who dealt in ideas and hard truths. Such was true in the South as it was in the England of which Matthew Arnold wrote: "Criticism first, a time of true creative activity, perhaps . . . hereafter, when criticism has done its work." The critical power, Arnold had written, creates "an intellectual situation of which the creative power can profitably avail itself." Bold social criticism introduces a new "order of ideas" which, if not absolutely true, is "true by comparison with that which it displaces." When new ideas reach society "there is a stir and growth everywhere; out of this stir and growth come the creative epochs of literature."[44]

Words of high seriousness and ones with which Johnson would have agreed. But he also would have smiled, for the simple reason that much of what he had written of the South in the 1920s and 1930s had been undertaken as much out of sheer exuberance as out of moral uplift. The exuberance sometimes led to excesses, to the practice of dramaturgy— "truth magnified by ten diameters." Sometimes, indeed, Johnson seemed a writer who was short on research, preoccupied with the lilt of his own style. He was not without other failings as a Southern prophet. For all of his insight into the direction of Southern literature, he tended in the 1930s to classify the greatest of Southern writers, Faulkner, with T. S. Stribling and Erskine Caldwell and to see him as little more than another "horror-monger-in-chief."[45] But who in the 1930s did not? Nor did he appreciate the Southern Agrarians. But neither did they appreciate him. He shared, finally, some of the limitations of his fellow Carolinian, Cash—principally a tendency to view the entire South from a distinctly Tar Heel point of view. Darkest Mississippi seemed at times as foreign to him as the Congo of his early imagination.

Johnson, in his eighties, acknowledged this last shortcoming. North Carolina, as he had predicted, had led the Southern social and economic revival; Odum and his lieutenants had "created a highly-industrialized agricultural state" to which there was "nothing comparable . . . in the Union." It had also led the intellectual revival. But "in beautiful letters," he wrote in 1972, "the Deep or Low-Down South has put it all over us." And if Johnson in his heyday had viewed the South with Tar Heel blinders, what Southerner did not have his own special set of blinders? The Agrarians saw Dixie from a trans-Appalachian, mid-South point of view, William Alexander Percy from the Delta perspective, and so on. About all we can ask of any Southern prophet is that he understand *his* South, and Johnson certainly knew his. One is tempted to consider what might have happened if, like Cash, he had spent his entire life contemplating that South; whether, if he had not moved to Baltimore, he might have written something like *The Mind of the South*. He had all of the component parts in the essays of the 1920s. But

Johnson was not, like Cash, a one-book man. He was not even, like his friend Odum, a one-region man.

Finally, as he said of Sir Thomas Browne, how he could write! Johnson was not only the social critic preparing the way for the literary artist; he was, in many respects, the literary artist himself. But he was a literary artist in a field in which scholars—the doctor-professors, Mencken called them—do not usually acknowledge literary artists. The field was journalism, and although eighteenth-century British journalists such as Addison and Steele qualify as literary figures, twentieth-century American ones such as Mencken, Lippmann, and Johnson generally do not. The field was equally social criticism, and although nineteenth-century British critics Carlyle and Arnold are studied in literature courses, twentieth-century American practitioners of the art usually are not. Social criticism, like journalism, it seems, should be a century in the past and preferably across the ocean before it qualifies as *belles lettres*.

In Johnson's case, it should not be, for he wrote of events past and present with a grace that can only be called literary. His writing was metaphysical in the sense that Samuel Johnson intended the word: in his essays "the most heterogeneous ideas are yoked by violence together" and "resemblances in things apparently unlike" are discovered.[46] He created a persona in his essays, he engaged his reader in the manner of Goldsmith and Irving, and he wrote with the wit and irony of a literary master. The human subjects of his essays were particular, but they were also universal, at times almost allegorical. He viewed Southern life, American life, of the twentieth century as a particularly fascinating drama that he, nearly alone, had witnessed—at least, comprehended— in its entirety. Colonel William J. Simmons, Cole Blease, and Cotton Tom Heflin—as later "Bright John," "Dulcet Lyndon," and "oily Richard M."—were merely players on the stage who soon took their bows. Johnson, a sort of Greek Chorus, remained. Born at a time just before his native South fully descended into its dark age of segregation, he lived long enough to see it emerge on the other side. Born, too, in Victoria's reign, he remained in some ways the nineteenth-century moralist, albeit one at war with the twentieth-century ironist. History was philosophy teaching by example, and so, in the Southern essays of the 1920s and 1930s, was journalism. These essays constituted but a small part of his total output, but they may have been his most important work. In them he undertook one of the highest callings for any man of letters: the truthful examination of his own society in his own time.

NOTES

1. Donald Davidson, *Southern Writers in the Modern World* (Athens: University of Georgia Press, 1958), pp. 38, 47; "The Artist as Southerner," *Saturday Review*, 15 May 1926, p. 782; and "Mr. Cash and the Proto-Dorian South," *Southern Review* 7 (Summer 1941): 12.

2. H. L. Mencken, letter to Emily Clark (1922); and DuBose Heyward, letter to Emily Clark (August 1923); both quoted in Clark, *Innocence Abroad* (New York: Alfred A. Knopf, 1931), pp. 121, 242, 253.

3. Johnson, "Issachar Is a Strong Ass," *Journal of Social Forces* 2 (November 1923): 7; "Fourteen Equestrian Statues of Colonel Simmons," *Reviewer* 4 (October 1923): 22, 24; and "The Advancing South," *Virginia Quarterly Review* 2 (October 1926): 596.

4. Johnson, "Dixie, My Dixie," *New Republic*, 22 September 1958, p. 20.

5. Virginius Dabney, *Liberalism in the South* (Chapel Hill: University of North Carolina Press, 1932).

6. Johnson, "The Cadets of New Market," *Harper's* 160 (December 1929): 114.

7. Johnson, *American Heroes and Hero-Worship* (New York: Harper and Brothers, 1943), p. 12.

8. Johnson, "To Live and Die in Dixie," *Atlantic* 206 (July 1960): 31.

9. Johnson, *Hod-Carrier: Notes of a Laborer on an Unfinished Cathedral* (New York: William Morrow and Company, 1964), pp. 82, 84.

10. Mencken, *Prejudices, Second Series* (New York: Alfred A. Knopf, 1920), p. 136, and "Confederate Notes," Baltimore *Evening Sun*, 26 December 1922; Johnson, in "Why Not a Poetry Society for North Carolina?" *Carolina Magazine* 53 (December 1922): 2, and letter to Mencken, 26 December 1922, in Johnson Collection, Enoch Pratt Free Library.

11. Johnson, "The Congo, Mr. Mencken," *Reviewer* 3 (July 1923): 891.

12. Ibid., pp. 892–93.

13. Johnson, "Fourteen Equestrian Statues of Colonel Simmons," *Reviewer* 4 (October 1923): 20–26; "Greensboro, or What You Will," ibid. 4 (April 1924): 169–75; "Onion Salt," ibid. 5 (January 1925): 60–63.

14. Mencken, "Beneath the Magnolias," Baltimore *Evening Sun*, 20 October 1924.

15. Johnson, review of *Nigger* by Clement Wood, *Journal of Social Forces* 1 (March 1923): 335; Johnson, "Critical Attitudes North and South," ibid. 2 (May 1924), 578–79; and letter to Odum, 27 September 1923, Odum Papers, Southern Historical Collection, University of North Carolina Library.

16. Johnson, letter to Mencken, 10 December 1924, Enoch Pratt Free Library.

17. Johnson, "The Ku Kluxer," *American Mercury* 1 (February 1924): 207–11; "The South Takes the Offensive," ibid. 2 (May 1924): 70–78; "Saving Souls," ibid. 2 (July 1924): 364–68; and Johnson letters to Mencken, 16 July, 30 July, 10 August, 14 August, and 27 September 1923, and 3 May 1924, all Enoch Pratt Free Library.

18. Johnson, "Service in the Cotton Mills," *American Mercury* 5 (June 1925): 219–23; "Journalism below the Potomac," ibid. 9 (September 1926): 77–82; and "Chase of North Carolina," ibid. 17 (July 1929): 183–90.

19. Johnson, letter to Mencken, 27 October 1924, Enoch Pratt Free Library; and "Billy with the Red Necktie," *Virginia Quarterly Review* 19 (Autumn 1943): 551–61.

20. Johnson, "The Congo, Mr. Mencken," p. 892.

21. Johnson, "Issachar Is a Strong Ass," pp. 5–9; and "Mr. Babbitt Arrives at Erzerum," *Journal of Social Forces* 1 (March 1923): 206–9.

22. Johnson, "Behind the Monster's Mask," *Survey*, 1 April 1923, pp. 20–22, 55, 56.

23. Davidson, "Mr. Cash and the Proto-Dorian South," p. 12.

24. Robert Penn Warren, "T. S. Stribling: A Paragraph in the History of Critical Realism," *American Review* 2 (February 1934): 463–86.

25. Johnson, "The Cadets of New Market," p. 117.

26. Davidson, " 'I'll Take My Stand': A History," *American Review* 5 (Summer 1935): 313.

27. Allen Tate, "Last Days of the Charming Lady," *Nation*, 28 October 1925, p. 486; Davidson, "Spyglass," Nashville *Tennessean*, 1 March 1925, and "The Artist as Southerner," p. 782.

28. Johnson, "The South Faces Itself," *Virginia Quarterly Review* 7 (January 1931): 152–57.

29. Johnson, "No More Excuses," *Harper's* 162 (February 1931): 331–37.

30. Louis D. Rubin, Jr., Introduction, *I'll Take My Stand* (1930; New York: Harper Torchbooks, 1962), p. xi.

31. Owsley, letter to Davidson, 8 April 1931; Davidson to Fletcher (copy), 21 March 1931; both in Davidson Papers, Vanderbilt University Library. Also, Davidson to Mims, 24 January 1934, quoted in Michael O'Brien, *The Idea of the American South* (Baltimore: Johns Hopkins University Press, 1979), p. 201.

32. Johnson, "The Battling South," *Scribner's Magazine* 77 (March 1925): 303.

33. Percy, letter to Davidson (January 1930?), Davidson Papers.

34. Johnson, *By Reason of Strength* (New York: Minton, Balch and Company, 1930).

35. Gregory, review of *By Reason of Strength*, *New York Evening Post*, 15 November 1930; Daniels, review of *By Reason of Strength*, *Saturday Review*, 13 December 1930.

36. Davidson, *Southern Writers in the Modern World*, pp. 38, 47.

37. Johnson, *Number Thirty-Six* (New York: Minton, Balch and Company, 1933), p. 210.

38. Johnson, *Andrew Jackson: An Epic in Homespun* (New York: Minton, Balch and Company, 1927); *Randolph of Roanoke* (New York: Minton, Balch and Company, 1929); *The Secession of the Southern States* (New York: G. P. Putnam's Sons, 1933); *The Wasted Land* (Chapel Hill: University of North Carolina Press, 1937); *America's Silver Age: The Statecraft of Clay-Webster-*

*Calhoun* (New York: Harper and Brothers, 1939); *Woodrow Wilson* (New York: Harper and Brothers, 1944); and *The Making of a Southern Industrialist: A Biographical Study of Simpson Bobo Tanner* (Chapel Hill: University of North Carolina Press, 1952).

39. Johnson, "Billy with the Red Necktie," pp. 551–61; "Old Slick," *Virginia Quarterly Review* 26 (Spring 1950): 204–13; "The Horrible South," ibid. 11 (January 1935): 201–17.

40. Johnson, *The Man Who Feels Left Behind* (New York: William Morrow and Company, 1961); *Hod-Carrier: Notes of a Laborer on an Unfinished Cathedral* (New York: William Morrow and Company, 1964).

41. Johnson, "After Forty Years—Dixi," *Virginia Quarterly Review*, 41 (Spring 1965): 199.

42. Johnson, "To Live and Die in Dixie," pp. 29–34.

43. Ibid., p. 30; and "No More Excuses," p. 336.

44. Johnson, "Southern Image-Breakers," *Virginia Quarterly Review* 4 (October 1928): 519; and Matthew Arnold, "The Function of Criticism at the Present Time," *Lectures and Essays in Criticism*, vol. 3 of *The Complete Prose Works of Matthew Arnold* (Ann Arbor: University of Michigan Press, 1962), pp. 261, 269.

45. Johnson, "The Horrible South," p. 211.

46. Samuel Johnson, "Abraham Cowley," *Lives of the Poets*, in *Johnson, Prose and Poetry*, selected by Mona Wilson (Cambridge: Harvard University Press, 1967), p. 798.

# The Savage South

# The Congo, Mr. Mencken

In Johnson's first essay in the *Reviewer* (July 1923) he contends that H. L. Mencken had chosen the wrong figure in his famous essay, "The Sahara of the Bozart." Southern literature, Johnson claims, was as bad as Mencken had charged, but it was bad in a different way. The South was not sterile; rather, it was overflowing with verbose, flowery writers. It was a jungle, "The Congo of the Bozart."

> The greatest mystery of religion is expressed by adumbration,
> and in the noblest part of Jewish types, we find the cherubims shadowing the mercy-seat. Life itself is but the shadow
> of death, and souls departed but the shadow of the living.
> All things fall under this name. The sun itself is but the dark
> *simulacrum*, and light but the shadow of God.

I wish that I could write like that. Some inconvenient remainders of common sense restrain me from trying to do so, but in the bottom of my heart I wish that I could write in the manner of Sir Thomas Browne. It is not that I am especially impressed by the weight of his philosophy for I am quite sure that I have no more idea of what he meant than he had himself; but the man could boom so!

This may be one of those confidences that should be given to none but the family alienist, but I think not. On the contrary, I begin to believe that it indicates no more than that I come of a family that has lived for a century and a quarter in the United States below the fortieth parallel. It does not indicate that I am insane, but merely that I am Southern; for the Sir Thomas Browne complex lies heavily, not upon me alone, but upon sixteen sovereign commonwealths. For proof, I refer the reader to any volume of the titanic set of books published in Atlanta under the title of "The Library of Southern Literature."

On my desk as I write lies Volume One, A–Bo. In it (pp. 373–374) is to be found this resonant bit:

> His life was one continued and benign circumnavigation
> of all virtues which adorn and exalt the character of man. Piety,
> charity, benevolence, generosity, courage, patriotism, fidelity, all
> shone conspicuously in him, and might extort from the beholder

Copyright © 1923 by the *Reviewer* and reprinted with permission.

the impressive interrogatory, "For what place was this man made?" Was it for the Senate or the camp? For public or private life? For the bar or the bench? For the art which heals the body, or for that which cures the infirmities of the State? For which of all these was he born? And the answer is, "For all!" He was born to fill the largest and most varied circle of human excellence; and to crown all these advantages, Nature had given him what the great Lord Bacon calls a perpetual letter of recommendation— a countenance not only good, but sweet and winning—radiant with the virtues of his soul—captivating universal confidence; and such as no stranger could behold—no traveler, even in the desert, could meet, without stopping to reverence, and saying, "Here is the man in whose hands I could deposit life, liberty, fortune, honor!"

The circumnavigator of all the virtues was, it appears, a gentleman named Linn, who at the time of his death held a commission as United States senator from the State of Missouri; and the eulogist was his colleague, Benton,[1] born, let me patriotically add, in my own native State, North Carolina, a commonwealth singularly prolific of such Sons of Thunder. Benton not only desired to write in the manner of Sir Thomas Browne, but actually tried it; and so, alas, have innumerable others. So they continue to try, and succeed only in releasing upon us the outrageous Mr. Mencken, who makes remarks about the South too painful to bear repetition.

What is the explanation of this curious obsession with sound to the exclusion of sense? It certainly is not a racial characteristic brought from Europe, for the South is predominantly Anglo-Saxon, with strong infusions of German, Scotch and Huguenot blood; not by any means conspicuously bombastic peoples. Why have the descendants of English, Scotch, German and French settlers in the Southern States varied so far from type as to produce a literature unrivalled in English for empty sonority?

If the Sir Thomas Browne complex is an acquired characteristic, an adequate explanation of its existence is not far to seek. Southerners have been subjected for a time varying from two to ten generations to an environment differing radically in only one particular from the environment in which the rest of the population has lived. That difference lies in intimate daily contact which Southerners of necessity have made with the most potent personality on the continent—Mister Nigger. If there is

1. Lewis Field Linn, Democratic senator from Missouri, 1833–43; Thomas Hart Benton, Democratic senator from Missouri, 1821–50.

any conspicuous difference between the intellectual and artistic life of the South and that of the rest of the country, is it unreasonable to believe that it is connected with the single conspicuous difference in the environment of the Southerner and that of the other people of the country?

That such a difference exists is hardly to be doubted by anyone who has read with attention the hereinabove mentioned pointed remarks of Mr. Mencken. "The Sahara of the Bozart" he called the South. I think, as I shall explain later, that his figure was ill chosen; but it must be admitted that he supported his assertion with an impressive wealth of detail. Any doubts that survived his whirlwind attack must be resolved by this indisputable fact: such Southerners as have achieved national reputation in letters have, with rare exceptions, done the bulk of their good work elsewhere than in the South. The New England school flourished and perished in New England. The Far Westerners thrive on the Pacific coast. The Indianans find Indianapolis quite habitable. William Allen White and Ed Howe manage to survive even in Kansas. But the South seems to be afflicted with some tremendous centrifugal force that hurls artists across her borders like stones from a sling. The heavier the man the farther he flies. Lafcadio Hearn landed in Japan.[2]

There have been exceptions, of course, but the rule holds good; and where such a rule holds good there is obviously something highly peculiar in the artistic and intellectual life of the region.

It is not to be explained by poverty and ignorance, for Elizabethan England was far poorer and more ignorant than the South ever was. It is not by our illiterates that we are differentiated sharply from the rest of the country. Cole L. Blease is no illiterate, nor Vardaman of Mississippi, nor William Joseph Simmons, founder of the Ku Klux Klan. Benton, the eulogist of Senator Linn, was no illiterate, and John Temple Graves is educated, not to say learned.[3] These men have gained more than local notoriety by widely varying means; but they have in common a certain wild fantasticality, whether it be expressed merely by the employment of rolling, sonorous periods, or swashbuckling defiance of the civilized world, or meeting by the light of the moon in weird garb to

2. William Allen White, editor of the Emporia (Kansas) *Gazette*; Ed Howe, formerly editor of the Atchison (Kansas) *Daily Globe*, editor of *E. W. Howe's Monthly*, and author of *The Story of a Country Town*; Lafcadio Hearn, a transplanted European who came to New Orleans in his late twenties and made his reputation as a writer of travel literature in the 1880s and 1890s.

3. Cole L. Blease, governor of South Carolina, 1911–15, and Democratic senator, 1925–31; James K. Vardaman, governor of Mississippi, 1904–8, and Democratic senator, 1913–19; John Temple Graves, Southern journalist, later to become editor of the Birmingham *Age-Herald* and author of *The Fighting South*.

mutter spells and incantations in unknown tongues. They are Southerners, and their mad success in the South is certainly indicative of the fact that they embody Southern ideals much more successfully than such comparatively matter-of-fact persons as—to choose three ejected North Carolinians—Joseph G. Cannon, Walter Hines Page and Benjamin N. Duke.[4]

Whence have we derived this taste for turgid eloquence, for grandiloquent defiance, for masks and flowing white robes? Perhaps we might be helped toward the answer if the Rev. Baltimore Criddle would emerge from his Coffin Club and tell us where he got his love of mouthfilling vocables; or if Ander, whose "eyes is white as snow, his gums is blue," could inform us why on the trifling provocation "he retch an' fotch his razor fum his shoe"; or if we might know the idea underlying the regalia of the Sons and Daughters of I Will Arise. We are Nordics, to be sure; but Nordics whose need of color is no longer satisfied with mere purple and gold, Nordics who demand saffron and crimson and emerald, whose cool Northern temperament has been inflamed and excited by acquaintance with the phantasmagoria of the jungle.

Mr. Mencken spoke of the South as "The Sahara of the Bozart."[5] I submit that he could hardly have chosen a worse figure. The Sahara, as I am informed and believe, is for the most part a treeless waste, denuded alike of animal and of vegetable life. The South resembles more Sierra Leone, where, according to Sir Harry Johnston, "the mammalian fauna of chimpanzis, monkeys, bats, cats, lions, leopards, hyenas, civets, scaly manises, and large-eared earth-pigs, little-known duiker bushbuck, hartebeeste, and elephant, is rich and curious." So is the literary flora; and if Mr. Mencken presumes to doubt it, I invite him to plunge into the trackless waste of the Library of Southern Literature, where a man might wander for years, encountering daily such a profusion of strange and incredible growths as could proceed from none but an enormously rich soil.

The South is not sterile. On the contrary, it is altogether too luxuriant. It is not the Sahara, but the Congo of the Bozart. Its pulses beat to the rhythm of the tom-tom, and it likes any color if it's red. Vachel Lindsay struck the tempo:

---

4. Joseph G. Cannon, U.S. representative from Illinois, 1873–1923, and speaker of the House of Representatives, 1903–11; Walter Hines Page, North Carolina journalist who became editor of the *Atlantic Monthly* and *World's Work*, a successful publisher, and U.S. ambassador to Great Britain under Woodrow Wilson; Benjamin N. Duke, pioneer Southern industrialist and philanthropist.

5. H. L. Mencken, "The Sahara of the Bozart," *Prejudices, Second Series* (New York, 1920).

"Fat black bucks in a wine-barrel room

  .    .    .    .    .

Pounded on the table,
Beat an empty barrel with the handle of a broom,
Hard as they were able,
Boom, boom, BOOM,
With a silk umbrella and the handle of a broom,
Boomlay, boomlay boomlay, BOOM."

Can anything rare and exquisite survive under such conditions? Certainly. Orchids. Edgar Allan Poe grew them long ago, and Sidney Lanier later, and James Branch Cabell grows them today. But in the tropics one soon wearies of orchids. There the exotic would be a trim, English garden * * * or, if we must have luxuriance, the stately, ordered luxuriance that Sir Thomas Browne could create.

Before there can be fair gardens in the South, though, there must be Herculean labor performed in clearing away the jungle growth—labor involving the use of sharp steel, swung vigorously. It is within the bounds of probability that some laborers will perish miserably, stung to death by noxious insects, or rent limb from limb by the mammalian fauna. But such things must be at every famous victory.

Furthermore, this very negroid streak that gives to the bulk of Southern writing at present the startling appearance of an African chief parading through the town arrayed in a stovepipe hat, monocle, frock coat and no trousers, may prove in the future an asset of first-rate value. The chances are that it will at least prevent us from falling into drab monotony. North Carolina a few years ago produced one immortal whose works were not included in the Library of Southern Literature; yet Miss Peterson—for such was her name—in her "Vision" produced two lines that I will set up against the best of that J. Gordon Coogler so enthusiastically admired by Mr. Mencken. They read,

"I seen Pa coming, stepping high,
Which was of his walk the way."

He who has the vision to see Southern literature coming at all—and I profess to have it—needs must see it stepping high, for that is of its walk the way. It could not be otherwise. It has the pulse of the tom-toms in its veins, the scents of the jungle are in its nostrils and the flaming colors of the jungle in its eyes. It will be colorful beyond belief, instead of a discreet maquillage it will come wearing smears of paint like a witch-doctor. It may be outlandish, but it will not be monotonous. It may be gorgeously barbaric, but it will not be monotonous. For all I know, it may be in some manifestations tremendously evil—it may wallow in filth, but it will not dabble in dirt. I think we may even have a hint of it now in Clement Wood's ghastly, soul-sickening and damnably true "Nigger."[6] That, at least, is a possible line along which it may come.

In the meantime, though, we have with us today a public fascinated by the flashy, even though it may be false. Instead of poets and authors we have poetesses and authoresses, poetets and authorets. At Richmond, Cabell plucks abstractedly the strings of his medieval lyre; at Charleston, away off to one side, DuBose Heyward and Hervey Allen[7] are tentatively trying out their harp and 'cello combination; at the University of North Carolina the Playmakers are trying to play a fantasia on toy trumpets. Others are scattered here and there with rare and beautiful instruments. But the centre of the stage and the attention of the audience are engaged by a literary equivalent of Isham Jones' jazz band engaged in a spirited rendition of "Bang Away at Lulu."

Jazz is wonderfully moving * * * I wish I could write like Sir Thomas Browne.

.

6. Clement Wood's novel, *Nigger* (1922), is a sympathetic treatment of a Negro family's struggles in Alabama in the early twentieth century.

7. DuBose Heyward and Hervey Allen, Charleston poets and novelists, founders of the Poetry Society of South Carolina in 1921.

# Fourteen Equestrian Statues
## of Colonel Simmons

In the *Reviewer* (October 1923) Johnson proposes, tongue in cheek, that the South erect statues to Colonel William Joseph Simmons, founder of the Ku Klux Klan, because Simmons has aroused the Southern consciousness and has shown the Southern "literate minority" the thinking of one particular mind of the South.

Colonel William Joseph Simmons, founder of the Ku Klux Klan, probably will go to his grave without receiving from a grateful South that tribute of weeping, honor and song prescribed as the just due of a citizen whose services to the state have been of extraordinary value. Colonel Simmons, it is true, has not gone altogether without reward. He has an imperial title, an imperial palace and, if rumor lieth not, an income rather better than imperial. But these, except the title, are material things and probably dross to a spirit avid not of gain but of glory. Ironic fate has contrived that even the title, doubtless most precious of the Colonel's possessions, is of a style that gives the lie to the Colonel's most important work in the world. He is Emperor of the Invisible Empire, and no association of ideas can connect the word "emperor" (except unfortunately) with the names of Brutus, Kosciusko, Marco Bozzaris, Lincoln and Enver Pasha; yet if history is to classify men according to the net result of their work in the world it is into this list of the great Liberators that the name of Simmons must go. There is a steady increase of the evidence that his work will put him there, willynilly, and due acknowledgment of the fact might as well be made before his epitaph is written.

The sober truth is that Colonel Simmons is swiftly winning a just claim to recognition as the Deliverer of the South. Not from negro domination. That was purchased long ago at the inconsiderable price of a Presidency of Rutherford B. Hayes. Nor has he freed us from danger of domination either by the successors of Peter or the seed of Abraham, since no such danger ever existed in the South. It is a menace more subtle and insidious than negro, Jew or Catholic that the knights of the Ku Klux Klan are attacking with every promise of success. It is a spiritual bondage of the South that they are breaking; and if they suc-

Copyright © 1923 by the *Reviewer* and reprinted with permission.

ceed, who could in justice deny their present Emperor the more illustrious title of Emancipator?

The careless superficiality with which the Ku Klux Klan phenomenon has been examined by most of those who have written on the subject is incredible. Most of the accounts of its origin and increase might have been written by scandalized Catholics, Israelites, or negroes for the light that they throw upon its more profound cause and its less immediate effects. Without exception so far as I know, the writers have assumed that the order owes its existence to a contempt for established authority in the South. The truth is exactly the reverse. Far from proving that Dixie is fierce, haughty and intractable, the Klan is merely the latest demonstration of the amazing docility of the masses of the South.

The evidence is so obvious that it is astonishing that it has been overlooked. The thing that the investigators have ignored unanimously is the fact that, while Colonel Simmons did found the order, its principles were not original with him. He did no more than organize an agency to carry into effect, in due form and order, the prevailing social, political and religious doctrine of the region. White supremacy certainly did not originate with him. Detestation of Jews is still more remote from Atlanta in its beginnings. Admirers of Dr. Martin Luther will hardly concede that Colonel Simmons was the first man ever to hold the church of Rome in slight esteem. And suspicion and dislike of foreigners was a prominent characteristic of the people with whom history began. Long before William Joseph Simmons became Imperial Wizard, long before he became even a Colonel of Woodmen of the World, long before he practiced as a local preacher of the Methodist persuasion, in fact, long before he was born, the principles of the Ku Klux were fixed and established among native white gentile Protestants in the South. Press and pulpit harped upon them daily. For scurrilous abuse of the Catholic church, for instance, no kleagle, klud, titan, cyclops or goblin ever could hold a candle to many a backwoods preacher or peripatetic evangelist performing regularly in the South. For vilification of foreigners and surly suspicion of new ideas the propagandists of the Klan found precedents in the campaign speeches of candidates for every elective office in the South for the past thirty years. The Klan's crazy idea of what constitutes Anglo-Saxon civilization was not conceived by William Joseph Simmons in a fit of delirium tremens, but is precisely the conception presented for years by a considerable proportion of the Southern press, and but rarely challenged by those Southern journals that are fairly intelligent.

The vast success of the organizers of the Klan is absolute proof that they went to the masses in the South with no brand-new philosophy.

Neither did they propose any startling innovation in procedure. Stepping outside of the law to achieve a laudable end is not regarded as a serious crime in the South. The South discovered nearly sixty years ago what was revealed to the North only when the Eighteenth Amendment gripped it, namely, that the law is an ass. Therefore the proposal of the Ku Klux organizers that enforcement of the current religious, social and political code be removed from the hands of the peace officers and undertaken by a masked secret order was not particularly shocking to the average barber or cotton mill hand. The soundness of Ku Klux doctrine seemed to him to be beyond debate, for had not its essentials been expounded for years by his pastor, his paper and his political boss? The methods of the Klan seemed only slightly irregular, for had they not been winked at in the South ever since Reconstruction? On the other hand, the possibilities of the Klan as a purveyor of pleasurable excitement are obvious even to a moron, and its capability of being used as an instrument of private vengeance is clear to a knave of rudimentary intelligence. It was bound to flourish.

But the greatness of its success has had the effect of rousing the intelligence of the South to a realization of the thralldom under which it has lain. It has revealed to the South that its lack of keen and relentless self-criticism, the only effective social prophylaxis, has laid it open to invasion by any sort of disease. It has shown how an intelligence not vigorously on the alert to resist every attack will eventually be laid by the heels while kleagles and wizards triumph over it.

Many and many an intelligent Southerner has sat somnolently in his pew while his pastor, snorting prodigiously, applied to the Pope all the curses in the Apocalypse. He has read in his newspaper miles of editorial belchings about the immorality, treachery, poltroonery and fantastic wickedness of all the nations of Europe. He has heard reports of the way in which the honorable gentleman from Stinking Quarters, candidate for coroner subject to the action of the Democratic primary, has risen in his campaign speeches to heights of imbecility that Bedlam never dreamed when he paid tribute to the beauty, the chivalry, the godliness and the wisdom of this Our Southland. Yet it has actually never occurred to him that it is his manifest sacred duty as Christian, scholar and patriot, to strive for the unfrocking of the Rev. Andrew Gump on the ground that he is preaching diabolism in the name of Christianity, to cancel his subscription to his newspaper unless and until it discards the custom of seeking its editor among the inmates of a madhouse, and to greet the candidate for coroner with an enthusiastic kick.

But Colonel William Joseph Simmons has revealed to him in startling fashion the imperative nature of that duty. Colonel Simmons has organized those who take seriously the empty gabble of political, religious and journalistic blatherskites, thereby filling that vacuity with possibilities of infinite mischief. The deliverances of the lower orders of Southern divines on Romanism may be, regarded strictly as sermons, as futile as they are ignorant and foolish; but they may be fearfully effective as incitations to the gas-house gang to beat up old Father O'Connor. Editorials on the total depravity of Europe written by Greeleys[1] who have never crossed the State line may be worth slightly less than the ink required to print their final exclamation point if they are valued strictly as editorials; but they have power to move a platoon of masked barbers to wreck Pete Skalchunes' banana stand while Pete is foregathering with his brother Shriners at his lodge meeting. Even the ultimate imaginable achievement of fatuity, the campaign speech, may so intoxicate the inferior classes with a false sense of their dignity, wisdom and worth as Southerners that they may presume to use their secret organization to censor the morals and manners of their superiors.

These outrages are to be prevented only by removing their cause. This cause, it cannot be asserted too emphatically, is not the Knights of the Ku Klux Klan. Unassisted, they are as incapable of understanding the desirability of pogroms directed against Catholics and negroes as well as Jews as they are incapable of understanding the theory of relativity, or Beethoven's Fifth Symphony, or that two and two make four. If their minds ever worked, except as they are goaded and guided into working, they would almost immediately work out the absurdity of the whole preposterous business. In fact, in most communities the organizers did gather in a few men capable of voluntary cerebration, which explains the wholesale desertions of the Klan that almost invariably have occurred a few months after the organization of a new klavern. The fact that a man remains a knight for any considerable length of time is conclusive proof that that man never thinks. The knight is no peculiar being; his intellectual and spiritual brethren swarm in the ranks of every fraternal order in the republic, including the Knights of Columbus, B'nai B'rith and the Sons and Daughters of I Will Arise.

The cause of the sinister record of the Ku Klux Klan is not to be found in its personnel, which is as harmless as that of the Junior Order of United American Mechanics. It is to be found among those agencies that have pumped the empty skulls of the knights full of hatred and suspicion of other creeds, other races, and other nationalities than their own. The fight of the intelligent South must be made on these agencies. But these agencies include large and influential sections of the Southern

1. Horace Greeley, founder and editor of the New York *Tribune*, 1841–72.

press, pulpit and political organizations. To attack these, the Southerner must burst all bonds of conservative tradition, break with the past and defy the present with the bald, unequivocal and conclusive assertion that lying is wrong.

The revolutionary character of such a declaration is derived, of course, from its lack of modification. It is traditionally wrong for the cook to lie about the eggs she stole, or for any salaried employee drawing less than five thousand dollars a year to vary in the least from strict accuracy in his reports. It is only in businessmen known to Bradstreet that lying becomes acumen; only in editors that it becomes the creation of healthy public opinion; only in politicians that it becomes patriotism; and only in holy orders that it rises to the crowning dignity of defense of the faith. It is by revealing to the literate minority in the South that a liar in any of these positions is really more pernicious than a lying cook or clerk that Colonel William Joseph Simmons has wrought his great work of liberation. It required some such work as his to do it; therefore if there is any sense of justice in the South it will in years to come hold his memory in esteem.

Uproarious patriot that he is, Colonel Simmons probably will not share in the regret of others that circumstances apparently are going to confine the liberating influence of his career to his native section. If there were any way of getting rid of the Ku Klux except the arduous and painful way of turning honest the South unquestionably would adopt it. The Southerner is no more than human. In his objection to having his own weaknesses and follies thrust upon his attention he is indistinguishable from a New Englander, and almost as much inclined to overestimate his own virtues.

But Simmons and circumstances have left him no choice. Elsewhere the Knights of Columbus, the tribal orders of Israel, and the National Association for the Advancement of Colored People may be relied upon to define and delimit the activities of the klansmen. Recent history has proved that buckshot may furnish an effective cure when exhortation and admonition fail, and that that remedy is pretty certain to be applied. But the situation in the South is different, for none of the three powers cited above possesses in many communities below the Potomac strength enough to cope with the Invisible Empire. If she is not to turn entirely imperialist the South must escape by strengthening her republican institutions with practically no assistance from K. of C., B'nai B'rith, or W. E. Burghardt Du Bois. The hard-pressed South is under the necessity of restoring law and order by strictly lawful and orderly means!

In view of the fact that the South is thoroughly American, one might reasonably conclude that it can't be done. But such a conclusion, after all, gives small credit to the celebrated ingenuity of the American; the fact that he has never done anything of that sort before is surely no conclusive proof that he never will do it. Besides, the effort required in this particular instance is not superhuman. To suppress the Ku Klux it is not necessary for the South to achieve and maintain anything remotely approaching absolute intellectual integrity. She has merely to become a little more honest, intelligent and liberal than any section of the country is at present.

Yet this accomplishment, relatively trifling as it may seem, would be of such vast importance that the man through whose agency it came to pass is entitled to the grateful recognition of the section. The least that is due Colonel Simmons is the erection by each Southern State of an equestrian statue of the Emperor-Emancipator as the chief ornament of its capitol grounds. Let no one raise the foolish objection that the Colonel is unaware of what he is doing. What liberator ever foresaw the final result of his efforts? Did Garibaldi expect to raise Mussolini to the throne of the Caesars? Did Lincoln expect to open the way to fame and fortune for John Arthur Johnson?[2]

2. Jack (John Arthur) Johnson, boxer, first Negro heavyweight champion of the world.

# The Ku Kluxer

In Johnson's first contribution to Mencken's *American Mercury* (February 1924) he investigates what was becoming known as the benighted or "savage" South. He is severely critical of the Klan, yet seeks to explain why one hypothetical white Southerner—who has listened too closely to the words of fundamentalists and demagogues—might be attracted to the Klan. Johnson anticipates W. J. Cash in his emphasis upon the role that chivalry and honor played in the Klan.

I think that my friend Chill Burton is an Exalted Cyclops, although he may be only a Fury, or a lesser Titan, for my knowledge of the nomenclature of the Ku Klux Klan is far from exact. At any rate, he is an important personage among klansmen in our town, but rather insignificant in the State organization. He may therefore be classified as a klansman ranking slightly above the average, but not far enough above it to be in any way identified with the Atlanta potentates, who are a breed different altogether from the ordinary members. So if one might determine what made Chill Burton a member of this curious organization, I believe that the secret of its rapid growth would be made plain; for an argument that would convince him would unquestionably convince millions of other obscure and worthy Americanos.

In the first place, the lurid imaginings of many writers on the Klan, particularly in the North, may be dismissed at once. It was not the prospect of participating in a celebration of some revolting Witches' Sabbath that fetched Chill, for he isn't that sort of man. He is fifty years old, a pillar of the church, an exemplary husband and the father of six head of healthy children. He believes in the verbal inspiration and literal interpretation of the Scriptures, and accepts the Athanasian Creed and the Democratic Platform with unquestioning faith. You might entrust your purse or your daughter to Chill with quite as much confidence as you might entrust either to the right reverend ordinary of the diocese, or to the pastor of the First Baptist Church. He will *not* take a drink, and he *will* pay his debts. In brief, if Pope was right, Chill is one of the noblest works of God.

But he is incurably romantic. Doubtless that is an inheritance. His name indicates as much, for he was christened Achilles, which, con-

Copyright © 1924 by the *American Mercury* and reprinted with permission.

sidering the abbreviation as a guide to the pronunciation prevailing in the House of Burton, certainly indicates a disposition on the part of his immediate forebears to reach out for the undiscovered. His occupation proves it, too, for he has been on the road for thirty years representing a tobacco company, and a man who can sell snuff and plug tobacco for thirty years without even attempting suicide is obviously endowed with the romanticist's ability to create around himself a world of dreams to mask or replace reality. Again, his conversation demonstrates it, for he is perpetually discovering mare's nests of the most awful nature—conspiracies among municipal officials to loot the city treasury, conspiracies among Negro school-teachers to incite the pickaninnies to pillage, rapine and massacre, and daily new proofs that someone—formerly German spies, later I. W. W.'s, and later still Russian Bolshevists, with Mr. J. Pierpont Morgan playing in the interludes—spread the cotton boll-weevil through the South by casting the insect from moving trains.

Chill goes through life surrounded by the machinations of occult and Machiavellian intelligences. He walks briskly, planting his square-toed shoes with decision. He is sturdy, the least bit stooped, decently garbed in clothing of inconspicuous cut and neutral tint, and his iron-gray hair is growing thin on the top of his head. Occasionally his eyes light up with a pale blue flame, and his mouth tightens into a grim slit; but otherwise he gives no outward indication of the fact that his soul is tormented by tremendous and ghastly visions and his mind appalled by the perils that threaten the very existence of true religion and unpolluted Anglo-Saxon blood.

These visions and perils, and nothing base, were the considerations that made of Chill what is colloquially known in North Carolina as a "klucker." He certainly does not thirst for the heart's blood of Mary Amanda Emmeline Seymour Pleasure Belle Caroline Kearns, who presides in his kitchen. He is on perfectly friendly, if not intimate, terms with J. Leroy Goldstein, the pawnbroker, and Chris Skalchunes, who keeps the fruit stand, and he treats the Rev. Father Paul O'Keefe with faultless, frosty courtesy. Chill would sincerely deplore the lynching of any of these individuals; most emphatically would he refuse to have anything to do with their molestation, even in as mild a form as a cowhiding, or a coat of tar and feathers. Yet from the bottom of his soul he believes that the dominance of the Anglo-Saxon is hourly imperilled by the Negro; that if the Nordic strain is polluted by infusion of any other blood, American civilization will collapse and disappear; that if the Protocols of Zion were fraudulent, then something worse exists still unrevealed; and that secret agents of the Pope, infiltrating the Bureau of

Engraving and Printing, strove treacherously to convert America to Catholicism by introducing crosses, snakes and pictures of His Holiness among the decorations on the dollar bill of 1917. Therefore, when less scrupulous brother knights of the Invisible Empire commit outrages under cover of darkness, Chill's attitude is that while lawlessness is always to be regretted, it is better that a few individuals should suffer injustice than that our civilization, our religion and our very race should be exposed to the secret assaults of foes without scruples and of super-human cunning.

Nor is his belief a proof of insanity any more than it is a proof of insanity for his small son to believe that Caesar overcame the Nervii. The boy has no legal evidence that Caesar or the Nervii ever existed in fact; the schoolmaster has simply taught him that the battle occurred, and that settles it for him. Equally oracular authorities, the pastor and the politician, had filled Chill with fear and distrust of Negroes, foreigners, Jews and Catholics long before William Joseph Simmons, of Atlanta, began to dream of a throne. The explanation is absurdly simple. Devil-drubbing is always easier and safer if the particular devil selected for chastisement is feeble, or far away. In the South, where the Ku Klux Klan originated, foreigners, Jews and Catholics are relatively few and far between, and Negroes are politically and socially impotent. Therefore every Southern demagogue, sacred or profane, has for generations covered his significant silence on industrial slavery, on race hatred, on baronial estates supported by legalized peonage, and on election frauds by thundering denunciations of the carpetbagger, St. Peter, Judas Iscariot and Lenin, none of whom was then and there present or likely to demand embarrassing explanation.

The Cause was furthered in the South by other circumstances. It happens that the South actually was under Negro domination once, and after half a century the memory of that experience still keeps its racial sensibilities abnormally acute. A Northern observer recently pointed out that the Negro is all that it has to worry about so it has made up for the lack of other major troubles by worrying itself into a pathological condition about the race problem. Thus, in view of the diligent tillage that had been going on for many decades, it is no marvel that the Invisible Empire reaped a rich and instantaneous harvest in the Southern field.

Yet it is commonly reported now that the banner Ku Klux State is not Georgia, but Indiana. It is evident, therefore, that the strongest appeal of the Klan is not to prejudice against the Negro—an assumption borne out of the significant fact that only in rare instances in the South have men wearing the regalia of the Klan attacked a Negro. Nor have Catholics, Jews and foreigners furnished the majority of the victims, except at such times as they have offered themselves as candidates and been politically massacred at the polls. The whippings, the tar and feathers, and similar attentions have usually been administered to known or suspected criminals or social outcasts. To this sort of work the klucker of a grade slightly lower than that of my friend Chill goes forth joyously, sublimely confident that he thereby serves the larger cause of white, Gentile, Protestant supremacy, just as the county chairman stuffs the precinct boxes with the county ticket only, thoroughly convinced that he is thereby helping God and the national committee to save the country.

The necromancy by which the guardian of the sacred fires of civilization, race and religion is transformed into a whipper of prostitutes and a lyncher of bootleggers is no mystery. It is no more than the familiar psychological phenomenon of "taking it out on somebody." Chill is profoundly convinced that the Nordic Protestant is in imminent danger; what could be more natural, then, than for him to regard with tolerance, if not with approval, the extra-legal chastisement of anyone who violates Nordic Protestant standards in whatever particular? No doubt some Gray Eminence is the man higher up; but he is not within reach, or even identified as yet. In the meantime, this strumpet also violates our Protestant Nordic Standards. Go to, let us deal with her now, and catch His Eminence when we can!

But who impressed Chill with the notion that his duty to obey the law is less than his duty to defend racial, social and religious purity? Who but those who set up the great American fetish of equality, not merely before the law, but in every respect? Chill has been assured from childhood that in the United States of America every man is a king in his own right and so naturally he assumes royal prerogatives. The energy of a monarch in cutting legal red-tape in the cause of justice may very well be a virtue; but it is a virtue that cannot be democratized without disaster. To have a rigid and exacting standard of manners and morals set by an aristocracy may be of great benefit to a nation; but when the proletariat undertakes to confer that benefit—well, we have the result before us in America.

The Ku Klux Klan has swept beyond the racial boundaries of the Negro and flourishes now in the Middle West because it is a perfect expression of the American idea that the voice of the people is the voice of God. The belief that the average klansman is consciously affected by an appeal to his baser self is altogether erroneous. In the voice of the organizer he hears a clarion call to knightly and selfless service. It strikes him as in no wise strange that he should be so summoned; is he not, as an American citizen, of the nobility? Politics has been democratized. Social usage has been democratized. Religion has been most astoundingly democratized. Why, then, not democratize chivalry?

The klansman has already been made, in his own estimation, politically a monarch, socially a peer of the realm, spiritually a high priest. Now the Ku Klux Klan calls him to step up and for the trifling consideration of ten dollars he is made a Roland, a Lancelot, a knight-errant vowed to the succor of the oppressed, the destruction of ogres and magicians, the defense of the faith. Bursting with noble ideas and lofty aspirations, he accepts the nomination. The trouble is that this incantation doesn't work, as none of the others has worked, except in his imagination. King, aristocrat, high priest as he believes himself to be, he is neither royal, noble, nor holy. So, under his white robe and pointed hood he becomes not a Chevalier Bayard but a thug.

The shocked surprise of many prominent publicists and educators in the presence of the phenomenon of the Klan is the crowning absurdity of the farce. These men have spent years and gained great renown making just this thing possible. They have stuffed millions of youths, and filled miles of bookshelves with twaddle about the glory of the masses. By dint of herculean labor they have at length deprived the adjective "common" of its legitimate connotation when it is used to modify the noun "people." To do them justice, they seem to have produced an *un*common people, a people incapable of perceiving any essential difference between St. George and a butcher, a people unwilling to admit that spearing a dragon is a feat requiring mental and spiritual qualities not necessarily possessed by a pig-sticker.

Chill is no more to blame for his delusions than the Knight of the Rueful Countenance was for his. The romances are to blame. Chill, indeed, has an excuse that Quixote could not plead, for Chill's romances were offered and accepted as sober narrations of fact, as histories, as lectures, as sermons. They were offered by and accepted from authorities whom Chill respected too much to question; and whom it is not profitable in any case, and not safe in many cases, for anyone else to question.

Thus they are not merely woven into the fabric of his thinking—they are the very warp and woof thereof. The *chansons de geste* of the Republic are as real to him as were the details of the combat in Roncesvaux to a French peasant of the Fourteenth Century. He is no more firmly convinced that the sun rises in the east than he is that Washington, not Rochambeau, won the Revolutionary War, or that the War of 1812 was bravely waged and gloriously won by the patriots of America, or that the struggle of the sixties was notable among all wars for the brilliant strategy of the officers and the magnificent discipline of the troops on both sides, or that the battle of San Juan Hill was a terrible fight, or that Sir John Pershing's helpful hints were what enabled Foch to turn the trick. He has been taught such things from his youth up, so of course he believes that to doubt them would be to reduce his percentage of Americanism away below par. He has been taught romance in the name of history to the end that, glorying in the proud record of American arms, he might present an unfaltering front to any foe when his every instinct commanded him to go away from there. But instead of making a patriot of him, it has served merely to convince him that as an American he is "a mighty tur'ble man," one born to command, and disobedience to whom partakes of the nature of mutiny in the ranks.

The cult of the Nordic he accepts with the same sublime faith. It is not merely that he is totally unfamiliar with the arguments that may be advanced in favor of, say, Slavic, or Latin, or Semitic culture. He does not believe that any such arguments are possible. It simply never has occurred to him that there can be anything to say on the other side. This romance under the label of ethnology has been foisted upon him partly by fantastic imbeciles who believe it themselves, but largely by the economic overlords of the country, who are desperately afraid of what might happen if the nimble-witted economic soothsayers that the Slavs and Latins and Semites are producing in hordes ever began to inject their theories into the stolid Nordic brain. The idea was to make of the American proletarian an economic, as well as a political patriot. The result has been to make him a racial bully.

As for the impressions that Chill has received from his spiritual instructors, they are so nearly incredible that it is hard to believe that they were implanted with any sane object in view. I hesitate to attempt to outline his beliefs, but some conception of them may be conveyed by certain matters of fact. I have seen garbled extracts from the curse of Ernulphus, as quoted in "Tristram Shandy," circulated in pamphlet form with the information that they were part of an oath sworn by every Catholic priest at the time of his ordination. The "Protocols of the Elders of Zion" are still read with avidity by klansmen, and the exposure of their fraudulency is quite honestly believed to be Jewish propaganda. As for Protestant solidarity, I have known of a special prayer-meeting called for the purpose of offering supplications for the conversion to the Baptist faith of a merchant who was, in the literal sense of the word, a damned Methodist. This appalling travesty of Christianity must, it seems at first, have been inspired by no less malignant a genius than Satan himself; it is unquestionably the strongest evidence ever offered to prove the existence of a personal devil. But it is only the inevitable result of the labors of pious romancers who, with the sanctified object of inducing Chill to "put on the whole armour of God," have not hesitated to embellish the truth by assuring him that there is only one style of equipment that is regulation stuff, only one issue creed, only one genuine, o. d. church. The intention was to make a well-drilled soldier of Armageddon; the result seems to have been to produce a spiritual bushwhacker, with no stomach for fighting the common enemy, but delighting in every opportunity to raid the dugouts of the allies.

To inculcate patriotism, to immunize against foreign radical ideas and to strengthen the bulwarks of true religion are certainly prominent among the aims of the current program of Americanization, which is absorbing enormous quantities of money and time and the energy of innumerable massive brains. I submit that the magical rise of the Invisible Empire, Knights of the Ku Klux Klan, is one outstanding proof of the tremendous effect of that program. No romance that apparently tended to strengthen respect for the flag and the faith has been rejected by the Americanizers on the ground that it was blatantly false. But outraged truth has an uncomfortable habit of avenging itself. Spurious history, spurious ethnology, spurious religion have produced a spurious patriot, none the less existent because unexpected and undesired. The fact that nobody foresaw that Chill would blossom into a klansman does not alter the fact that the klansman is one of the flowers of our democracy.

But there is nothing spurious about the tragedy of my friend Chill Burton. That is as authentic as fear. The fact that he is the target of objurgations of the most violent sort is a trifle. What is important is that the man walks through a cloud of unseen presences, terrible and repulsive. The Negro Dominant is a *poltergeist* not unfamiliar to most Southern whites, but he is only one of Chill's invisible attendants. Salathiel creeps ever at his heels; the non-Nordic skips nimbly about, varying his hues chameleon-like, from swarthy white through yellow and brown to black; the Bolshevist, draped with bombs and attended by hordes of nationalized women, hovers near; and above them all looms Antichrist, just now equipped with mitre and crozier but capable, I suspect, of assuming at need the form of any sect other than Chill's own. It is a serious thing to be a warrior, priest and king all rolled into one. It entails responsibilities. Democracy has armed, anointed and crowned Chill, but it has also sent him abroad attended by this ghastly train.

On the whole, I think that it would have been kinder to him and safer for the country if America had told him no lies to begin with.

# Saving Souls

Johnson and Mencken corresponded throughout 1923 and 1924 about other articles Johnson might write for the *Mercury*. Johnson suggested essays on Southern evangelists and Southern Baptists. He wrote in December 1923 that he intended to "devote some consideration to the growth of ritualism in the religion of the South," and in another letter he explained to Mencken in detail the procedure of baptism. One article on evangelists and tent revivals appeared in the *Mercury* of July 1924. Here, as in his essays on the Klan, Johnson treats his subjects not as abstractions—as Mencken often did—but as flawed and pitiable humans.

Along with the peach-blossoms and the first jonquils of last Spring there came to the city of Raleigh, capital of the State of North Carolina, a Great Moral Awakening. This, of course, was nothing remarkable *per se*, since Great Moral Awakenings, in Raleigh and elsewhere, not infrequently mark the season of the rising of the sap, when dandelions star every grassy bank with "patines of bright gold" and chautauqua tents blossom in vacant lots, also with some reference to bright gold. Perhaps, indeed, it is this very stirring of renewed life in blade and leaf, this resurrection from the dust of Nature's immortal hope, that directs men's thought in Spring to occult and transcendental things, and so leads them easily into spiritual adventures. Or perhaps it is a darker influence—the season's sinister power to make, as the Negroes say, "a man's gall quit wukkin"—which turns him annually to calomel and meditations upon death, hell and the grave. Be the cause what it may, Great Moral Awakenings shortly after the vernal equinox are not sufficiently rare in the Republic to deserve much remark. But the one that was visited upon Raleigh early this year was so ineffably beautiful a specimen, it exhibited with such charming completeness the skeletal structure of the whole phenomenon, that it was worthy of and will here get a favorable mention.

The Great Moral Awakening at Raleigh was superinduced by the labors of an evangelist who copes successfully with the inordinate name of Ham.[1] This fervent and determined brother had striven valiantly

1. Mordecai Ham, Baptist evangelist and prohibitionist prominent in the 1920s.

Copyright © 1924 by the *American Mercury* and reprinted with permission.

against the patron devil of the place for six long weeks, and had striven in vain, but at the end of that time he suddenly converted a bootlegger, and instantly hell's Hindenburg line was blown up by the explosion of its own ammunition dumps. Within forty-eight hours Raleigh was more intensely moral than any other town within a radius of a hundred miles —more moral, even, than it had been itself since January 29, 1920. The process whereby this benign change was effected was simplicity itself. The convert, being persuaded to forswear his life of shame, celebrated his new and passionate devotion to the true, the beautiful and the good by playing Judas to his former companions in evil-doing. He told everything he knew—and he knew much. Within a few hours after his long-delayed but earnest adhesion to the hosts of light one citizen of more or less prominence was apprehended by the watch, along with 180 quarts, and warrants were out for many others. The appalling news that a man thitherto considered perfectly reliable, honorable and trustworthy had suddenly become a Christian spread swiftly throughout the town, and bootleggers, gamblers and too-complaisant ladies stood not upon the order of their going, but went at once. In the twinkling of an eye, almost, Raleigh was so thoroughly sterilized morally that it is doubtful that liquor would have been sold to a justice of the Supreme Court, not to mention the parching drummers in the city's hotels, and there was hardly a game of penny-ante in progress within the corporate limits.

This Great Moral Awakening, so sudden, so complete, offered a fine example of the way in which an accomplished evangelist functions. It is idle to inquire how much sterilization accomplished by Pastor Ham will continue to protect Raleigh against sin. An evangelist does not guarantee a permanent cure; he does not indeed, guarantee anything. He merely undertakes to do his darndest to scare the hell out of a given community for the time being. The task of keeping it out he then relinquishes to other hands. No doubt he earnestly wishes that they may prove equal to the task; but if they fail, he is always willing—for the usual consideration—to return and do his work all over again. Obviously, this is no labor for lily-fingered men. It calls for mental and physical robustiousness. The ranks of the orthodox clergy, products of depressing colleges and theological seminaries, supply few virtuosi of the required virulence, so evangelism is recruited mainly from professions less fastidious. When the renowned Al Jennings, of Oklahoma, came to Washington last Spring to testify before a congressional investigating committee, Eastern newspapers made much of the fact that he was originally a train-robber, then a politician, and finally an evangelist. Easterners seemed to have the idea that it was remarkable that a train-robber could become an evangelist. As a matter of fact, success in both professions depends upon precisely the same talent, to wit, ability to convince the client that instant, horrible death hangs over him, and that escape is possible only through implicit obedience to the professor's orders. The trick of terrorization that served him well as a train-robber was equally useful to Jennings as he stood at the foot of the sawdust trail.

Few of Jennings' competitors, however, have had an early training as advantageous as a career of train-robbery. Dr. Billy Sunday, no doubt, laid up a reserve of physical energy during his days upon a baseball field, but the Rev. Cyclone Mack, before he became an evangelist, was a lowly barber, and other celebrities of the profession include locomotive engineers, watchmenders, race-track touts, bartenders and drummers.[2] Several political lame ducks have heard the call within recent years, and there is even one Oxonian, but he preaches only in churches and so he can hardly qualify as the real thing.

But whatever his origin, the successful American evangelist of today —there is a tradition that a different technique obtained a generation ago—employs a method that is standardized in its essentials. He works in a specially constructed "tabernacle," or in a circus tent, because no ordinary church could hold a crowd large enough to be worth his time. His approach, as the go-getters call it, is carefully stage-managed. The meeting is usually opened by the chief of his attendants, the singer. A good singer is to the circus ballyhoo man what Duncan Phyfe was to a carpenter: he has taken the craft of the barker and developed it to something close to perfection, something akin to magic. The singer, then, with the assistance of a large choir recruited locally, proceeds with the preliminary song service. This consists of one song after another, the first two, perhaps, separated by a prayer. Sometimes the first song is an ancient and noble hymn, familiar to generations of church-goers. But that is a mere concession to convention, not properly a part of the song service at all. This consists of music of a markedly different type, occasionally tuneful, but usually monotonous and musically worthless. Commonly it is the setting for words so puerile, so utterly inane, that even a convert would realize their triviality were he to speak, not sing, them. Nevertheless, the song service, far from being foolish, is diabolically clever, considering the purpose it is intended to serve. Whatever else may characterize the music, one feature is common to all of it: the rhythm is strongly, very strongly, marked, and the tempo is quick. That is what counts.

2. Al Jennings, Billy Sunday, and Cyclone Mack: popular evangelists of the 1920s.

Consider the effect upon massed thousands of human beings, mainly morons, of chanting in time to the gestures of a magnetic leader. Words and music, indeed, might be dispensed with altogether without any loss of effectiveness. It is a reasonable assumption that the I. Q. of a crowd of college students is appreciably higher than that of any mob ever assembled in an evangelist's tent, yet it is no trick at all for cheer leaders, simply by employing a rapid, strongly marked rhythm, without words or music, to convert such a crowd into a frenzied pack, without intelligence or volition of its own, and apparently without any emotion save mere bloodlust. The singer's task is rather more delicate. Having got his mob yelling in unison, it is his business to heat it up as hot as possible without making it too hot for the evangelist to handle. Therefore, he nurses it along dextrously, watching it keenly, making the women sing one stanza and the men the next, making the people to the left of the centre aisle sing against those on the right, making the boys sing a stanza and the girls another, while the whole congregation swings in on the chorus; and finally, just at the moment when the crowd is, so to speak, cherry-red, he quickly brings the song service to a close and retires. Then the evangelist steps to the front and takes command. The salvation of souls is on.

The situation that confronts him is no ordinary one, and is not to be dealt with by ordinary means. The regular clergyman, at work in his own church, rises to address an audience soothed, not to say narcotized, by a service of prayer and praise designed to invoke the spirit of reverence. The evangelist rises to address one deliberately and skillfully incited to a state bordering on frenzy. The clergyman's congregation looks to him for the bread of life. The evangelist's is roaring for red meat. Obviously, the evangelist's sermon must be such a discourse as never rattled a stained-glass window, or resounded under a Gothic vault. Fear and rage: these are the only emotions of man under the hypnosis of the mob spirit. The evangelist sets out deliberately to arouse them: fear of hell and wrath against the wicked. In achieving the former object he follows the classical models that have come down to him from Jonathan Edwards and the other theological cavemen of the Golden Age. But for the latter, he has a technique of his own, based on a sort of burlesque of the old Roundhead diatribes against Curlilocks. It consists simply of vilifying in the most unbridled language whatever group in the community fails to meet with his transient approval.

Being human, he cannot approve, of course, that which he does not understand, and he can approve only with difficulty that which he envies. The arts and sciences, alas, stand little chance of coming within the understanding of barbers, bartenders, racetrack touts and locomotive engineers, or even within that of drummers and train-robbers. It is easily comprehensible, also, that even a modest degree of material luxury is capable of arousing their bitter envy. Thus, it is by no means to be taken for granted that they are playing the hypocrite when they assail furiously the better educated and more civilized folks of the community they address. Doubtless they are sincerely convinced that a man who can and does read a French book, pay money for opera tickets, and unblushingly confesses that Discobolus delights him, is certainly damned as an enemy of God and the People. But it is equally plain that the language of a barber-shop Jeremiah rebuking sin is not precisely the sort that would be countenanced and encouraged in a young ladies' seminary. The evangelist's conception of a sinful act is usually the sort of adventure that may be reasonably expected to result in lues, delirium tremens or a jail sentence, and his denunciation of it is not less gross than his concept. But lurid, blasphemous, scurrilous and occasionally downright obscene as that denunciation sometimes becomes, it fails to strike harshly upon the consciousness of the hearers, for their sensitiveness has been deadened by the singer's preliminary greasing. They have been carefully and skillfully prepared to receive just that sort of dose, and they take it avidly. You cannot judge the sermon by reading it; the effect as it is delivered is entirely different. Has not your sainted maiden aunt, seduced into attendance at a football game, been known to nod approvingly when the fat alumnus, sitting in front of her in the roaring stands, swore like a pirate when somebody fumbled the ball? The effect upon her was entirely different from that of precisely the same language, employed by the ashman when he got a hot clinker in his shoe.

Your aunt, however, speedily recovers from her debauch because she recognizes it as a debauch, a mere interruption of her routine of life, not part of its serious business. Therein she differs from the voluptuaries of the sacred tent; they do not recover quickly. They remain under the spell for days and weeks, sometimes for months on end. Not infrequently they are filled with a self-righteous officiousness that makes them public nuisances, and a sullen hatred of their unevangelized neighbors that makes them public menaces. Impressionable children, caught in one of these orgies, may never recover; many a proud American freeman has gone through life a psychic cripple, his self-confidence blasted and his intelligence withered by the curse put upon him in infancy by some yelling warlock whose very name he has forgotten.

The tremendous effectiveness of these evangelistic operations in the hinterland is due, of course, to the fact that they have relatively little competition. The South and the Middle West are the two most fertile fields for evangelists, and both sections are notoriously ill-provided with decent public amusements. For the same reason the Ku Klux Klan flourishes in the same regions. The drab monotony of existence demands some relief. If the poverty and sparseness of the population make it impossible to support theatres and concert halls, and if the communal *mores* prohibit horse-racing, cock-fighting and dancing, the range of emotional outlets is sharply restricted. Evangelism furnishes one—and that one is the public making of war medicine. The evangelist, in the last analysis, is the eternal Medicine Man. The roll of the tom-tom in the Congo jungles, the rhythm of the Hopi snakedancers' stampings and yells—these he makes use of, but slightly modified, in his preliminary song-service. His own ceremonial dress, of course, he has altered. The necklace of shark's teeth, the girdle of human skulls, the festoons of phalanges and metatarsal bones and the coat of white paint he has had to abandon. But he whoops and dances in the old, ecstatic way, and to the same end that his colleagues in the jungle have always danced and whooped—the propitiation of the tribal deity and incitation of the braves to a proper pitch of fury against the enemies of the tribe.

It would be a foolish and mistaken judgment, however, to infer from the fact that he is only a witch-doctor with clothes on that the evangelist is exclusively, or even primarily, an evil influence. It seems more than probable that witch-doctors, as a class, have never received justice from publicists, because practically all the reports of their activities that have come to us have been made by persons whom they have felt bound by conscience to oppose—explorers, missionaries, commanders of expeditionary forces, and other such alien agitators and revolutionaries. If the truth were told, no doubt it would be found that Gagool was not only a sincere conservative, but one of the most powerful agencies for law enforcement and one of the stoutest supports of the existing system in all the region round about King Solomon's mines. Certainly it is true that the evangelist's work tends toward the suppression of such evils as spread syphilis and cirrhosis of the liver, fractured skulls and involuntary bankruptcy. By providing bored communities with a better show attended by less personal danger, it tends also to discourage lynching. By exhausting the honest workman's capacity for emotion of any sort it tends to discourage strikes, as astute cotton manufacturers in the South have discovered.

But against these high services to humanity are to be written down the facts that the evangelist frequently sows factional strife and discord in the communities he visits, makes life a burden for Christians of the Roman communion, and hurts business for the Israelites. In fact, a town driven *juramentado* by an evangelist is a highly uncomfortable place of residence for any but a Fundamentalist until the effects of the hasheesh have worn off. There is also the less practical, but, to some people, highly important additional consideration that he employs the name of Christianity to describe what is essentially a purely demoniac religion. There are Christians who can forgive all else save the use of the name of the Nazarene to preach hatred, bigotry and all uncharitableness. Not a few of them are orthodox clergymen who see in the goatish gambolings of the hedge-priests the destruction of their labor of years. But of one charge frequently brought against him the evangelist can be acquitted. He is not a hypocrite. Contrary to a somewhat wide-spread belief, Mr. Pecksniff cannot long put it over *hoi polloi* if *hoi polloi* can actually see and hear him. You can fool all of the people some of the time, and educated people, perhaps, all the time, but you cannot fool the riffraff all the time. You may get away with one harangue, or two but not with a series delivered daily for six weeks. Like Harold Bell Wright,[3] the evangelist must believe his own stuff, or he can't put it across. If you doubt that, try it some time.

The witch-doctor, to be sure, seldom believes in all his own tricks. But he does believe in the fundamental theory of the thing, and his American colleague believes likewise in the fantastically horrible idol whose savage gospel he preaches. He is on excellent terms with that idol. When He so far forgets Himself as to send a thunderstorm to interrupt the services, the evangelist does not hesitate to bawl Him out, although of course in a polite way. So believing, he is perhaps as near to perfect happiness as it is given to mortals to attain. He is well-paid—it is the poor evangelist who cannot pull down $500 a week while he is working—for no more distasteful labor than bullying his audiences and abusing people he dislikes, and in addition to the cash his work assures him a harp, a crown, and a mansion on high when his labors on earth are ended.

3. Harold Bell Wright, minister and author of popular novels.

# The Horrible South

In the *Virginia Quarterly Review* of January 1935 Johnson announces that what he had prophesied in 1923 in "The Congo, Mr. Mencken" had indeed turned out to be true: Southern literature had become violent, grotesque, gothic. The "beat of the tom-toms" was loud and clear in writers such as William Faulkner, Thomas Wolfe, T. S. Stribling, and Erskine Caldwell.

Far back in the Dawn Age—*circa* 1924—the lamented *Reviewer*, of Richmond, published an article relating to the development of belles-lettres in the South which ended with this passage:

> North Carolina a few years ago produced one immortal whose works are not included in "The Library of Southern Literature"; yet Miss Peterson—for such was her name—in her "Vision" produced two lines that I will set up against the best of that J. Gordon Cooglar [sic] so enthusiastically admired by Mr. Mencken. They read:
>
> I seen Pa coming, stepping high,
> Which was of his walk the way.
>
> He who has the vision to see Southern literature coming at all—and I profess to have it—needs must see it stepping high, for that is of its walk the way. It could not be otherwise. It has the pulse of the tom-toms in its veins, the scents of the jungle in its nostrils, and the flaming colors of the jungle in its eyes. It will be colorful beyond belief; instead of a discreet *maquillage* it will come wearing smears of paint like a witch-doctor. It may be outlandish, but it will not be monotonous. It may be gorgeously barbaric, but it will not be monotonous. For all I know, it may be in some manifestations tremendously evil—it may wallow in filth, but it will not dabble in dirt.

Regarded merely as a specimen of English prose this, I must admit, has little to recommend it; but regarded as prophecy, I submit that it is what our modern *précieuses* term a lallapaloosa. Mark you, this was written before many Americans were aware of the existence of such people as Laurence Stallings, Paul Green, Julia Peterkin, Frances New-

Copyright © 1935 by the *Virginia Quarterly Review* and reprinted with permission.

man, DuBose Heyward, Thomas Wolfe, ~~William Faulkner~~, Erskine
Caldwell, or even T. S. Stribling, for although Mr. Stribling had pub-
lished several novels, "Teeftallow" was still two years in the future.
Mr. James Branch Cabell, Miss Ellen Glasgow, Miss Mary Johnston,
and Mr. Irvin S. Cobb very nearly constituted the full list of living
Southerners whose fiction was read beyond the Potomac. Thomas Nelson Page, Joel Chandler Harris, and George W. Cable were as dead as
Edgar Allan Poe. Here and there a lonely scholar, such as Archibald
Henderson or Ulrich B. Phillips, was breaking into print with a volume
of history, criticism, or biography. Hervey Allen, living then in Charleston, had won a prize with "The Blindman" and had set Heyward and
Josephine Pinckney to singing, while occasional pipings were heard
from the direction of John Crowe Ransom, in Tennessee, William Alexander Percy, in Mississippi, and John McClure, in New Orleans. Granting that these were good people; granting that one or two of them even
touched greatness, and that several others have become much more
significant in the last decade, can any rational man maintain that their
work in 1924 bore any obvious relation to the characteristic Southern
literature of 1935? Yet if you admit that it did not then you must admit
that the prophet quoted above did a really remarkable bit of prophesying.

Whereat I modestly rise and take a bow. For I wrote that article in the
Reviewer.

But having made an honest confession so far, I might as well strain
honesty a little further and admit that when I wrote, I never dreamed of
anything like "God's Little Acre" or even "The Hard-Boiled Virgin."[1]
Nobody has been more astonished than I have at the trend Southern
writing has taken since Emily Clark fled to infidel parts and The Reviewer yielded up the ghost. Nobody expected less than I the development of a situation in which it is left to Mr. Joseph Hergesheimer, of
Pennsylvania, to write of Southern swords and roses, while the Cava-
liers and their ladies apply themselves assiduously to loving delineations
of hell and damnation, and little else.[2]

Oh, yes, of course I have heard of Herbert Ravenel Sass and "Peter
Ashley" and James Boyd and Roark Bradford and Stark Young.[3] Nor

1. *God's Little Acre* (1933), Erskine Caldwell's satirical novel treating poor whites in
Georgia; *The Hard-Boiled Virgin* (1926), a satire by Frances Newman at the expense of
Southern womanhood.

2. Emily Clark, editor of the *Reviewer*, an iconoclastic little magazine in Richmond,
1921–24; Joseph Hergesheimer, Pennsylvania author of historical novels.

3. Herbert Ravenel Sass, Charleston novelist, journalist, and historian of South Carolina; *Peter Ashley* (1932), a novel by DuBose Heyward; James Boyd, historical novelist
from North Carolina; Roark Bradford, Southern journalist, novelist, and short-story writer

do I yield to any in my admiration of the delicate, yet powerful, artistry of Ellen Glasgow. Indeed, for sheer excellence of craftsmanship I believe—and I say it with a sidelong glance at Mr. Cabell—that "The Romantic Comedians"[4] takes rank above any other novel that has come out of the South in my lifetime. Of course, if you were to push me into a corner with "Jurgen" I might take refuge in the technicality that "Jurgen" is described by its author as a biography; but I am sure you are too polite to press the issue. All these people, however, are outside the main current of Southern writing. The point will be granted without question as regards Mr. Cabell, who never has been in any current; but I think it is equally true of the others. Above the Potomac and west of the Mississippi, at any rate, the impression is general that the characteristic Southerners are the horror-mongers.

This is bitter medicine for conservative Confederates and many of them refuse to swallow it. Dixie is full of spirited old women of both sexes who decline to recognize any merit in men and women who have scandalized them. Indeed, it is safe to say that if the Southerners who are now attracting most attention had been restricted to their sales in the South, they would never have survived. But that is true of Miss Glasgow and Mr. Cabell as it was true of Thomas Nelson Page and Joel Chandler Harris. "She never was much given to literature" remains among the truest words ever spoken of the South. If the condition needs correction, it is not for the benefit of the authors; as long as they can sell to the benighted Yankees, they will do very well. It is the South itself that loses when it fails to pay careful attention to these people.

For, difficult as it is for the old women to believe it, they do not write that way merely because they are full of original sin. One man might, or two, but not a whole school. They set down what they see, or what they honestly think they see, around them; and if what they see is dreadful, it is for the South to look to it. The mere advertisement of our defects is not a fault—on the contrary, it is a virtue, for a man does not emit agonized yells unless he is hurt. There are men who have walked through some of the scenes described in "Sanctuary" without turning a hair, but William Faulkner screamed until he curdled the blood of half the country. Who is the more civilized, Faulkner or the men who were never horrified by a real lynching half as much as they were by his

---

whose best work dealt with Negro life; Stark Young, Mississippi-born novelist and drama critic, author of *So Red the Rose*.

4. *The Romantic Comedians* (1926), Ellen Glasgow's satirical novel set in a city resembling Richmond; *Jurgen* (1919), James Branch Cabell's controversial and highly acclaimed novel.

description of one? When is the South more civilized—when its young men view its horrors impassively, or when they are so revolted that they howl until the continent rings again?

Perhaps, though, our genuine conservative Confederate would describe his sorrow's crown of sorrow not as anything the men have done, but as what the ladies are doing to themselves. Without doubt, the Southern lady has suffered much at the hands of her sisters within the past decade. Ellen Glasgow began the work of demolition long ago; with a smile and a scalpel she has been operating relentlessly for many years. But just about ten years ago Frances Newman went to work with a yell and a poker. The walloping she gave "The Hard-Boiled Virgin" stands as one of the most magnificent tantrums in all literature. The South was properly shocked, and closed its eyes to the inconvenient fact that if the Southern lady under attack had been stuffed with anything but sawdust, Frances could never have knocked her to pieces so easily.

As a matter of fact there is, or there was, a Southern lady whom Newman's shafts never touched. This lady literally had everything—grace, dignity, intelligence shot through with humor, astounding endurance, a spice of malice, and a courage that might have put Bayard to shame. But she was not a product of the ante-bellum South. She was the woman who was a young girl during, or shortly after, the Civil War; and far from being a hot-house flower, her existence was about as sheltered as that of Molly Pitcher, who served the gun at Monmouth. Southern women were not sheltered from 1865 to 1880. On the contrary, like the ladies of doubtful reputation in Scripture—but in a very different sense—their "feet took hold on hell." The South, between 1865 and 1880, had no room for hot-house flowers. It was a storm-beaten land, a land of blood and fire. Even the most privileged of its women in those days were intimately acquainted with the three great verities, poverty and love and war; and any one of them who survived at all, survived because she was a harder-boiled virgin than anything that Frances Newman's heroine ever imagined. Perhaps she had never heard of the Freudian *libido*, but in dealing with the newly-liberated blacks she learned plenty about rape, incest, and sadism. In the course of time, though, her hair grew white and her once erect spine bowed under the weight of years. She mellowed and refined into an appearance of great daintiness and fragility, and it took much more than casual observation to detect the truth that under her frail exterior she was all whipcord and steel. The dear old ladies in lace caps became the ideal of Southern womanhood, and a great many women who had not been tempered in the furnace heats of Reconstruction assumed the rôle of Southern ladies.

Unfortunately, though, the appearance was nothing and the temper was everything. A generation of "Southern ladies" grew up that were not Damascus blades, and not even good, honest Barlow knives, but brummagem goods unable to withstand any real test. Nevertheless, so strong was the tradition, they were accepted for a long time as the real thing, in the South. It is this sort of "Southern lady" that Ellen Glasgow has dissected and Frances Newman has mangled. Perhaps the ablest inquiry ever conducted into her genesis, etiology, and pathology is in a book to which too little attention has been paid in the South, Sara Haardt's "The Making of a Lady."[5] Haardt, however, has ignored the first rule of dramatization, which is to magnify everything by ten diameters; her book, as a result, is too calm, dispassionate, and accurate in its reporting to command much attention, and her too-quiet voice has been largely ignored.

Newman, however, was too loud to be ignored. Even if the South had been able to pass her by with a sniff, it would have done no good; for the benighted Yankees instantly and gleefully recognized her lovely nymphomaniac as, feature for feature, the very "Southern lady" to whom they had been introduced during the last twenty years. The benighted Yankees had rarely encountered the real thing, for the Southern lady who was really great and wonderful, and who established the title as a thing to command the reverence and admiration of every manful Southern man, was usually too poor and too busy to travel until she grew too old to travel. Consequently, the female Southerners who have invaded the North carrying the name of Southern ladies have too frequently been cheap little tarts really much below the level of Katharine Faraday, who was dignified to a certain extent by her intellectual curiosity. This is the sort of thing we find it difficult to acknowledge. It is much easier and more satisfactory to attribute the slight esteem in which the rest of the country holds the "Southern lady" to prejudice. It is much easier to attribute all unfavorable opinion to prejudice. But it is also false and idiotic.

It is certainly not my purpose to try to start a cult of Newman worshippers. The truth is, I never liked the woman's work; its finish is too hard and glossy. But she was important if only as a reminder to the world that the South still produces not "ladies" only, but also women equipped with intelligence, energy, courage, and resolution. She deserves better things of her native section than the denunciations that the scandal-mongers of Atlanta have heaped upon her.

Julia Peterkin has fared somewhat better. After all, contrary to popu-

---

5. *The Making of a Lady* (1931), novel of Southern life by Sara Haardt (Mrs. H. L. Mencken).

lar opinion in some sections, literate Southerners do read the newspapers, and practically everybody below the Potomac knows that Julia Peterkin once won the Pulitzer Prize. So, while some of us may cherish the suspicion that Mrs. Peterkin's books are not as ladylike as they might be, still we regard her as important enough to be introduced to Governors. There is a delicious story of how a flustered secretary, ignoring her protests, once dragged her up to an Excellency and presented her as "the author of that magnificent book 'Porgy'." And when the novelist, aghast, murmured that unfortunately the honor was not hers, but belonged to Mr. DuBose Heyward, the unabashed secretary straightened it out with the explanation, "Well, Mrs. Peterkin has written—ah—well, Mrs. Peterkin has written *something*!"

I have always cherished a suspicion that this lady was remarkably right. Mrs. Peterkin has not only written something, but it may be argued plausibly that it is something that ought not to be mentioned to Governors of Southern States. For Governing is a practical business. Governors should be men of action. And what, pray, can a Governor do about "Scarlet Sister Mary"? Or "Black April"? Or "Green Thursday"? There is something to be said for the theory that the minds of public officials, like those of young children, should be protected from too early and too intimate acquaintance with the Facts of Life. For when a Governor has heard what Julia Peterkin has to say of the pain and frailty, the poignant humanity of black people struggling in the clutch of circumstance, he is likely to develop an enfeebling skepticism of the hangman's noose and the penitentiary bars as effective social agencies. Yet without liberal use of these agencies it is probable that the business of governing the bi-racial South would be even worse conducted than it is now.

Peterkin, DuBose Heyward, and Paul Green exemplify the method of the new school of Southern writers in dealing with the Negro. Stribling, Faulkner, Wolfe, and Caldwell concern themselves with the black man only incidentally; and with Howard W. Odum, writing about the Negro is an avocation.

The case of Dubose Heyward is peculiarly interesting because his work, like that of Robert Louis Stevenson, represents a triumph of acute observation and—if I dare employ an outmoded phrase in the presence of the new psychology—intuitive insight. Mrs. Peterkin has managed Negro servants all her life, and has observed field-hands in the country. Green has worked, and worked with, Negro farmers from his youth up. Odum, too, knows the farm and country Negroes. But Heyward is not only an aristocrat, but a city man at that. His acquaintance with the Negro has been confined almost entirely to observation of city types, and if there is one thing about the blacks on which all Southerners are agreed, it is that the town Negro is psychologically far more complicated and difficult to comprehend than the unspoiled primitive of the fields.

Nevertheless, the perfection of detail in "Porgy" has rarely, if ever, been excelled by any white man writing about Negroes; and at the same time this intense realism has been successfully combined with a poetic treatment that makes an essentially squalid and blood-curdling melodrama emerge as a glittering and exquisite romance. The sea-change that Stevenson worked upon cut-throats, the American has worked on the dwellers in Negro slums. Obviously Heyward's strength and his weakness alike are attributable to the fact that he is a poet, and a good one. The magic that informs "Carolina Chansons" gleams in all his books, making "Porgy" great, ruining "Angel," popularizing "Mamba's Daughters," and completely depopularizing "Peter Ashley." Doubtless the relative failure of "Ashley" is due to the fact that it was mistaken for a novel because it looks like one; whereas it is in reality DuBose Heyward's finest poem, written without rhyme or meter because it needs neither.

There is no finer English style in the South than Heyward's; there is no keener eye, no more discerning mind than his; there is no more honest and truthful writer. And yet I hesitate to set him up as the most important man who has emerged in the region within the last ten years. For he is not only a poet, but a lyricist. He is William Morris' necromancer, who can conjure up outside every window a vision of delight,

> While still, unheard, but in its wonted way,
> Piped the drear wind of that December day.

He can evoke Paradise, but he cannot, or he will not, raise hell; and that is both his strength and his weakness.

Paul Green can, but he always does it *à la manière de* somebody or other. The result is that while he is a triple-threat man, he has remained more or less a threat. He is a good dramatist, but Heyward is better. He is a good scenario writer, but Stallings[6] is better. He is a good storyteller, but several other Southerners are more popular, and Wolfe, at least, is more powerful. Yet there isn't a more sincere, conscientious, and courageous artist in the South. Green has been deprecated as being too derivative. I don't believe it. His ideas are not library ideas, smelling of the lamp. He derives from the soil of North Carolina, and no-

6. Laurence Stallings, Southern journalist and playwright, author (with Maxwell Anderson) of *What Price Glory?* (1924).

where else. Yet the fact remains that he has not struck the imagination
of the public as several essentially lighter men have done. To the observer his seems to be a hobbled talent, obviously capable of far greater
things than it has actually achieved. What is the impediment? Certainly
not lack of honesty, or courage, or energy; or the presence of emotional
anemia. Probably it is based on too much respect for his betters. He has
read too much, and understood too well the excellence of what he read.
He knows exactly how Sophocles did it, and he is incapable of imagin-
ing that there are any circumstances under which Paul Green could do it
better than Sophocles. But, as a matter of fact, there are. Occasionally
Green lights on a theme for which there are no precedents, so he is
compelled to use his own judgment. For example, he published in
Harper's a few months ago a sketch called "Fine Wagon"—relating
how a Negro teamster gloried in his recently-acquired wagon, which
broke down at the first test. It was extremely slight, but it told more
about the real Negro problem than can be found in fifteen pounds of
sociological investigations of race relations. As for its artistic quality,
well, in half a dozen pages it presented man contending with destiny—
pride prostrated by its own absurdity, love helpless to aid the beloved,
aspiration defeated by the aspirant's own faults, hope doomed from the
start. It was so perfectly the tragedy of human existence that for three
months I have been striving earnestly to forget the cursed thing, and
finding it as irrepressible as Banquo's ghost. But it owes nothing to
Sophocles. It is art in North Carolina, not in Athens.

There is no more enigmatic figure among Southern writers than
Howard W. Odum. He is a sociologist by trade and a novelist only on
the side, so to speak. On my desk as I write is a pamphlet he recently issued on regional planning for some learned society in California. The
second sentence in it reads:

> To the extent that propositions submitted may constitute
> evidence in support of these premises they may be considered
> as hypotheses basic to the conclusions which follow.

Well, now, I ask you—could Herbert Hoover beat it? Yet the man
knows English. Not only does he speak it fluently, but he writes it with
extraordinary effectiveness. You may think I lie, but this is the very
man who, in "Rainbow Round My Shoulder," caught the essence of a
Negro vagrant's speech, caught and fixed on the printed page one of the
most elusive cadences known, caught and preserved its caesuras, its
syncopations, its retarded beats, all its queer, shuffling, light-hearted
rhythm. As an artistic *tour de force* it is amazing; but not more amazing
than the English that Howard Odum turns out when he lapses into the

sociologist again. However, it is as creative critic more than creative artist that Odum has figured importantly in the revival of letters in the South. He has to an extraordinary degree the faculty of stimulating others to work. In the brave days before 1932, when a panic-stricken Legislature wrecked the public school system of North Carolina and murdered the State University outright at the behest of a combination of farmers and industrialists tired of paying taxes, Odum was one of the galaxy of scholars who made the village of Chapel Hill the intellectual capital of the Confederacy. Since that time more than two-score of his colleagues have fled the devastated region for their livings, if not their lives, but Odum hangs on. It is encouraging to believe that his work is not yet done—that he may still write something other than sociological treatises, and still spur others on to write well.

Yet, the people thus far considered all together have not done as much to establish in the North and West a certain reputation for Southern writing as has been accomplished by four men, to wit, T. S. Stribling, Thomas Wolfe, William Faulkner, and Erskine Caldwell. These are the real equerries of Raw-Head-and-Bloody-Bones, these are the merchants of death, hell, and the grave, these are the horror-mongers-in-chief. These are they who drive the conservative Confederates into apoplexy.

And these lads, if you must have it, have very nearly been too much for me. If I have seemed to speak disparagingly of Southerners who dislike this quartet, candor compels the admission that I am not much better. I make no boasts of my physical prowess in other respects, but I have always cherished the belief that I have a right strong stomach; yet perusal of the works of these four has shown me very definitely that there are limits beyond which I dare not go. Yet, despite the queasiness which they have caused a great many of us, is it not clear to every Southerner who has paused to give the matter real consideration that each of these has made a contribution to the advancement of civilization in the South? Take Mr. Stribling, for example. Year before last he won the Pulitzer Prize with a novel warranted to make any conservative Confederate gag; more than that, it was the second member of a trilogy, of which the first was almost as appalling and the third was worse; and more than that, as early as 1926 he had stripped the hides off our much-coddled mountaineers in "Teeftallow." A rough and obnoxious fellow this, beyond a doubt; and yet "The Forge," "The Store," and "Unfinished Cathedral" were the very antidote needed for too much Thomas Nelson Page. The original Page, I still think, was an artist of high attainments; but his excellencies had been copied to a nauseous excess.

It is an undeniable fact that in forty-odd years nearly all spent in the

South I have rarely seen anybody as vile as everybody is in Mr. Stribling's books; but then I have rarely seen anybody as noble as everybody is in Mr. Page's books. The fact is that there is no realism in either; they are both great romanticists, only Mr. Page took his out in loving and Mr. Stribling his in hating. Nevertheless, since we had had Page, Stribling was an absolute necessity if we were to regain something like balance. And to my mind, every Southerner who has read the earlier novelist is under an obligation to read the later one. In "Unfinished Cathedral" he has performed the immensely important service of reminding us that if we dig around the foundations of every great fortune, in the South as elsewhere, we are pretty sure to release stenches that are beyond all credibility. Money in great piles is acquiring far too much sanctity in the South; if Stribling helps release us from the evil spell of millions, is he not a laborer worth his hire? With all the noisome odors he has released, he is a sign of health; for we have no right to shut our eyes when Colonel Miltiades Vaiden comes by simply because Colonel Carter of Cartersville is handsomer.

Thomas Wolfe fired one broadside and then fell silent—at least until this spring: a new book by him is announced as this is written. But he need do no more. "Look Homeward, Angel" is enough to justify half a dozen lives. I admit that the book is full of faults and flaws; but remember, my lords and gentlemen, so is "Don Quixote," so is "David Copperfield," so is "Les Misérables"; and the defects of Wolfe's huge tome are of the same order, that is to say, the defects of overabundant vitality, of too tremendous an internal pressure, of too mighty a struggle for expression. It is full of confusion, but it arises from the swirl of too many ideas all trying to reach expression at once, not from futile groping for any idea at all. It carries too great a spate of words, but that is due to its headlong rush, not to idling and dilly-dallying along the way. It is roaring and cacophonous, not dulcet, but is it reasonable to expect Polyphemus in his agony to flute sweetly?

Here, at any rate, is size. Wolfe's book may deserve any or all of a dozen derogatory adjectives, but no one can call it petty. And the South has needed size. She has produced many graceful men—Page and Cable come to mind at once—and occasionally she brings forth such a sinewy fellow as Cabell; hearty bucks on the order of Cobb and O. Henry[7] she has known fairly frequently; but the sober, unflattering truth is that her average product is of lesser stature than these—not a man, but a mannikin. I have never seen Mr. Wolfe in the flesh; for aught I

7. O. Henry (William Sydney Porter), popular short-story writer of early twentieth century; Irvin S. Cobb, Kentucky journalist and humorist of early twentieth century.

know to the contrary, he may stand five feet two in his socks and wear a thirteen collar; but as an artist he is shod with number twelve brogans and swings John Henry's sledgehammer.

His protest is not against the machinations of what General Hugh Johnson would call "slight men."[8] The devilment of bankers and industrialists and politicians and the reverend clergy does not worry, or even interest, him. He roars against the immortal gods. He girds at Fate, he grapples and goes to the mat with Destiny. They talk about the baneful effect of his long study of Greek on his style, but the fact is he has brought Greek tragedy into the lives of the hill people of North Carolina. And in so doing he has touched them with a new dignity, a larger significance. He has frightened them, enraged them, depressed them, grieved them; but he has also established a link between them and the mighty past; and who can deny that this Greek has come bearing a gift that may be terrible, but is royal, too?

Some say that William Faulkner, when he wrote his two most celebrated books, was indulging in the exercise known among purists as kidding. Certainly there is no discoverable plan or purpose in "As I Lay Dying" or in "Sanctuary." And Mr. Faulkner has come to an untimely end, apparently having gone respectable in the very flower of his life. But if his motive remains obscure, his accomplishment is as plain as a pikestaff. It may be true that, having written two or three pretty good books which created not even a ripple of interest, he determined to jar the natives off their perch at any cost, simply as revenge on their complacency. At any rate, he did it. I am one who yawned over "Dracula" and was never able to finish it; I have read books about the interesting rites of the South Sea cannibals, and eaten hog jowls and cabbage right heartily immediately thereafter; I have even dipped into "Untrodden Paths of Anthropology" with only a few mild shudders. But "Sanctuary" put me under the weather for thirty-six hours. Never a conservative Confederate of the lot, never a simpering old woman of either sex, was any more profoundly shocked.

But the shock has worn off, while a profound admiration of the cleverness of this artist in horror remains. There is a page in "Sanctuary" which mentions no murder, or rape, or lynching, or sexual degeneracy, or blood, or ordure, but which sticks in my mind as the most devilishly brilliant passage in the book. It is nothing more than a description of a group of college students on a train; but the casual, almost inadvertent, way in which the author reveals the smallness of

8. Hugh S. Johnson, colorful soldier and author, administrator of the National Recovery Act under Franklin D. Roosevelt.

their souls, the pettiness of their minds, the damnable worthlessness of the whole lot, makes tremendous writing. However, even in its less subtle horrors, "Sanctuary" has done well for the South in revealing the fact that there are rotting spots in our civilization that are capable of producing things so revolting that the mind recoils from their contemplation. Does that discovery do us any good? Well, it depends on whether we feel strongly enough about it to do something. The novelist has done his part.

Mr. Erskine Caldwell, evidently, is a much more solemn fellow than Mr. Faulkner. His horrors are by no means so incomprehensible, and his reaction to them is very purposeful. But the monstrosities he dredges up from Southern social depths are even more frightful, for they lack the aura of unreality that hangs about the Faulkner books. One sees here the direct and appalling results of a slipshod social and economic system, the final effect of that rugged individualism which some of us have been foolish enough to praise. Old Jeeter Lester, of "Tobacco Road," is no such emanation from the Pit as Popeye, but he is a much more sharp reproach to American civilization; while Ty-Ty, of "God's Little Acre," is the ruin of a man indeed.

It is true that Mr. Caldwell tills a field that is both narrow and barren. One soul may be as precious as another in the sight of God, but in the sight of history what happens to the half-wits has not often had an appreciable effect on the fate of nations. The destiny of the South, as far as the measurable future is concerned, is being worked out in the Stribling, rather than in the Caldwell, stratum of society. As far as social effectiveness is concerned, Mr. Caldwell is for the most part wasting a fine talent; but his artistic effectiveness is great enough to create beauty in the most unlikely places—to spread an iridescent shimmer over the slime.

These, it seems to me, are the people who have played the leading rôles in the pageant of Southern letters. Of course they are not the only Southerners who are doing good work; all the way from Lizette Woodworth Reese, in Maryland, to those excellent yarn-spinners, Maristan Chapman,[9] in their new home in Florida, one finds able people scattered about. But they are not under the big top. The performance that all the rest of the world regards as the main show in the South lists on its program Popeye and Ty-Ty, Colonel Miltiades Vaiden and Oliver Gant, Porgy, Scarlet Sister Mary, Black Ulysses, Abraham McRae, and Kath-

---

9. Lizette Woodworth Reese, popular Baltimore poet; Maristan Chapman (Mary and Stanley Chapman), pseudonym for a husband-wife team who produced sentimental novels set in the Southern mountains.

arine Faraday.[10] "The pulse of the tom-toms in its veins, the scents of the jungle in its nostrils . . . colorful beyond belief . . . wearing smears of paint like a witch-doctor . . . outlandish but . . . not monotonous, . . . gorgeously barbaric, but . . . not monotonous." That was written in 1924, but I think I'll let it stand—yes, I'll let it stand.

Furthermore, having provided myself with a gas-mask in case of another "Sanctuary" or "God's Little Acre," I find myself able to swell with patriotic pride as the show proceeds. Do you demur, on the ground that it is a horrible South these novelists are parading before us? Then you are looking at it with blind eyes. You are seeing only the lame, the halt, and the blind; the morons, the perverts, the idiots, the murders, the satyriasis and nymphomania, the lust and lues. You are overlooking the horror and pity these things have aroused in some of the best minds of the South. You are overlooking the burning indignation that such things should be in the land we love, and the fierce determination that the South shall see at any cost, shall see although her soul is sickened, shall see in spite of a thick crust of prejudice, hypocrisy, laziness, arrogance, and fear; shall stand, like Faust, and for her own soul's salvation, gaze into perdition. And you are overlooking the towering compliment to the South implicit in these people's belief that if she sees, she will act.

The horrible South was the South that was morally, spiritually, and intellectually dead. The South that fatuously regarded every form of art, literature included, as a pretty toy, but in no sense one of the driving forces of civilization—that was the horrible South. The ghastly, cadaverous South that for forty years after the Civil War groped in the twilight region between civilization and barbarism was a figure of horror; and yet more horrible was the South that began to grow fat at the turn of the century, and that through prosperous years grew fatter and fatter, especially in the head, until it seemed likely that both her brain and her heart were doomed to drown in her own grease. The South whose young women were silent except for giggles, and whose young men were silent except for brays—that was a horrible South.

But a South full of bitter, muscular men with swords—that may be alarming, but it isn't horrible. A young man who raves and curses with the voice of Stentor and venom of Jeremiah, may be described by any number of adjectives, but no rational man will intimate that he is dead. If a good deal of the South's recent literature stinks—and in my opinion it does—it is with the odors of the barnyard, not those of the charnel-

10. Fictional characters in works by William Faulkner, Erskine Caldwell, T. S. Stribling, Thomas Wolfe, DuBose Heyward, Julia Peterkin, Howard W. Odum, and Frances Newman.

house. The pretty literature of thirty years ago had a different smell; it reeked of tuberoses, funeral flowers. An undertaker's parlor, banked with floral designs, smells sweeter than a compost-heap; but death is in the midst of one, and the promise of a golden harvest in the other.

If I believed that the horror-mongers were the South's last word, I might be as deeply chagrined as anyone. But they are not. On the contrary, they are almost the first, but they will be far from the last Southerners to grapple courageously and vigorously with the problems of the modern South. And the grappling is the thing of importance, not the incidental noise. Dixie, far from standing aghast, ought to hail this uproar with the triumphant shout of the Father broadcasting the return of his Prodigal Son; for her youth "was dead and is alive again, was lost and is found."

# That Newest of New Souths

# Greensboro, or What You Will

Perhaps Johnson's finest examination of New South boosterism and Babbittry, this essay appeared in the *Reviewer* (April 1924). The city he describes is Greensboro, but it could be Roanoke, Spartanburg, or any other emerging Southern city of which it might be said: "There is no God but Advertising, and Atlanta is his prophet." The essay shows how greatly the Southern Agrarians were in error when they found Johnson an uncritical advocate of progress.

This is a chant of the city that is to be, and you may name it what you please—Charlotte, or Raleigh, or Winston-Salem in North Carolina, Greenville or Spartanburg if you go south, Danville or Roanoke if you go north, or any one of a hundred other names of a hundred other towns precisely like it scattered from the Potomac to Mobile Bay, from Hatteras to the Rio Grande. I name it Greensboro, North Carolina, because I am a citizen of Greensboro, and our muezzins summon us to prayer with the sacred formula, "There is no God but Advertising, and Atlanta is his prophet." Nevertheless, we are resolutely broad-minded. We gulp, and admit that there are other towns in our class known to some people besides Mr. Rand and Mr. McNally. Therefore, if it pleases you to strike out Greensboro and write in another name, by all means proceed to do so; we of Greensboro shall be secretly outraged but just to prove that we are no Mainstreeters we shall smile from the teeth out and acquiesce too heartily.

But from one thing, I pray you, refrain. Do not curl your lip because Alias Greensboro comes shouldering its way into the grave and dignified company of its elders. If the reviewer's ambition is to present a complete series of Southern types, this one cannot be neglected. The word "city" does not mean in the South Richmond, Baltimore, Charleston, New Orleans, Louisville and no more. Nor may the collection be regarded as complete if Atlanta be added. By a merciful dispensation of Providence Greensboro has never been able to imitate Atlanta as closely as it would like. It is still distinctly different, still of an independent type; and to many hundreds of thousands of Southerners the word "city" means just such a town as Greensboro. A town that may be identified by so many Southerners as their own certainly is of right to be included in any gallery of pictures of Southern cities.

Copyright © 1924 by the *Reviewer* and reprinted with permission.

O. Henry once wrote that he was born in a "a somnolent little Southern town," and in so doing a man to whose nature malevolence was foreign left to his city a legacy of bitterness. A considerable portion of Greensboro's stock in the advertising trade is O. Henry. It earnestly desires not to be ungrateful to him, but how those words "somnolent" and "little" do rankle! Greensboro is enormous, and so wide-awake that it is pop-eyed. Why, did we not have a special officer of the census bureau down last year to count us after the cotton mill villages had been taken in, and did he not report a total population of 43,525? Everyone knows it. None can escape the knowledge, except the wholly illiterate, for both the morning and evening newspapers still print the magic figures in large, black type every day. And as for alert modernity, does not a seventeen-story office building spurt up suddenly and unreasonably from the middle of town, like Memnon among the dunes singing the glory of its creators when the rays of the rising sun touch it in the morning? It is really too bad that O. Henry wrote that line, for his worshippers still come here in numbers, expecting to find a quaint Southern village, with the scent of honeysuckle and the sound of guitars filling the suave air at dusk. And they generally fail to appreciate at its true worth the progress that Greensboro has made. Some have been known to go away peevish.

Nevertheless, Greensboro is more representative of the present South than would be the somnolent little town for which these pilgrims seek in vain. Change is the breath of its nostrils, indeed the very texture of its soul. It was created by the sudden transition into an industrial region of the vast plateau that parallels the Blue Ridge from Atlanta to Lynchburg, Virginia. Here is established headquarters of one division of the new invasion of the South, which has occurred since O. Henry was a boy, and which has relegated the South that he knew to the pages of romance. Where Sherman came up and Grant came down to grind the Confederate armies between them, now Cotton and Tobacco have established their armies of occupation, and Greensboro and a long line of towns like it have sprung up with a speed comparable to the speed with which the cantonments grew in 1917.

But while the cantonments have already vanished, Greensboro will remain and nothing is more important to the South at the moment than to examine it, to inquire what manner of thing this is which has been thrust upon it, and which threatens to dominate its future. Inspection of its material phases is only too painfully easy. But whisper your inquiry, and our Chamber of Commerce will fall upon you ecstatically, snowing you under with pamphlets, casting recklessly into the air handfuls of popping statistics like Chinese firecrackers, hustling you into a motor car to exhibit to you endless miles of asphalt and endless rows of unlovely skeletons of houses in process of construction.

It is a subtler and more difficult thing to catch a glimpse of the spirit of the place. It is not the business of the Chamber of Commerce to know that such a thing exists, and such things as it is not its business to know it painstakingly forgets. It cannot possibly remember, for instance, that Greensboro has only one railroad; why even inquire of it whether or not the city has a soul?

If the inquiry were made, the inquirer would almost certainly be misdirected. He would doubtless be sent to look at one of the suburban developments, which would be pleasant, but not profitable. They are merely additions to the pamphlets, the statistics, the automobile trip about the city. True, they are delightful to visit, all smooth-shaven lawns, broad streets with parkways running along them, and handsome homes all new and shiny inside. Some of them contain books and flowers and music as well as velours and mahogany and Oriental rugs; but they all have concealed plumbing, electric washing machines and vacuum cleaners. In other words, they are both new and complete. They have arrived, and the only story connected with them is a story of achievement. Greensboro, on the other hand, is new, but it is not complete; and the only story connected with it that is worth the telling must be a story of aspiration, a story of hopes hardly formulated, of ideals dimly perceived.

They wandered down Elm street on Saturday afternoon, when the mill villages on the outskirts of the town pour their populations into Greensboro's main thoroughfare. The inadequate sidewalk swarmed with people in a hurry, but they were untroubled by the incessant bumps and shoves of speeding pedestrians on business bent. They had obviously come to take in the town, and they were taking it in, leisurely and with immense satisfaction.

He carried in his arms a child of some eighteen months. She wheeled a perambulator. First one, then the other, grasped the hand of a toddler of three and slung it along, its feet rapping the pavement staggeringly and ineffectually. His suit certainly had been purchased, some time ago, at a fire sale in New Jerusalem, down by the railroad station. His shirt might have been the cause of the fire. Her shapeless shoes, cotton lisle stockings, and dress of neutral tint were topped by a hat that reminded one of a startled hen balancing on a board fence and ready to fly at the slightest alarm. The characteristic pallor of the cotton mill operative lay upon them both. Their faces were equally vacant, but hers was pinched by a hunger not of physical food.

Their direction carried them into the stream of traffic nearest the curb, but suddenly before a shop window she turned at right angles, thrust the perambulator straight through the line of people going in the other direction without the slightest interest in the ensuing disturbance of traffic, and brought it to a halt before the sheet of plate glass. Languidly he joined her, and they stood at gaze.

The window advertised a sale of silks, and the decorator had followed the custom of fixing bolts on high and permitting the fabric to cascade to the floor in shimmering streams. The window was a riot of colour blended with artful carelessness, a debauch of loveliness, voluptuous, enticing, exquisite. It fairly cried aloud for great ladies, imperiously it demanded wonderful bodies, soft and flawless skins, perfect contours, dignity and utter grace, for which these wonderful and costly things might furnish a worthy setting.

Outside he and she stood, not enraptured, but calmly and judicially admiring; indefinitely far from suspecting the irony that might have set Olympus a-roaring; and when they soon tired of it, they moved on, having spoken only a harsh word or two to the squirming toddler.

Yet for a moment there had been a gleam in her eyes.

Greensboro is the Master Key to the South's Best Markets. If you don't believe it, ask the Chamber of Commerce. It has published a booklet saying so, and it ought to know, for that is one of the things it is supposed to know about. Perhaps you may have been deluded into believing that the master key is Danville, or Roanoke, or Winston-Salem, or Charlotte, or Raleigh, or Greenville, or Spartanburg, or Macon, or Augusta, or some other of those Southern towns that are always making preposterous claims. But it isn't. It's Greensboro. Greensboro thought of the phrase first and can prove it.

Greensboro has the biggest denim mills, and—and—and, oh, well it's all in the pamphlet. The point to remember is that Greensboro has the biggest.

Greensboro has a proud list of illustrious sons. She has named a cigar and a mattress and a hotel after O. Henry, and if Wilbur Daniel Steele[1] ever gets a big enough reputation she will doubtless name a cigar and a mattress after him. We have no new hotel to name just now.

Greensboro has many varied industries employing many thousands of workmen and the payroll amounts to so much monthly, and twelve times that in the course of a year.

---

1. Wilbur Daniel Steele, North Carolina–born novelist and short-story writer.

Greensboro, as was said of Cedar Rapids, Iowa, is equidistant from all points of the horizon and is therefore a natural distribution centre.

Greensboro has practically the same climate as North Carolina, but being thirty miles east of Winston-Salem, and ninety miles north of Charlotte, and eighty miles west of Raleigh, and fifty miles south of Danville, she is protected on all sides from blizzards, sand-storms and beating rains.

Greensboro has the absolutely unique distinction of being the third city in size in North Carolina.

Greensboro is infinitely preferable as a place of residence to New York, London, Paris, Berlin, or Vienna. I forget why, but you can find that and many more such absorbing items of information in the pamphlet.

No, that is inexact—I forget the reason given in the pamphlet, but I am well aware of many reasons for living in Greensboro that the pamphlet curiously omits. For instance, a good business man has served this city for three years as mayor without stealing a cent and without getting anything for his labour but a prolific crop of enemies. A big lawyer has spent $50,000 worth of his time trying to get—and getting—decent schoolhouses for the city's children, including the negro children. An insurance man for years has lived on half the income he might have made because half his time was taken up in a heart-breaking struggle to keep real estate brigands from putting garages in people's front yards, and in securing parks and playgrounds for the city. I might multiply instances of the kind, but these are suggestion enough.

Why do they do these difficult and profitless things? Well, they seem somehow to see, as through a glass darkly, a shimmer of magnificence in the future of this commonplace little town. They have the impression that somewhere beyond their reach, but within sight, there is such splendor, such grace and dignity and beauty as the town has never dreamed of; and arrested by the vision they stand spellbound. They allow themselves to be jostled and pushed aside by hurrying passers-by without protest, rather than turn away from the loveliness they expect never to touch. And he who strives to create unattainable beauty, regardless of his medium, has he not the artist's soul?

The irony of it is not subtle. He must be humourless indeed who fails to perceive the incongruity of Greensboro's critical appraisal of the apparel of queenly cities. I do not challenge your right to laughter who have seen her only as you passed by and have had time barely to note that she is well fed and musicless, dramaless, destitute of painting and sculpture and scantily endowed with architecture meriting a second glance. Languidly chewing gum and inspecting rich brocades woven for mistresses of empires and broad seas, she is perhaps justly an object of derision. But I pray you pardon me if I do not join in your mirth, for I am somehow not in the mood for laughter. I have seen the gleam in her eyes.

# Onion Salt

In the *Reviewer* (January 1925) Johnson advances the thesis—common enough fifty years later but rare in his day—that the South would never fully give in to American standardization, would not be absorbed by the American average. Rather, it would be the other way around: Ku Kluxism, religious fundamentalism, and white supremacy were already moving north, and the South, like onion salt, would continue to flavor the whole. This was Johnson's final essay in the *Reviewer*. In the October 1925 issue the editors promised another, an essay about Mencken to be entitled "The Gentleman With a Meat Axe." But the *Reviewer* died that autumn, and Johnson's anticipated essay, which was to discuss Mencken's contribution to Southern literature, never appeared in the *Reviewer* or any other magazine.

Pessimists who see the South as being steadily engorged and assimilated by a nation standardized to the limit have yet to establish their thesis. Absorption proceeds, but it is still a question whether the result will be a South indistinguishable from the rest of America, or an America strongly flavored with the South. Onion salt is readily absorbed, but rarely lost. One may not be able to distinguish it from the rest of the mass, but the most undiscriminating palate knows that it is there.

Certain elements of Southern civilization are so astringent or pungent that their individual savor may be detected in the farthest confines of the Republic. Notable is the bundle of emotions—the Freudians have embezzled the word "complex" and converted it to their own uses so thoroughly that it is no longer available in the general vocabulary—outwardly manifest in the Ku Klux phenomenon. The most notable victory of the Ku Klux in 1924 was won in the state of Maine. Another of the banner Ku Klux states is Oregon. The leaven of Atlanta has leavened the whole lump.

So the influence of the South spreads from within outwardly. But it is potent also to tincture with its characteristic hue invading ideas of the most uncompromising Americanism. Nothing occurred in the South in 1924 more characteristically American than the establishment by Mr. James B. Duke of a foundation endowed with $40,000,000, the interest on which is to be employed for educational and charitable purposes.

Copyright © 1925 by the *Reviewer* and reprinted with permission.

In no other country is the establishment of such foundations by men of great wealth so much the mode. The fact that a Southern multimillionaire falls in with the custom of Northern and Western multimillionaires is indisputably evidence of the similarity of Southern thinking to that of Northern and Western thinking.

And yet the Duke foundation, while generally in accord with the American tradition, is characterized by a distinctly individual feature. There were many precedents for the establishment of Duke University. There were precedents for the extensive hospitalization scheme, which will absorb a third of the funds of the foundation. The feature that is unique for a foundation of such great size is the establishment of a sort of *Congregatio De Propaganda Fide.* A tenth of the income of the foundation will be used for the erection and maintenance of Methodist Episcopal churches in rural sections of the Carolinas. Furthermore, two per cent of the total income will be used for pensioning old preachers of the same faith who have served in the conferences of North Carolina. Mr. Duke's purpose is not simply to civilize, or even to Christianize, the Carolinas. He intends to Methodize them.

Is moral certainty that rises so near to the sublime to be encountered frequently outside the South? There are Mormons in Utah and Mennonites in Pennsylvania and Dr. John Roach Straton[1] in New York, to be sure, but all three are conspicuous by reason of the striking contrast to the environment that their existence affords. Mr. Duke's concept, on the contrary, merges so perfectly into the philosophy of the South that hardly a commentator has seen anything noteworthy in it.

As long as such rigidity of conviction persists, the danger that the South will lose its individuality may be considered remote indeed. As long as its local pride is warm, its patriotism fiery and its religion incandescent, it will remain distinctively individual in a federation otherwise populated by Laodiceans. It will continue to spawn prophets and martyrs, demagogues, saints, heroes, fakirs, and religious, social and political whirling dervishes like the grasshoppers for number. It will continue to stand ready to die at the stake for its ideals and equally ready to burn negroes and non-conformists. It will at any time unhesitatingly and cheerfully march through a slaughterhouse to an open grave behind the banner of anybody named Davis.

Since the fateful day of November last, the South and Wisconsin have maintained a political party each. This state of affairs is something

1. John Roach Straton, Baptist minister, lecturer, and writer, pastor of the Calvary Baptist Church, New York City.

new and strange for Wisconsin, and it seems unlikely to last beyond the
quadrennium, but for the South it was a return to normalcy. Being
politically separate from the rest of the union has not disturbed her in
the memory of this generation. One continually hears of this movement
or that, this leader or the other, as destined to break the Solid South, but
on the morning after election day that solidity always shows up intact.
The political individuality of the section resists every effort at assimilation. The experience of more than fifty years all goes to show that if
political coalescence is to be secured, it is idle to talk of bringing the
South back to the union; the only practical mode of procedure is to bring
the union to the South. In 1884, in 1892, in 1912 and in 1916, that
method was adopted; and then, and only then, the South has found itself
politically in agreement with the rest of the nation.

This singularity rests, of course, on the peace without victory of
1865. Out of that affair the South emerged with the conviction that
unqualified adherence to the theory of the rule of the majority is altogether wrong. If your majority happens to consist of negroes, then your
theory collapses. The Democratic party was in position to make of the
negro, as well as of the tariff, a local issue, for it had always been the
traditional protagonist of states' rights. Naturally, it received the adherence of the South. It will doubtless continue to receive it indefinitely
unless the South loses its moral certainty on the negro question, or until
another party accepts the Southern view.

Unfriendly critics describe this state of mind as mere bigotry and
prejudice. That description may, or may not, be correct. In any case, it
has been applied to every individual, or group, that has affected the
history of the world immediately and profoundly. Conquerors are always bigoted and prejudiced, from the viewpoint of the conquered.
Neither Mohammed nor Martin Luther was filled with sweet reasonableness. If William Lloyd Garrison[2] had been open to conviction, he would
never have convinced enough others to win his fight.

The only really dangerous man in the world is the man who knows
beyond peradventure that he is right. If it is true—and who can overlook
the impressive array of evidence that supports the theory?—that the
South is the only section of the country that is blandly certain of its own
righteousness, then it is folly to talk of the danger of any loss of its
distinctive individuality, by its absorption into an amorphous mass. The
danger lies all the other way. Ku Kluxism, Fundamentalism, White
Supremacy, to mention only three ideas once distinctively Southern

---

2. William Lloyd Garrison, American abolitionist of the mid-nineteenth century.

which are now national, prove that that South, so far from being be-leaguered and at the point of surrender, has developed a sort of von Hutier attack, is apparently conquering by infiltration.

Whether or not this will prove a good thing or a bad thing for the nation and so eventually for the South itself is altogether beside the point. The point is that the Philistines be upon, not the South, but the rest of the nation.

There is only one glaring weakness in this line of argument. That lies in the fact that the South is rapidly beginning to educate her children, and it is rare indeed that moral certainty can stand long against educa-tion. It is conceivable that, like Henry Adams, the South may eventually become so learned that she will discover that she knows nothing at all, not even that she is always right; in which case her hands may fall and Amalek begin to prevail.

# The Battling South

In a somewhat upbeat essay written for *Scribner's* (March 1925) Johnson maintains that even in the midst of unfavorable publicity given the South because of the Ku Klux Klan and religious fundamentalism, some Southerners were still fighting to resurrect the civilization of Washington, Jefferson, and Lee. He hails such earlier Southerners as Charles B. Aycock and Edgar Gardner Murphy and contemporaries such as William Louis Poteat, president of Wake Forest College.

Beyond peradventure, the most startling contribution made to American history by the South since the beginning of the century is the origination of the Ku Klux Klan. Not a few critics have assumed that it is the only noteworthy contribution, which is not the case; and some have concluded that it is the first of a series of similar contributions, which is unduly pessimistic. The activities of the singularly unknightly knights have centered upon the South innumerable searchlights of criticism, some of which illuminate it and some of which merely bathe it in the color of the critic's individual prejudices, but all of which tend to make it squirm. The South went into shadow in 1865. It is unaccustomed to occupying the centre of the stage. In the sudden and unflattering prominence which the Klansmen have achieved for it, it shows to little advantage. It has forgotten the art of make-up, and in consequence all its warts stand out terrifically.

One result of the section's inability to put its best face foremost has been the growth of a theory that the States which Mr. Mencken designates as "the late Confederacy" are of a distinctly different order from the remainder of the forty-eight in that they have diverged from the highroad of American development and have followed a bypath which has led them into fens and quagmires; and that this erratic course was their deliberate choice to begin with, and has not been regretted since. This reasoning leads inevitably to the conclusion that the South must be dismissed as a possible field of development of American culture.

To substantiate this theory there is the Ku Klux Klan, and behind the Klan a group of incredible hoodlums sent from the South to Washington with commissions to high office, and behind the hoodlums the hideous record of lynchings in the United States for the last fifty years. There are the illiteracy statistics, from the standpoint of an educated people ab-

Copyright © 1925 by *Scribner's Magazine* and reprinted with permission.

solutely damning in their implications. There is the notorious artistic sterility of the region. There is its prevailing impermeability to ideas. There is its political Bourbonism.

Unhappily, these are not matters of opinion, but facts, all too easily demonstrable. The history of the South as a part of the republic is now divided into two almost equal parts by the Civil War. The disparity in the record of visible Southern achievement in those two periods is astounding. The former included the gift to the nation of a group of giants almost unrivalled in its history. What other group of leaders has influenced the nation more profoundly than George Washington, Thomas Jefferson, John Marshall, James Madison, James Monroe, Andrew Jackson, Henry Clay, and Abraham Lincoln? But since 1860 almost the only Southerner who has impressed the country as powerfully as the least important man in that list is Woodrow Wilson, and he went into the service of the nation by way of New Jersey.

Great Southerners simply have not appeared above the national horizon since the Civil War, which lends color to the theory that the civilization that produced them is to be counted one of the casualties of the war, along with the doctrine of secession and the institution of human slavery. The fact that the assumption is painful to Southerners does not make it any the less the natural view for others to take. No candid Southerner can review the record of the last fifty years without realization of the fact that the positive alarm with which his section is viewed by the rest of the country is not altogether unjustified. That alarm is real enough, for it is based on the known frailties of other sections. The astonishing and sinister success of the Ku Klux Klan in the North and West is amply sufficient evidence that religious fanaticism of the most unenlightened type is no monopoly of any section. Were the South to devote its energies to the organization of bigotry and prejudice, it would unquestionably find a great following north of the Potomac and west of the Mississippi. The results might easily prove disastrous. America—not the South alone—lacks as yet sufficient enlightenment to be immune to social poisons administered with the skill which Southern demagogues admittedly possess.

Then if the typical Southern demagogue can mobilize and captain the energies of the South, the outcome will be portentous for the rest of the country and tragic for the South, for those energies are immense. Because the section was prostrated by a fearful war and lay for a generation quiescent, some superficial observers assumed that it was moribund. That has been proved an error. It was convalescent. The last quarter of a century has witnessed its material and physical regeneration. By comparison with the best-endowed sections of the country, the South is still poor; but by comparison with its own condition forty years ago it has recently gained enormous wealth. By comparison with Pennsylvania, New Jersey, and New York, it is sparsely populated; but, except in Florida and Texas, its population per square mile is well above the average for the United States and far above the average for the whole area west of the Mississippi. A section possessed of great wealth and a huge population is necessarily powerful. But, theoretically at least, it is as powerful for evil as for good.

In so far as material progress is concerned, the recovered strength of the South is admittedly being used wisely and fairly efficiently. In 1857 a North Carolina insurance company wrote into its policies a clause cancelling the contract if the policy-holder, between June and October, travelled below the southern boundary of South Carolina and Tennessee. The explanation was the prevalence of yellow fever and pernicious malaria in the Gulf States. These are two horrors that have been abolished by the energy and intelligence of Southern health officials. With them have gone the hookworm and typhoid fever, while chronic malaria has been driven into the more stagnant backwoods communities. Insurance companies now make no invidious distinction against any Southern State. Much the same story can be told of other public works. The greatest construction companies in the North and West now regularly arrange to shift a considerable proportion of their personnel and machinery to the South during the winter months, on account of the great demand for engineering work which there can be carried on all the year. Many Southern cities are as handsome as any towns of similar size anywhere in the country. Within the last ten years a marvellous change has come over them in the matter of hotels, for instance, and excellent paving has come to be the rule, rather than the exception. There is a rapidly increasing group of philanthropic Southern millionaires, to endow hospitals and schools. The mushroom-like growth of hydroelectric plants has brought modern conveniences, not only to every city and village but to many isolated farmhouses as well.

"All this," as the Lord of Montaigne remarked of the Cannibales, "is not verie ill," but in an otherwise attractive polity the essayist found a fatal defect—"but what of it? They weare no kinde of breeches nor hosen." Haberdasheries, indeed, cover the South in every direction, and pantaloons are worn universally, but of the moral and spiritual investiture of the natives there is more to be said. The veracious Mr. Lewis assures us that George F. Babbitt lives in a house of excellent architectural lines, tastefully furnished by a well-known firm of decorators, and located on a beautiful boulevard in the handsome city of Zenith. No doubt he patronizes a good tailor, too, but the moral and spiritual nakedness of Babbitt has become nationally symbolical. The financial and material development of the South may be admitted without invalidating the inquiry into whether or not its spiritual nudity is assuming the proportions of an American scandal.

In other words, the South is proved capable of producing millionaires, forests of smoke-stacks, Rotarians, clean, comfortable cities, and advertising clubs. It is also proved capable of producing the Ku Klux Klan, lynchings, persecutions of biologists, and ignorant, ruffianly politicians. To put the most charitable construction upon it, the account, thus far, is about balanced. There is in the account here presented no perceptible sign of the existence of the civilization which was illuminated, during the first half of the republic's existence, by the long line of illustrious Southerners from Washington to Robert E. Lee. If that civilization is extinct, smoke-stacks and Rotarians can never replace it. If that civilization is extinct, the South is dead, and its material activity is not a genuine revival, but a species of galvanism, the horrible twitching of a cadaver stimulated by electricity.

The Southerner who would accept such an interpretation would be a pessimist indeed, but in the face of the facts those who reject it are under the necessity of furnishing some explanation of the faith that is in them. This is easier said than done. There are reasons, and they are understood by most Southerners; but to make them intelligible to the rest of the world is a task of some difficulty, because the rest of the world is for the most part ignorant of all save the superficial aspects of history in the South since Appomattox.

The South's losses in wealth and manpower during the conflict of the sixties are known of all men. What is rarely understood outside the South is the fact that the most prodigious loss did not occur until after Lee had surrendered. That was the loss of the tradition of government in accordance with the law administered by the people's representatives, which the South had inherited in common with the rest of the American people. It is evident that the stability of any form of self-government depends upon the respect of the people for the institutions that they have erected for their own governance. If there is any Anglo-Saxon inheritance from the seven centuries that have passed since Runnymede, that inheritance is comprised in the individual's willing submission to the institutions that the people have set up.

But it is just this inheritance that was wiped out of the Southern States by the aftermath of the Civil War. The blast of hatred that seared the country through four murderous years incinerated whatever remnants of mutual understanding may have survived the controversy over slavery. When the war ended, neither section was capable of harboring decent sentiments toward the other. A crazy fanatic shot Lincoln. A Northern general manacled Jefferson Davis. Each instantly became the archetype of his section in the minds of the people of the other section. The fact that these mental images were equally false is entirely irrelevant, because it was upon the images, not upon the truth, that men based their actions in those bitter days. And the actions were real enough.

The North had the upper hand, and the North acted upon the assumption that it was dealing with a treacherous and ignoble foe, who would hesitate at nothing, not even at assassination, to escape the admission of defeat. One does not argue with the rattlesnake; therefore the North proceeded to make a vigorous and determined effort to murder the autonomy of the South. With bayonets at their throats, the Southern States were compelled to subscribe to the Fourteenth and Fifteenth Amendments, which the North believed would assure to the negroes equal participation in government. Not content with that, the victor then disqualified the white South to participate in its own government, thereby turning control over to the blacks.

The South, equally blinded by its bath of hatred, promptly assumed that nothing short of total destruction of Southern civilization would slake the blood-thirst of the North, and that appeals to Northern reason, justice, and generosity would be so much wasted breath, as no such qualities existed north of the Potomac. One does not argue with a homicidal maniac, armed to the teeth; therefore the South abandoned the theory of government by the will of the majority and resorted to government by trickery.

The result of these misapprehensions was the horror summed up for Southerners in the word "Reconstruction." All the fruit of the toil of statesmen, all the structure of government, from the magistrate's court to the organic law of the republic, was corrupted and tainted for the South. So it was forsworn. Those bulwarks of democracy, respect for the orderly processes of the law, acceptance of the sanctity of the ballot, loyal support of the institutions of popular government, instead of being the marks of the good citizen, became disreputable when the law, the suffrage, and all the institutions of government were in the hands of newly freed slaves, who had had no part in their creation, and no training in their proper use. When all men of proved character, ability, and trained intelligence were debarred from participation in government, who could respect it? After all, respect for government is predicated on government's being respectable, which it was not in the South in the late sixties.

The Constitution of the United States, the Congress, the courts, and the federal army all decreed that Southern white men should not rule in their own country. So Southern white men consigned to hell the Constitution of the United States, the Congress, the courts, and the federal army, and ruled anyhow. But to do it they had to terrorize negro voters, stuff ballot-boxes, horsewhip judges, and in general violate the principle of submission to the constituted authorities which is the foundation of orderly and enduring government by the people.

None the less, by this process the South lost more than the war had cost her. Destruction of the citizen's belief in his government was destruction of the moral values accumulated through seven centuries of training in self-government. Nobody knows this better than thoughtful Southerners; but at the time when the damage was done nobody in the South looked far beyond the immediate necessities of the moment, for it was then apparent that the end of all things was at hand. After a few years the leadership of the South did wake up to a realization of the abyss to which the rule of violence was leading. The moment of its awakening is easily fixed in history—it is marked by the sudden subsidence of the wilder manifestations of revolt and the dissolution of the original Ku Klux.

But work of the sort that went on in the South in the late sixties and the early seventies is never easily undone. Reestablishment of the prestige of the repudiated institutions has been tremendously difficult. It has been so difficult that the effort has absorbed the energies of the ablest men in the South to the exclusion of well-nigh everything else. The leadership that it might have supplied to the nation has been fully occupied in recapturing the leadership of the South itself, trying to sweep back the tide of demagogy, ignorance, stupidity, and prejudice that the dynamiting of civilized government loosed upon the luckless country.

But a leader, no matter how able, who confines himself to advocacy of public education, obedience of the law, and respect for the sanctity of the ballot, will hardly impress the country as a brilliant and original captain of democracy, seeing that those things are taken for granted in sections not chained to such a body of death as Reconstruction fastened upon the South. Passionate advocacy of the theory that two and two make four is not calculated to impress the faculty of mathematics; yet if that theory had been seriously and resolutely challenged, it might be far more difficult to prove it than to establish the Einstein hypothesis. The theory that every honest man owes obedience to the law, respect to the courts, and support to the institutions of popular government has been challenged in the South; and the fight to re-establish it has been the main concern of the best minds of the section for two generations.

There is nothing brilliant, nothing spectacular, about this battle. It is a sort of fighting as dull and obscure as it is murderous. An Edgar

Gardner Murphy[1] can wear his life out in it, and beyond the boundaries of his native Alabama hardly any one will know that he has lived and died. Who was Murphy? Only a theologue, who stood manfully against negrophobia and child labor. It rarely occurs to a Northerner that in Alabama twenty-five years ago such a stand required a chevalier as stainless and as fearless as Bayard. A Charles Brantley Aycock can lash himself to his work until outraged nature revolts, and apoplexy strikes him dead with his boots on, in the midst of a plea for the common schools. But few will note his passing. Aycock? Only a North Carolina politician, who, as Governor, in the beginning of the century argued rather ably for public education. But the man had the gift of swaying the mob, and he might have had any office he chose, simply by swimming with the tide. On the contrary, he chose to champion huge expenditures for education in a State that had been completely looted in the name of public works, including education, some twenty years before. It was political suicide, and, as the event proved, physical suicide from over-work.

Here are two Southerners who will never have a place in any national Hall of Fame. They might easily have deserted and gone North, where their brilliant talents would have been recognized and fittingly rewarded; but the very fact that they chose poverty, obscurity, and apparent defeat in their native section is as heroic as any exploit of the military idols. The Jackson at New Orleans, or the Jackson in the Shenandoah Valley, never fought better for the South. Nor do I believe that the man who wrote the Declaration of Independence, or the man who established the authority of the Supreme Court, laid foundations more enduring; for, while Murphy is dead, Tuskegee exists in Alabama, in spite of the Ku Klux Klan, and the State has a good child-labor law. While Aycock is dead, North Carolina now spends annually for common schools twenty-three times as much as she spent when he was Governor, and votes $13,000,000 for a single building programme at the State university and two State colleges. They flung their lives away, but they broke the phalanx. The South has never lacked men who would die for it on the battle-field. These are two who gathered the spears of ignorance, suspicion, and prejudice to their breasts and died like Winkelried.

The number of their peers is beyond computation, for the hardest part of these men's lot in life is that often they must go unrecognized even by their neighbors—nay, distrusted, disliked, sometimes persecuted, by their own people. But the conclusive evidence of the power of their

---

1. Edgar Gardner Murphy, Alabama minister, author, and child-labor reformer of late nineteenth and early twentieth century.

opposition to the forces of disintegration is the very fact that the South has not lapsed completely into barbarism. On the contrary, she emerges steadily into the light. Demagogy is still rampant below the Potomac, it is true, but where has it been completely stamped out? Fantastic and unbelievable ruffians still appear in Washington from Southern States, but Oscar Underwood has Alabama behind him, regardless of the Anti-Saloon League, and Virginia stands to Carter Glass, even though he dared speak and vote against the bonus. Perhaps most significant of all, six years ago when the guns were still thundering, North Carolina re-elected Claude Kitchin, who spoke and voted against war with Germany;[2] and this in spite of the fact that the National Defense League declared that the spy-hunters found less evidence of disloyalty in North Carolina than in any other State of the Union. If these facts are not convincing proof of the growth of a liberal spirit below the Mason and Dixon line, consider this: William Louis Poteat is both a biologist of repute and president of a college supported by the Baptist denomination in North Carolina[3]—this with the Kentucky solons legislating Darwin out of the schools, and Bryan raging like a pestilence through Florida. Furthermore, at its last meeting the Baptist State Convention gave President Poteat an overwhelming vote of confidence, evolution and all!

It would be too optimistic to assert that the end is in sight, and that the date when the South will come once more under the sway of the spiritual heirs of Jefferson and Marshall can be fixed, even approximately. But it is not too much to say that the fight for moral domination of the region veers now toward men of the old school. This material prosperity helps. The South makes too much of it, no doubt. Every section that attains it makes too much of it for a while. But it is giving Southerners the leisure that is essential to the production of an aristocracy. It is, in Mr. Wilson's phrase, releasing the generous energies of the superior minds of the section, and by giving to inferior men property, it gives them a stake in social stability and orderly government, which makes them wonderfully amenable to reason. With increasing leisure comes also increasing interest in the graces of civilized life and in the beautiful arts, an interest that enables the Carolina Playmakers to establish a state theatre that actually pays its own way, that enables Nashville, Tennessee, to set up a symphony orchestra, and that finds

2. Oscar Underwood, congressman from Alabama, 1895–1915, senator, 1915–27; Carter Glass, congressman from Virginia, 1902–18, senator, 1919–46, secretary of the treasury under Woodrow Wilson, 1918–19; Claude Kitchen, North Carolina congressman, 1900–1923, and House majority leader in the Wilson administration.

3. William Louis Poteat, president of Wake Forest College.

expression in a dozen poetry societies and in such magazines as the Richmond *Reviewer* and the New Orleans *Double-Dealer*.

Small gains, if you please, but gains; and the fact that there are any gains at all is sufficient evidence that the destructive forces now operative in the South are not unopposed. The social order that produced William Joseph Simmons and his Ku Klux Klan, that sent To-Hell-With-the-Constitution Blease to the United States Senate, that lynched fifty-four negroes in 1922, and that persecutes scientists who repudiate the medieval theology of hedge-priests, is challenged every year with increasing sharpness and vigor by the civilization that produced the Declaration of Independence, the Bill of Rights, and Robert Edward Lee.

# Service in the Cotton Mills

"Bedeviled by the government, conspired against by labor organizers, belabored for no reason that he can understand by the liberal press, portrayed to the world as a tyrant, a bloodsucker, an ogre, he is bewildered and decidedly peevish." Thus, in one of his first articles for a national audience (*Survey*, 1 April 1923), Johnson had described the Southern cotton-mill owner. Mencken wanted to see more, and in a letter in 1924 Johnson promised an essay for the *Mercury* on mill owners "as apostles of Service." In this essay, published in June 1925, Johnson goes "behind the monster's mask." He anticipates W. J. Cash—and like Cash, draws on economist Broadus Mitchell—by suggesting that the Southern movement to build cotton mills was an economic equivalent of war (if the Yankees could not be defeated one way, they could be defeated another), and by suggesting that the mill baron saw himself as the successor to the plantation owner who treated his workers paternalistically.

Right-thinkers in the North, East and West seem to hold it as axiomatic that all the Southern cotton mill owners ought to be hanged. This is not the conclusion, but the premise of most of the current argumentation about social and industrial conditions in the South. From that premise conclusions are drawn that to Southerners are strange and wonderful indeed.

Now, it is doubtless true enough that manslaughter, practiced upon a number of Southern cotton mill owners discreetly selected, might purify the atmosphere below the Potomac and make that heroic region a better place to live in; but the same thing, obviously, is true of an equally large proportion of the cotton mill owners of Rhode Island and Massachusetts. As much might be said, indeed, of the lawyers of New York, or the coal dealers of Ohio, or the clergymen of California. There is no large group of men anywhere that would not be the better for an occasional decimation. The Southern cotton mill owners, as a class, have not escaped the common human folly, but it is a far cry from that admission to the assumption that all of them ought to be hanged.

Yet that assumption, or something closely approximating it, passes unchallenged in the North, East and West. Attend a sociological conference anywhere, and listen to the reports upon human existence in the

Copyright © 1925 by the *American Mercury* and reprinted with permission.

South. Note the unanimity with which the Northern press ascribes the rejection of the child labor amendment by Georgia and North Carolina to the machinations of the cotton mill men—in the face of the plain fact that the amendment would have been rejected by both States had there not been a cotton factory in either. Did the Southern mill men furnish the overwhelming popular vote against the amendment in Massachusetts? Yet mark the inevitability with which they are held up as horrible examples everywhere. They are fair game for every uplifting hunter and there is no closed season.

There must be a reason for this. It is incredible that it should have come to pass by chance, or by mere malicious intent. I believe it is the product of a collision of two moral superiorities. The Northern uplifter who comes South encounters something new in his experience. Being hated does not trouble him, for he is used to that. Being feared he not infrequently finds luxurious. If the Southern cotton mill owner merely hated and feared him, he would understand it perfectly, and to some extent condone it as an involuntary tribute to his own moral superiority. But the feeling he encounters is nothing so simple as a mixture of fear and hatred. It is sophisticated with loathing, contempt and white-hot moral indignation. The Southern cotton mill owner looks upon the Northern uplifter with much the same emotion that stirs within the plain man who observes a Gila monster in a zoo—he knows that it is unlawful to kill the thing, yet from the bottom of his soul he feels that it is contrary to reason and the natural rights of man to permit such a creature to live.

Now, the uplifter knows beyond peradventure that he is doing the work of God. What, then, is he to think of men who regard him as these Southerners do? Those who merely oppose him are in the nature of things doing the work of the devil; but what is to be said of those who not only oppose him, but regard him and his work as utterly vile and loathsome, who look down upon him from a Himalaya of moral superiority? Obviously, they are in a category of their own, amenable to no known laws, entitled to no sanctuary. Wicked men may be converted, or at least restrained; but arch-fiends, who make good evil and evil good, are beyond hope. Extermination is the only recourse.

What has happened is plain: the uplifter, knowing his own moral superiority, has collided with a man even more belligerently superior. The impact of the collision is the most terrific the world has ever known, and it generates heat enough to vaporize the eternal rocks.

Where the uplifter gets his consciousness of moral superiority is a problem for psychologists, psychiatrists, psychoanalysts and other delvers into the mysteries of the aberrant mind. But where the Southern mill owner gets his is easy to see. He inherits it. True, his inheritance bears some similarity to the royalty of Sixtus of Bourbon and the Russian lady friend of the Monday Opera Club, in that the course of events has invalidated his claim, but just as surely as Bourbon and Romanoff once held sovereignty, so he once had a fair color of title to moral superiority in the South.

The subject has been treated extensively by Dr. Broadus Mitchell in his study, "The Rise of Cotton Mills in the South"[1] [sic] in which the interested inquirer may find a carefully documented discussion of the social, civic and religious elements that contributed to the founding of the industry. The notion that textile manufacturing was introduced into the South by shrewd and far-sighted business men intent solely upon capitalizing the double advantage of proximity to the raw material and a huge supply of pauper labor cannot survive the perusal of this work. Those advantages, in fact, were only vaguely understood by the participants in the Cotton Mill Campaign of the early eighties. There were weighty authorities, notably Edward Atkinson, of Boston, who argued shrewdly and persuasively that such advantages were more apparent than real and that the textile industry in the South could never become important enough to offer serious competition to the New England mills. The fallacy of Atkinson's arguments was demonstrated only after the industry had been established. There is plenty of evidence that not a few of the men who put up capital for the first mills were more than half persuaded that he was right, and that they never expected the industry to return dividends, even if it survived at all.

Nevertheless, they put up the money, and a new industrial order was created out of hand between 1879 and 1881. The venture turned out profitable beyond the dreams of its most optimistic promoters, and its development has been prosecuted ever since with increasing energy and enthusiasm; but that the motivating force of its founders was not altogether profit-seeking is proved conclusively by the fact that in repeated instances subscribers sold their stock at a loss as soon as the factories to which they had subscribed were completed.

The philosophy underlying such subscriptions was nothing less than that of *noblesse oblige*. It was the sense of moral superiority in the Southern aristocracy that impelled it to seek a remedy for conditions already deplorable and rapidly becoming desperate. Lee had surrendered less than fifteen years before the Cotton Mill Campaign began,

---

1. *The Rise of the Cotton Mills in the South* (1921), by Broadus Mitchell, a Johns Hopkins economist.

and the South, since Appomattox, had undergone the process which by a ghastly irony, was labeled Reconstruction, with the result that socially and politically it was far below the level of 1865, and as far as the public treasury was concerned, worse off financially, too. But by 1879 the worst of political misrule was over. The last Southern State had swept out the carpet-baggers and the natural leaders of the South were leading again.

The political situation made momentarily secure, their attention was necessarily turned upon the economic situation. It could hardly have been worse. The condition of the poor whites, in particular, was lamentable. Their sole means of subsistence lay in competition with the newly-freed Negroes in agriculture, with the inevitable result that they were swiftly sinking to the Negro's standards of living, which were far lower then than they are now. To men without social conscience, this might have been no more than an interesting phenomenon, worthy of attention merely as a study in societal evolution. But to men of highly conscious moral superiority, men accustomed to thinking of themselves as belonging to a master class, it was a sheer impossibility to regard the situation so comfortably. They were as incapable of avoiding a sense of responsibility in the circumstances as they would have been incapable, twenty years earlier, of permitting their Negro slaves to die of starvation. They had to do something to provide these people with some means of subsistence. They did do something. They built cotton mills.

The student of the origin of textile manufacturing in the South is usually dumbfounded by the blithe disregard of rudimentary business principles displayed by the early *entrepreneurs*. Aspiring hamlets built cotton mills without any sort of investigation into the advantages of the locality for textile manufacturing. Only in rare instances was the enterprise headed by a man of any experience in business, save perhaps cotton buying. The usual plan was to select that man in the community who possessed the people's confidence in the highest degree and draft him into service, regardless of his previous training. Thus the new mills were headed by doctors, lawyers, teachers, planters, and even clergymen. "What did the doctor, lawyer, or fertilizer man know about running a mill?" one of the pioneers of the business said, talking it over thirty years later. "Yet it got to the point where, if he were prominent in the town and did not become a cotton mill president, he lost his social position."

This procedure is as inexplicable as the ravings of the wildest Bedlamite until one remembers the spirit in which the whole venture was conceived, but then it becomes understandable, if not logical. This was not a business, but a social enterprise. Any profit that might accrue to the originators of the mill was but incidental; the main thing was the salvation of the decaying community, and especially the poor whites, who were in danger of being submerged altogether. The record of those days is filled with a moral fervor that is astounding. People were urged to take stock in the mills for the town's sake, for the poor people's sake, for the South's sake, literally for God's sake. In Salisbury, North Carolina, a certain Mr. Pearson, described as "a lean, intense Tennesseean who preached powerfully," held a revival in the course of which he scorched the souls of the richer residents on account of their neglect of their poorer neighbors; so immediately after the meeting a group of them organized a cotton mill with a preacher, the Rev. F. J. Murdock, as its secretary and treasurer. Later he became president and, as one commentator remarked, "the mill was religion-pervaded from the outset."

There was talk of profit in connection with the founding of the mills, but in these early years it never became the dominant motif. Always it was the prospect of civic and social salvation that was stressed. All the money return looked for was expected to accrue to the poor whites and to drag them back from the edge of the abyss obviously opening to swallow them. Such considerations are not potent to sway the minds of inferior men, and they were not addressed to men of that type. They were addressed to the master class, to men who felt their superiority to the common herd and acknowledged the attendant responsibility. Great numbers of them had owned slaves and had worn the uniform of the Confederacy. Fifteen years after the war had been lost, the bulk of the Confederate officers were drawing near the end of their active lives. Some of them, of course, were to survive for decades, but they were nearing the close of their effective leadership. The founding of the textile industry in the early eighties may therefore fairly be regarded as the last great effort of the old order, the final gesture of the slave-owning aristocrat before he left the stage forever. It was a worthy gesture. True, it was the cue for the entrance of an actor of a very different type, but in itself it was altogether in keeping with the history of a race of men who lived with an air. Even when they became industrialists, they did it quaintly, they did it becomingly, they did it in the grand manner.

Marvelous to relate, the enterprises which they founded succeeded. The old men did not last long. Their blunders, in many instances, were too glaring, too appalling, even for the lax business standards of their day, but in a surprising number of cases the advantages of proximity to the raw material, cheap power and cheap labor outweighed even their inexperience and incapacity. Many of them died with comfortable fortunes; occasionally they started their sons on the road to wealth. One encounters now and then a Southern cotton mill man who is obviously a man of birth and breeding, for there are not a few great families who have managed to cling to their properties through all the succeeding years and have thereby restored the tarnished splendor of their names.

But these by no means dominate the industry today. When the early mills had demonstrated the fact that textile manufacturing might be carried on in the South at a profit, promoters of a different type swooped in from all quarters. The go-getters arrived. Sometimes they rose from the ranks of the poor whites employed in the mills. Oftener they were hard-headed and hard-fisted individuals who had sternly refused to have any part in the movement so long as it was simply an effort for the common good, but who waxed enthusiastic when it was demonstrated that there was money in it. The field afforded incredibly rich pickings for such as these, and they were later increased by a horde of up-and-coming immigrants from New England. By this time a man of the right type could hardly fail to succeed in the business. All that was necessary was for him to get a job as bookkeeper for one of the trusting old gentlemen of the *ancien régime* and in a few years he owned the mill. It was not even necessary for him to steal it. By introducing efficient business methods he could double, triple, quadruple its profits, and the grateful stock-holders would nearly always split. By the time mills became so numerous that labor began to demand a wage that would enable parents to make a living for their families without working their young children, and competition with the mills of New England and Lancashire became brisk, the ancient aristocracy had relinquished the helm and the industry was manned by a crew hard-boiled enough to hold its own with the blood-thirstiest pirates of Lowell and Providence.

But note what an inheritance the modern Southern textile manufacturer has come into. The mills are only part of his legacy. He has the tradition, too. The pioneer cotton manufacturer had risked what small remnants of his fortune the war had left in an enterprise of doubtful future designed primarily to secure the happiness and well-being of his people. He sought first the common weal. He was therefore naturally and properly regarded as a public benefactor. His successor, becoming a cotton manufacturer, becomes *ipso facto*, in his own mind at least, a public benefactor in his turn. He forgets that he put *his* money into an enterprise no longer doubtful, but a demonstrated success. He forgets that he risked his capital, not in consideration of the common weal, but in consideration of the 50%, 60%, 75% and 90% that numbers of Southern cotton mills have returned as yearly dividends. But who of us is not inclined to forget the embarrassing points of dissimilarity that mark us off from the saints and heroes? It may not be logical, but it is certainly human for the Southern cotton mill man of today to regard himself as in all respects the heir of his distinguished predecessor.

More than that, he does possess something of the old slaveholder's spirit. He looks after his people with the passionate energy that characterized the care of the ante-bellum aristocrat for his Negroes. The amount of welfare work carried on by Southern mills amazes and appals the visitor from the North. Not merely lodging, but clubrooms, drug stores, Y.M.C.A. buildings, churches and funeral parlors are sometimes supplied by the mills. Teachers of the Bible, boxing and aesthetic dancing are on the company pay-roll. Pavements and community morals are looked after with equal assiduity.

Energetically as he invades it, however, the man of commerce is as ill at ease in this realm as the man of the master class was in commerce. The consequence is that he falls a ready victim to astounding frauds. Only occasionally has he the good sense to have scientific studies made of his personnel. Usually he trusts his own judgment, which is to say, he goes it blind, with the natural result that every sociological quack in the country has preyed upon him, selling him fantastic schemes of uplift for fantastic sums of money. The luckless working people suffer in silence; usually they recognize the excellence of the mill owner's intentions and try to be grateful. This work touches intimately the *amour propre* of the manufacturing tribe. Just as in 1850 a master who starved his Negroes, or worked them unmercifully, or kept in his employ a notoriously brutal overseer, was regarded by the neighboring gentry as an unspeakable totter, so the modern cotton mill owner who fails to put up without squawking for any amount of welfare work is regarded by his business rivals as a low fellow, outside the pale, and a menace to the good name of the South.

However, in the sociological world Lady Bountiful has for years been a fallen woman. Consequently, when earnest inquirers from the North, East and West come drifting into the South, they raise a hideous outcry over this very welfare work which the Southern mill owner regards as his through ticket to eternal bliss. To the Southerner it seems that they revile him for acting decently, kindly, generously, as a Christian gentleman should. Is it to be wondered at that his amazement and pain swiftly give way to towering rage? These blasphemers would estop him from doing the work of God! Every ounce of moral superiority in him—and it is measured by tons—crashes upon the head of the outlander. If that worthy were not himself endowed with a moral superiority approximating the weight of Mount Mitchell, highest peak east of the Mississippi, the impact would smite him clear off the earth and send his mangled frame whirling beyond the orbit of the moon.

But as it is, the irresistible force meets the immovable body and the result is a terrific conglomeration of flame, dust, smoke and most infernal noise. The inquirers are by far the better publicists, so the rest of the nation hears from but one side and comes to the conclusion that Southern cotton mill owners ought to be hanged. . . . Of that conclusion one may say only that it is probably as sound—as most other moral certainties.

# Journalism below the Potomac

In the *American Mercury* (September 1926) Johnson assumes the role of the complacent Southerner who maintains that Southern journalism is close to "perfection" because it adopts a business ideal and, with some few exceptions, does not dare rock the boat. The Southern publisher, at heart and in fact a Rotarian, was "content with an editorial page made up of thundering denunciations of the Republican Party and Antichrist." The year Johnson wrote this essay he himself left "Southern journalism" behind and joined the Baltimore *Sun*.

Southern journalism is now so near to perfection that the measure by which it has failed to attain the ideal is imperceptible to the naked eye. The Miami *Herald* last year published 42,000,000 lines of advertising. John Stewart Bryan, publisher of the Richmond *News-Leader*, is president of the American Newspaper Publishers' Association. Not a Rotary Club south of the Potomac now fails to include within its sacred circle some officer of the local newspaper publishing company. A score of Southern journals have recently occupied, and as many more are building, offices that cost more than a quarter of a million dollars each. The average Southern newspaper publisher today is much more respectable than a merchant, some are even more so than a banker, and a few are almost as holy as the owner of a cotton-mill.

There is no arguing against facts. Southern journalism today has reached a pinnacle that not even the wildest romantics of twenty years ago expected it ever to attain. At the turn of the century and for some years thereafter the words newspaper man brought to the mind's eye of the Southerner a starveling creature, skinny, sinewy, ferocious, the very antithesis of the American ideal of material, moral and spiritual well-being. All that is changed now. The typical newspaper man of the New South has an aldermanic paunch and a multiplicity of chins. His taste in cigars is apt to be as fastidious as that of a Wall Street operator. His bootlegger is the one who caters to the mayor. He submits to the revilings of the pro at the golf club as meekly as do the presidents of the First National Bank and the spinning-mills. In short, he has attained a place in the American nobility. He has become a Peer of the Realm, a Busi-

Copyright © 1926 by the *American Mercury* and reprinted with permission.

ness Man, and Bradstreet, our Western DeBrett, lists none sounder, fatter or greasier.

This applies, of course, only to men of seigniorial rank. As for the villeins, they have not altered perceptibly from what they always were and what newspaper villeins are the world over. They are, perhaps, somewhat more frequently sober than they used to be, and somewhat less seedy. But the proportion of them able to spell *maintenance* is about what it has been for generations; and today as it was in the Mauve Decade their words demonstrate flippant cynicism and their acts a pathetic eagerness to believe in the promises of a politician and the possibility of filling an inside straight. Their ranks are thickly strewn with wastrels, alcoholics, poets, philosophers, crusaders and other such riffraff. But they are the rank and file, and their quality is worthy of attention only as it serves the purpose of the captains; and the captains are in the main perfect. They wheel their battalions into line with marvelous precision and give battle for the sacred cause of Service with all the enthusiasm of Passaic textile manufacturers.

And why not? The causes that have brought the Business Man to his most perfect flower in other sections are now operating upon journalism in the South. More than that, certain hindrances to his full development in other sections operate less effectively in the South. Almost for the first time since the Civil War, the South is now enjoying a full share of the nation's wave of prosperity. Newspaper publishing in the region has become profitable. By comparison with the rewards of the business twenty years ago, it has become immensely profitable. It has created some millionaires and a great number of five-figure incomes. Southern journalism would not interest a Henry Ford, but when a newspaper in a city of less than 50,000 population can turn in a net profit of $90,000 in a single year on an investment of a quarter of a million at the outside, it is not a bad business. The individual who can extract dividends of 36% from his plant has ample reason to claim recognition as a Business Man. Southern journals have done as well as that, not once but repeatedly, within the last decade. With a good deal less than $90,000 it is possible, in a small Southern city, to live in a style that reflects no discredit on the peerage. Scores of Southern newspaper men are doing it on $20,000 a year; some in the smaller places on $15,000.

Furthermore, the development of Southern newspaper men into Business Men has not been subjected to the cross strains that are present in some other sections. A newspaper man with his pockets full of money in the North is frequently tempted to make of himself, not a Business Man, but an Aristocrat, or even an Intellectual. James Gordon Bennett, for instance, drifted off in the one direction, and the third Samuel Bowles in the other.[1] Neither would have presented good material to a modern Rotary Club. Neither had much desire to do the things that are required of the modern Business Man, if he would maintain his place in the hierarchy—such things as engaging in banana-eating contests at the luncheon club, singing booster songs, addressing high-school graduates, Bible classes, Dorcas societies and salesmen's conventions on the holiness of Service, playing golf at a dollar a hole, paying $90 a case for Scotch and roaring for Prohibition, and all the other dances, words and music that are part of the insignia of rank. Therefore Bennett went to Paris and Bowles to heaven, and both escaped.

But the Southern newspaper man has no such alternatives. Assuming that he is of a lively type, with a lust for power and an amiable weakness for *kudos*, he will not be attracted in the direction of Aristocracy, for it is withered to the root. The last conspicuous achievement of Southern Aristocracy was the precipitation of the Civil War, and while the psychology of defeat inhibited the South for a long time from realizing who it was that had caused its ruin, the realization penetrated at last and such prestige as Aristocracy had retained ebbed away.

As for the Intelligentsia, it doesn't exist and never has existed in the South as one of the ruling castes. The South has produced thinkers, but it has never honored them. Its heroes have ever been men of action, not men of reflection. Washington, the two Jacksons and Lee are its towering heroes. The intellect of Jefferson, indeed, was so gigantic that it impressed even the South, but Marshall it has held in slight esteem, and Wilson it venerates, not for his contribution to the theory of government, but because at the last he girded on the sword of the Lord and of Gideon and licked hell out of the Germans. The Intellectual in the South is merely an eccentric. His weight, in the estimation of the rulers, is scarcely that of a feather.

Therefore the Southerner who would sit in the seats of the mighty has one avenue of approach open to him, and only one. He must become a Business Man, for there is the kingdom and the power and the glory. It is no wonder, then, that the Southern journalist, when he is conspicuously successful, usually appears as the very flower of the modern business world, and conducts his newspaper in accordance with the requirements of his station in life.

---

1. James Gordon Bennett, editor of the New York *Herald*, 1867–1918; Samuel Bowles, editor of the Springfield (Mass.) *Republican*, 1878–1915, son and grandson of editors of the *Republican*.

Those requirements are rigid, but not at all complex. They are all
founded on an American adaptation of the doctrine that *noblesse oblige*,
and consist for the most part of a series of prohibitions. The newspaper
that wishes to be a worthy representative of its Business Man publisher
is not obligated to publish anything in particular except, perhaps, full
market reports; but there are a great many things that it must not publish, at least without vigorous editorial denunciation. These things are
such items as might tend to differentiate the publisher from other members of his caste. The mania of business is solidarity. Rotary and Kiwa-
nis are the resultant of this urge for all sticking together. But in the
nature of things a man who leads must get out in front; that is to say, he
cannot stick to the crowd. Consequently, anything that would tend to
make the publisher a leader would automatically cut him off from his
crowd, and is not viewed with enthusiasm by a publisher who has
become a Business Man.

It is not to be understood that the Chambers of Commerce exercise a
direct censorship over the Southern press. It is a matter much more
subtle and much more effective than that. When the proprietor of a
newspaper has been thoroughly assimilated by the business community,
when he becomes himself one of the Sanhedrin and helps direct the
destinies of the Chamber of Commerce, he is far beyond the need of a
censor. His own standing as a Business Man depends upon faithful
reflection by his paper of the spirit of modern business, and he would
feel disgraced if it reflected anything else.

If one of the villeins, for example, allows to go through the copy-
desk a story from the public health officer showing that the typhoid rate
has risen to a figure that is a disgrace to a civilized community, it does
not require a visitation by a wrathful committee of realtors to set the Old
Man on his ear. He will give a faithful imitation of a case of hydrophobia
the minute his eye lights on the story, for he realizes as keenly as any
realtor that the first duty of a Business Man is never to knock the town,
and, beside, is not the mayor a fellow Rotarian? If the cotton-mill hands
strike, nobody has to tell the newspaper proprietor what to do. He will
start without cranking, for all his higher instincts persuade him that
nobody but a foreign agitator paid with Soviet gold could have persuaded the mill-hands that the right length of a working day is ten hours
instead of the eleven hallowed by tradition. If anyone writes a long
article—longer, say, than the report of the day's transactions on the
realty market—about a book by Dreiser or an exhibition of etchings by
Pennell the proprietor recognizes the *faux pas* without being told, for
blank ignorance of all that concerns the fine arts and an attitude of
amused tolerance toward their practitioners is the accepted thing in the

circles in which he lives, moves and has his being. The Business Man knows beyond peradventure that the arts are at best effeminate and at worst disreputable, and therefore are not to be treated seriously by a newspaper intended for red-blooded he-men who cherish their respectability as sedulously as a high-class burglar cherishes his gentlemanly front.

The rigid elimination of everything that might excite fear, or wonder, or aesthetic pleasure makes the Southern newspapers uninteresting, of course, but what sort of Business Man would pose as a public entertainer, anyhow? Southern newspapers may be, in the main, as dull reading as so many insurance policies, but what of that? They bring in the cash.

Yet no review of their situation can be candid unless it includes some notation of the obstacles that stand between the Southern press and the absolute attainment of its ideal. Not all Southern newspapers are perfect, and some of them that seem nearly so occasionally fall from grace. Right in the Empire State itself, the Empire State in which business is most nearly Jehovah, Jove and Lord, even in Georgia, there are a few newspapers that are far from conforming to the standard. In Columbus, for example, there is a newspaper man so hopelessly out of step that even the Pulitzer Prize Committee has heard of him. This committee, which betrays a regrettable tendency to bestow its awards, not on sound business sheets but on chronic hell-raisers, picked for the 1925 prize the Columbus *Enquirer-Sun*. This newspaper is edited by a son of Joel Chandler Harris, out of whom it would have been hard indeed to make a Business Man; so perhaps Julian Harris was afflicted by inheritance with a contempt for ruling standards. At any rate, the *Enquirer-Sun* has for years been as a voice crying in the wilderness, and a particularly raucous voice, at that. The *Enquirer-Sun* is out of sympathy with practically every item of the regimen prescribed for Georgia by the ruling *Dreibund* of politics, religion and business. It has nothing but unpleasant words for darkness anywhere—whether the darkness in which the Ku Klux wields blacksnake whip and tar-bucket in the name of morality, or the darkness of the nigger in politics, or of feudalistic business whose methodology is that of the Dark Ages.

And Harris is not the only one. Niggerish politics and Ku Kluxism apparently do not sit well on the stomach of another Georgia sheet of prominence, the Macon *Telegraph*. The *Telegraph* also has a weakness for arts and sciences, and discusses books and music occasionally. So, of course, do the lordly newspapers of Atlanta, but not at all in the same manner. The *Telegraph* frequently discusses them intelligently. True, the paper made a strong bid for Georgia respectability when it laid on Laurence Stallings, who was born in Macon, a curse by comparison with which the curse of Bishop Ernulphus in "Tristram Shandy" seems eulogistic. Stallings, it appears, had referred in print to a Negro novelist as Mister. But cursing a Southern white man who called a Negro Mister is not in itself enough to gain merit for a Georgia newspaper, and the Macon *Telegraph* still lies under suspicion of undue fondness for the Intellectual.

Farther South there are also lapses that cannot be explained away. The Montgomery *Advertiser*, for example, maintains Grover C. Hall and is polite to Sara Haardt,—certainly not the sort of persons of whom the Chamber of Commerce would heartily approve. The New Orleans *Times-Picayune*, perhaps with some taint of Lafcadio Hearn still in its system, keeps John McClure[2] on its pay-roll; but it compensated for that recently when, in endowing a chair of journalism at Tulane University, it solemnly called to the attention of the university authorities the danger of allowing any person of radical tendencies to occupy that chair. Between the *Advertiser* and the *Times-Picayune*, however, lucky chance has sandwiched the Jackson, Mississippi, *News*. The Gulf Coast is safe.

Of Florida, it is enough to say that the Miami *Herald*, as noted above, carried 42,000,000 lines of advertising in one year. If any further description of the state of journalism there is needed, it is supplied by the additional fact that most of the 42,000,000 lines were real-estate ads. At present, the chief end of Florida journalism is to explain that the boom is not really busted. Until that matter is cleared up, it would hardly be fair to expect the State press to show interest in anything else.

In Memphis, Tennessee, the *Commercial-Appeal* fought the Ku Klux Klan so well that it, too, received the accolade of the Pulitzer award. But since then Dayton has risen to international fame. The modicum of intellectual force that any State press need exhibit to prevent a Scopes trial, the reader may estimate at his leisure. Tennessee has not that much.

In South Carolina exists almost the last faint trace of the old aristocratic prestige. It is almost gone now, but within the memory of living men it was strong enough to exert a dominating influence upon the Columbia *State*, which upheld the tradition so strongly and effectively that a Lieutenant Governor elected by the wool-hat boys felt called upon

2. Grover Hall, editor of the Montgomery (Alabama) *Advertiser*; John McClure, reporter and editor on the New Orleans *Times-Picayune* and a poet associated with the *Double Dealer* of New Orleans.

to shoot the editor. The *State* still clings more or less to its ancient ideas, but its futility is perhaps best demonstrated by the fact that no high State official has lately considered its editor worth murdering. The conspicuously non-conformist newspaper in South Carolina at present is the *Record*, also of Columbia, whose editor, Charlton Wright, seems determined to maintain his intellectual independence of all shibboleths whatsoever, with the exception, of course, of sacred Democracy, rejection of which would be journalistic suicide in South Carolina.

Bourgeois North Carolina has not acknowledged an aristocrat since 1585, when it swallowed up Sir Walter Raleigh's colony. Nevertheless, it has a newspaper tradition of its own, dating from Joseph P. Caldwell's editorship of the Charlotte *Observer*. Caldwell injected into North Carolina journalism the singular notion that Republicans are as much entitled to a fair hearing as other human beings, and in 1896 he said that William J. Bryan was not fit to be President of the United States. In Caldwell courage, pride and honesty overshadowed the higher qualities of salesmanship, so he died relatively a failure. He had little except the respectful admiration of all honest men in the State and the venomous hatred of all knaves and fools.

But he left a tradition. Somehow he gripped the imaginations of Tar Heel newspaper men, and that grip has not yet been completely shaken off. His own newspaper, indeed, has recovered entirely, although others have not. The Charlotte *Observer*, in connection with the Saklatvala case, uttered an encomium of Nervous Nellie that is alone enough to free it completely of any attainder that Caldwell might have worked. It read, in part:

> Senator Borah proclaims against the order barring the communist leader from the United States on the ground that it is a violation of the law of "free speech." . . . Secretary Kellogg takes the better American view that if free speech means the privilege of the American stump to agitators and plotters against the government, he is opposed to free speech. . . . There seems to be at least one public official at Washington alert to his duty.[3]

Somewhere in North Carolina, however, there has always been one newspaper—usually more—that clung to the tradition of Caldwell. Of late years the most conspicuous of them has been the Greensboro *Daily*

---

3. William Edgar Borah, U.S. senator from Idaho, 1907–39; Frank B. Kellogg, secretary of state under Calvin Coolidge, 1925–29.

*News*, edited by a pupil of Caldwell named Earle Godbey. Godbey is no crusader. He believes in few things, but peace is one of the few. However, he has the faculty of being intensely annoyed by nonsense in any form, and Fundamentalists, Ku Klux and politicians he apparently regards as the three most annoying sources of nonsense. Consequently, his paper enjoys among right-thinkers the reputation of an atheistical, non-Nordic, semi-Republican sheet, and is the radiant delight of the wrong-headed.

Then there is Josephus Daniels. Mr. Wilson's Secretary of the Navy has been the butt of more ridicule than any other high official of this century, but somehow he has survived. His newspaper, the Raleigh *News and Observer*, has done more deplorable things than any other sheet in the State, yet it, too, survives. Twenty years ago it did to John Spencer Bassett, the historian,[4] what the Macon *Telegraph* later did to Laurence Stallings, because Bassett, then a North Carolina college professor, called Booker Washington the greatest man, except Lee, born in the South within a century. More recently it proposed to settle a disputed point in Revolutionary history by popular vote. It rolls a soft-boiled eye at the Ku Klux and the Fundamentalists. It professes high respect for Thomas Jefferson, but obviously doubts that he intended the Bill of Rights to apply to Republicans, bootleggers, college professors and Socialists.

None of these things, of course, would constitute a blemish on the flower of Southern journalism, but the *News and Observer* does more. It has spoken disrespectfully of the American Tobacco Company, the Southern Railway, and even of the Textile Manufacturers' Association. It has discovered crooks within the Democratic party and has denounced them as vigorously as if they had been Republicans. It cannot be bought and it cannot be bullied, except, perhaps, by the Democratic executive committee. It has weird opinions, but they are its own opinions and it maintains them because they are its own and not because it is paid to maintain them or afraid not to maintain them. It is too honest and too bold to qualify as an acolyte in the temple of modern business.

But if North Carolina is shaky, the Old Dominion is as solid as Jackson at the battle of Bull Run. A man named Jaffé, editing the Norfolk *Virginian-Pilot*, has, indeed, apparently fallen out of the ranks to substitute for the goose-step a war-dance by the side of the road. But Norfolk is on the extreme edge of the continent, and if Jaffé grows too obstrep-

---

4. John Spencer Bassett, professor of history at Trinity College in North Carolina and, after 1906, at Smith College.

erous he can easily be shoved off. No, there is no serious trouble in
Virginia.

Viewed as a whole, the situation in the South thus seems to be
sufficiently reassuring, even with the exceptions noted. And yet a doubt
lingers. The more contumacious newspapers somehow have something
that seems to be missing among the perfect flowers of modern business.
For one thing, the best of the villeins clamor to get on their pay-rolls.
Without paying higher wages than other papers, they can pick and
choose, and whenever they snap their fingers at a smart young reporter,
he comes running. Some of them, moreover, are gaining a dangerous
prestige. Advertisers are slowly acquiring the notion that theirs is a
quality circulation, and if that impression should become widely established it might compel the adoption of their methods by others.

That seems to be a long way off as yet, but it is possible. At present,
Southern journalism is in the main controlled by the sublime slogan of
business: "Give the public what it wants." The Southern public, as a
whole, has not in this generation tasted leadership by the press, and so it
does not want it—as yet. It is content with the grist of the Associated
Press dispatches in the news columns. It is content with an editorial
page made up of thundering denunciations of the Republican party and
of Antichrist, variously personified in Clarence Darrow, the Pope, Harry
Emerson Fosdick[5] and the Elders of Zion, balanced by maudlin eulogies
of the Southern climate, the Confederacy, cotton manufacturers, and
successful realtors. It is content with features including book reviews by
estimable maiden ladies who accept Miss Rutherford[6] as a historian
inspired of God and infallible and who think Dreiser uncalled-for, music
criticism by the most oppressed of the cubs, dramatic criticism by the
third assistant advertising manager (he who handles the theater accounts), and, for the rest, canned stuff from the syndicates and the
comic strips.

But if the Southern public once tasted journalistic leadership? If it
were once given the notion that newspaper work might be made a
shrewd and honest criticism of life? In some Southern newspapers, as I
have said, it is already being shown a little of the battle of ideas, the
hard, vigorous, exhilarating clash of contending intelligences in the
great world beyond the county line, as that battle is interpreted by keen,
clear minds. Will it learn to like the dose, and begin to demand it of the

5. Harry Emerson Fosdick, liberal Baptist minister and author, pastor of Riverside
Church, New York City.

6. Mildred Lewis Rutherford, historian general of the United Daughters of the Confederacy, author of *Jefferson Davis* (1916) and other works in defense of the South.

newspapers that are now serving it a stale, suety hash of the news of last night, the politics of the last century, and the theology of the last Crusade? It is a disturbing thought.

But all that is mere speculation. The fact is that Southern journalism is now so near to perfection that the measure by which it has failed to attain the ideal is imperceptible to the naked eye.

# The Function of Criticism
# at the Present Time

# Critical Attitudes North and South

In a January 1924 letter Howard Odum suggested that Johnson write an essay on "our sensitiveness to outside criticism and some of our misinterpretations of Northern critics." The result was "Critical Attitudes" (*Social Forces*, May 1924), one of Johnson's best discussions of the nature of social criticism and of social criticism by Southerners in particular. Johnson the moralist emerges here (as he often does when he writes for Odum), calling for harsh criticism of Southern "bigotry, intolerance, superstition and prejudice" and defending those Northern critics who have critically analyzed the South.

Within the last few years the South seems to have become an object of deep concern to every publicist in the United States. It is difficult now to find on the news stands a serious magazine without an article on some phase of life below the Potomac, or a discussion of one idea or another that has come out of the South. Critical pilgrims are perpetually exploring the section and sending back to their publications reports varying in quality from the highly valuable to the worthless and mischievous. Change the apostrophe from "brither Scots" to "Southerners," and the remainder of Burns' renowned advice becomes apt and timely:

> If there's a rent in a' your coats,
>     I rede ye, tent it.
> A chiel's amang ye taking notes
>     And, faith, he'll prent it!

The noteworthy revival of interest in Southern affairs is based upon various events in recent history. But although the events are various, together they mark the final, complete return of the South to the Union. Southern historians have repeatedly and bitterly commented on the fact that when Lee surrendered the Congress of the United States promptly did what for four years the Confederate armies had striven in vain to do—put the South out of the Union. But as a matter of fact the resolution of Congress to treat the Southern states as conquered territory was only legislative recognition of a *fait accompli*. Morally and spiritually, the South had been out of the Union for four years. Congress could not legislate it out, and a few years later Congress was equally impotent to legislate it in again. Save in legislative fiction and administrative fact

Copyright © 1924 by the *Journal of Social Forces* and reprinted with permission.

the South was alien ground for many years after the breach of the sixties had been officially closed. Even commercially she had small part in the subsequent history of the nation until the rise of the textile industry diverted her attention and drew her from her exclusive preoccupation with cotton culture. This is not to be understood as an assertion that her people had no part in the building of the American nation between, say, 1860 and 1885. Their contribution to that work was immense, but it was made, so to speak, individually, and in large part by men who were Southern only by the accident of birth. As a section, the South was out of it.

As a section she has come back into the Union by such slow degrees that it is out of the question to settle upon any particular date as that of her return to the house of her fathers. All that can be stated positively is that she is now inside the Union again, and that can be stated positively only because within the last few years she has been influencing the life of the rest of the Union profoundly—so profoundly that the phenomena traceable to the influence of the South have attracted the attention of every publicist in the country.

Among these phenomena three stand out conspicuously. All three have been noted by the rest of the country with mingled emotions, among which distrust is conspicuous. The first of the three to be made manifest appeared in 1913 and continued through the late war. It was the demonstration then afforded the rest of the country that the South is still productive of political genius, and that it is of an aggressive type. Between the foundation of the government and 1850 that genius dominated the country, and elected a succession of Southern Presidents broken only by the Adamses and Van Buren. During the late war not only was a Virginian President, but five of his ten cabinet ministers were born below the Potomac. If that sort of thing is likely to continue, it would seem that the South is not only back in the house of her fathers, politically, but also that she has arrived there booted and spurred, with the power, and perhaps the will, to turn the rest of the occupants out of doors.

Critics, however, have no just cause for bringing railing accusations against the South on that account. If she has the political skill and energy to supply the country with able administrators, that is all to her credit. Less flattering to Southern vanity are two other phenomena that demonstrate her power to modify the destiny of the rest of the nation, surest proof that she is once more of, as well as in, the nation. These two contributions of the South to current American problems are the hegira of the Negroes and the rise of the Ku Klux Klan.

These two incidents are not unparalleled, by any means, but study of their parallels affords small comfort to the Northern or Western observer. The movement of the negroes is in many ways strikingly similar to the movement of Polish Jews after the collapse of the revolutionary uprising in Russia in 1906. It is estimated that almost a third of the seven million Jews then resident in Poland transferred themselves to the United States, either directly, or by way of Germany, within the eight years between 1906 and 1914; and that tide of immigrants, combined with the equally impressive flood from southern Europe, supplied the industrial North with a problem of assimilation which it has not yet begun to solve. Now the negroes, streaming north, are injecting a new, and still less assimilable, element. The Ku Klux Klan has its parallel in the Know-Nothing movement, and while Know-Nothingism finally wore itself out, it was not until after it had provoked profound social disturbances, attended by rioting and bloodshed. Thus the South has given birth to movements that have raised again two spectres that have affrighted the rest of the country before.

What wonder, then, that the rest of the country has discovered a sudden interest in the South? A section with a history of aggressive, dominant and skillful political activity, after a period of enforced quiescence, becomes active again, and exhibits unmistakable signs of the old ambition. A section whose societal organization has affected the nation hardly at all for half a century suddenly injects two appallingly difficult social complications into a situation already highly complicated. It is enough to make publicists in every part of the country abruptly turn their attention in this direction and set themselves to dissect and analyze every phase of Southern life.

Criticism of the South therefore is not only inevitable, but certain to continue and to increase, as the part played by the South in American affairs continues and increases in importance. It is a thing that cannot be avoided, and that should not be avoided. On the contrary, in so far as it is accurate and intelligent, it is valuable and should be welcomed by thoughtful Southerners.

What, then are the facts? Is the current criticism of the South on the whole accurate and intelligent, and is it, if not exactly welcomed, at least accepted and turned to good account by thoughtful Southerners?

Any answer to such questions must be doubly qualified, first by allowance for the wide margin of error inherent in generalizations, and second by allowance for an even wider margin of error chargeable to the account of human fallibility. But this entire inquiry is in the nature of the case an adventure into generalities, in which the risk of generalization must be accepted. Therefore, it may be said that the answer to both questions is Yes, in so far as human fallibility permits. Of course one sees now and then a belated flap of the bloody shirt; and one must admit that in the South, as everywhere else, the thoughtful are the minority. There still appears, occasionally, criticism that is born of bigotry and prejudice. There still occur, occasionally, bigoted and prejudiced reactions to criticism that is just. But Northern and Western critics in increasing numbers are writing of the South without conscious prejudice and after painstaking study; and their criticisms are commanding the attention of an increasing number of the leaders of the South.

A case in point that immediately comes to mind is that of Frank Tannenbaum's *Darker Phases of the South*,[1] which is ruthless criticism, but always intelligent and usually accurate; and which has received and continues to receive respectful and attentive reading, as well as vigorous denunciation, in the South.

Still, there is the factor of human fallibility to be considered. If it exceeds the irreducible minimum, on the side of the critics, or on that of the criticized, then current criticism of the South is relatively ineffective. If there is demonstrable susceptibility to error on the part of the critics their criticism necessarily loses value. If there is demonstrable obduracy on the part of the South as regards the critics now writing about the South then their criticism is equally ineffective. If both are demonstrable, then the allowance that must be made for error is needlessly great, and current criticism of the South is not, and cannot be, as effective as we may reasonably expect criticism to be.

Unhappily, the demonstration, in both cases, is all too easy. Despite her return to the Union, the misunderstanding that sent the South out of it, and kept it out for many decades, has not yet been entirely dissipated. Historians have never sufficiently emphasized the fact that the Bloody Chasm opened between two sections that were viewing the same problem from different angles. In 1860 slavery was regarded as a perplexing and difficult obstacle to the advancement of the nation and the race in the South, as in the North. But whereas the North regarded it as chiefly an economic problem, the South regarded it as chiefly a social problem. Uppermost in the mind of the Northerner was the thought that the negroes were slaves. Uppermost in the mind of the Southerner was the thought that the slaves were negroes. Naturally there was divergence of opinion as to what should be done about it; and that divergence of

---

1. *Darker Phases of the South* (1924) was a collection of essays of social criticism that Tannenbaum, a Columbia University professor, had first published in *Century* after travels across the South.

opinion as to methods of dealing with the problem, not a dispute over the existence of a problem, was what split the nation.

The divergence of opinion as to methods of dealing with the negro problem still exists. The Southerner who would go abroad proclaiming that there is no negro problem would be hastily taken into custody and locked in a padded cell by his neighbors; yet it is quite true that many a Northern critic has been unable to convince the South that what he considers the negro problem exists at all as a problem. Such critics, explicitly or—what is worse—implicitly, state the problem in some such terms as these: In the South the negroes are a dominated race; how can we release them? The Southerner is quite honestly unable to see in that any problem whatever. The negro problem, as he understands it, is more on this order: In the South the dominated race are negroes; how dare we release them?

Where there has been no agreement on definition of the question, the debate is foredoomed to end in futile recriminations. Thus the South has from time immemorial found itself attacked for refusing to listen to men who, from the Southern standpoint, argued from incomprehensible premises to abhorrent conclusions. Such attacks cannot be expected to promote sweet reasonableness in the minds of Southerners. They may be made in all sincerity by thoroughly conscientious men; but to the South they seem to be unprovoked, vindictive, senseless, and they are accordingly resented by Southerners who are themselves sincere and conscientious. Resentment, in turn, produces a steely rigidity of policy and opinion that cannot be affected by the sharpest and most accurate criticism. Something of the sort has certainly affected the Southern attitude toward all outside criticism. Any doubt on this score is promptly resolved by consideration of the reception accorded the efforts of the national legislature to deal with child labor. This was criticism of the most pointed, backed by the moral opinion of the nation as expressed in the heavy Congressional majorities for the various bills. But it was successfully resisted by the South. Greed profited by that resistance, but Greed did not supply its strength. The strength of the resistance was supplied by honest and humane men who resented, not the abolition of child labor, but interference by Washington with the conduct of their business.

Homogeneous peoples invariably resent outside criticism simply because it is of alien origin; but there can be little doubt that this predisposition to resentment has been intensified in the case of the South by the fact that much criticism of the section has been based upon psychological and historical concepts alien to her habit of thinking. It may be—in some cases it has been—the work of intellectual giants, but from the standpoint of the South it isn't intelligent because it isn't intelligible.

A minor, but appreciable, influence in this hardening of Pharaoh's heart is the development within the South itself during the last few years. It is difficult for the native born to keep track of the transformations being wrought between the Potomac and the Gulf, so rapidly do they occur; how then shall the visitor note them and understand their significance? A man in Birmingham, Alabama, is in the South. So is one in the cotton fields of southern Georgia, and so is another in the Carolina Piedmont; but a meticulously accurate report by one of them on the social organization of his community would be fantastically false as a description of either of the others. In too many instances writers have applied to "the South" descriptions that were true of one town or one county, but no more typical of the section than a faithful account of the civilization of Herrin, Illinois, would be typical of the Mississippi Valley. Politically there seems to be, up to this writing, still a South; but economically, socially, culturally and even, to a considerable extent, racially, strict accuracy exacts reference to "the Souths."

Let it be repeated for emphasis—it is next to impossible for the native to keep his information relative to any considerable portion of the section abreast of the transformations that constantly take place. The stranger, therefore, is in the very nature of things peculiarly susceptible to error of fact. Current criticism of the section indeed is constantly falling into glaring errors, which invalidates it further.

The factor of human fallibility, therefore, operates strongly to make the South believe that much of the current criticism of its social organization is unintelligent and inaccurate. And though it had been written by Solomon and checked by the Census Bureau, as long as the South believes it to be unintelligent and inaccurate, as far as its effectiveness is concerned it might as well be both.

The fact of prime importance, however, is the existence in the South of a thoughtful minority capable of making the necessary allowance for human fallibility, and in the North and elsewhere of publicists interested in finding out and publishing the exact truth about the South. There is at this hour more willingness on the part of the rest of the country to give the South a fair hearing than has been manifest for three quarters of a century. There is a new realization that Southern problems are necessarily American problems, that Southern progress is American progress, and that complete understanding of the South is essential to complete understanding of America. It is conceded that the South has a contribution to make to the spiritual and intellectual progress of the nation, and that the nation cannot hope to achieve its highest destiny without that contribution. America, at last, is ready to lend us her ears.

But shall she be required to lend us her tongue also? It is nothing to wonder at that the South has hitherto been silent. In addition to her moral exile, she has been engaged for two generations in the task of reconstructing a shattered civilization. Although the oldest section of the country, she was thrown back, by the cataclysm of seventy years ago, to something approximating frontier conditions, and the atmosphere of the frontier is notoriously inclement to the arts, especially to the highly sophisticated art of criticism. When the house has been knocked down, and it is imperatively necessary to construct some sort of shelter for the family, one able-bodied hod-carrier is worth a platoon of interior decorators. Up to the beginning of the century the South literally was unable to spare from the more immediately necessary work of reconstruction a single man of sufficient mental calibre to make an effective critic.

Those desperate and laborious days are over now. The civilization of the South has been rebuilt, and stands stronger and firmer than ever before. At last we can afford to take time off to answer questions, and to question ourselves as to what we intend to do and how we propose to go about it. At last we can afford to listen to what the neighbors think of our work, to obtain suggestions from them as to its improvement, and to explain to them its good points.

But who is to speak for us? Heretofore we have depended upon bringing in an outsider, showing him over the place, and leaving it to him to explain it to the rest of the world. That method has proved unsatisfactory. The man may do his best, but it is out of the question for him to know as much about it as those who have watched it all their lives.

If the work of building the new South is to go forward to best advantage, the South must develop its own critics. They can criticise most effectively, in the first place because they have the Southern viewpoint, and can therefore be understood, and in the second place because they have the most and the most reliable information, and therefore can most frequently spot the joints in Southern armor. For the same reasons they can best interpret the South to the rest of the nation.

But if they are to affect either the South or the outside world, they must be critics, not press-agents. Too much has been said of the South's need for "sympathetic" criticism. This demand has resulted in some so-called criticism that is sympathetic, not with the South, but with the South's least admirable traits, with bigotry, intolerance, superstition and prejudice. What the South needs is criticism that is ruthless toward those things—bitter towards them, furiously against them—and sympathetic only with its idealism, with its loyalty, with its courage and its inflexible determination. Such criticism will not be popular, for it is not in human nature to hold in warm affection the stern idealist who relentlessly exposes one's follies and frailties and continually appeals to one's better nature. But it will be respected and in the end admired. And above all, it will be effective.

The JOURNAL OF SOCIAL FORCES has faith to believe that there are in the South men and women who are capable of producing such criticism, and it is the wish of the magazine to afford them a mouthpiece. This endeavor has been misinterpreted, of course, and doubtless will continue to be misinterpreted; but that is of small importance if the magazine can continue to find contributors who are able and willing to present the facts as they exist, and to interpret them in the light of Southern conditions, Southern history, and—if there is such a thing—of Southern psychology. It is too much to claim that the South has nothing of which it should be ashamed; if that were true it would be a terrestrial paradise. But the worst that can be said truthfully of the South is by no means so bad as to justify a conspiracy of silence concerning it, for if we deny our faults no one will believe us when we admit our virtues.

# The South Takes the Offensive

In an essay written for the *American Mercury* Johnson speaks in a voice different from that of the *Social Forces* articles. In Odum's journal he was usually earnest, sometimes even hortatory. In the *Mercury*, he was usually ironic. Thus in May 1924—the same month in which he hailed Northern critics in *Social Forces* (see above, p. 85)—he adopts the persona of a Southerner who resents "the hordes of Yankeedom" that have descended upon the South, one who proclaims the superiority of Southern civilization. Johnson's irony, he wrote Mencken later, was not appreciated by all North Carolinians: "A good many people have been enthusiastic, but I was told today that in academic circles, notably the state university and Trinity college (Methodist), ["The South Takes the Offensive"] is much deprecated."

The murderer revisits the scene of his crime. On no other hypothesis can one account for the morbid interest which, for fifty years and more, Northern publicists have exhibited in the South. From the Hon. Albion W. Tourgée, author of "A Fool's Errand"[1] and—with collaborators—of the financial insolvency in which North Carolina lay for forty years, down to Frank Tannenbaum, who did, indeed, leave the spoons untouched, they have come for two generations, not single spies but in battalions. With Christian joy they have prowled among the ruins of Louvains which stand as memorials to an earlier von Kluck named Sherman. With vast perseverance they have baled out every cesspool they could find south of the Potomac. Every discreditable thing that the South has ever done, or said, or thought has been made the subject of detailed reports in the public prints.

The business of a critic, of course, is to criticize and the Northern critic who finds himself in the South naturally criticizes what comes under his observation. Were Northern criticism of the South confined to those who have been trained to the business and know what they are about, that would be a phenomenon strictly in the course of nature, not to be enjoyed, perhaps, but to be endured philosophically, as one endures hot weather in July or the insolence of Jamaica Negroes in New

1. Albion W. Tourgée, Northern author of *A Fool's Errand* (1879), *Bricks Without Straw* (1880), and novels of Reconstruction, was a carpetbag politician in North Carolina.

Copyright © 1924 by the *American Mercury* and reprinted with permission.

York. But it has gone far beyond that. It is not confined to professional writers. It is not confined even to professional uplifters, including the infinitely repulsive females who move Northern audiences to tears by accounts of their labors in the South, where their meddling makes life a burden to honest mountain moonshiners, or insures to young Negroes who would otherwise spend their lives as humble toilers in the cotton-fields a dignified and impressive end, quietly seated in the electric chair. Go to Asheville, or to Pinehurst, or to one of the Florida resorts which Northern squatters have converted into cities as typically Southern as Bangor, Maine, and listen to the comments on the wretchedness of the South. Travel every day for a month on one of the through trains between New York and New Orleans, and twenty-nine times one will be regaled in the Pullman smoker with a detailed account of all the errors, beginning with Secession, that the South has ever committed. Now and then, of course, one encounters a man of the North so sensible and so polite that were it not for his accent he would be indistinguishable from a Southerner. But he is a rare exception. The hordes of Yankeedom plainly regard themselves, not only as thoroughly competent critics, but in some measure as missionaries told off to preach the gospel violently in a heathen land.

This is remarkable. When the messianic delusion infects an entire population, causing it to spend fifty years, and incalculable tons of paper and ink, not to mention spoken words, in discussion of a section that but rarely pays the slightest attention to its critics, the thing is surely traceable to some definite cause. That cause I believe to have been stated in the opening words of this paper: the murderer revisits the scene of his crime.

To be sure, the South has not been murdered outright, but her survival is not due to any lack of homicidal intent on the part of her assailants. After she had been beaten and severely wounded on the field of battle, the gentle order of political Assassins was loosed upon the terrain whence the Northern hordes had withdrawn; and it was the work of their poisoned knives, not that of the sword of Grant, that kept the South financially and politically bed-ridden for half a century. It was murder in intent, if not in effect, and the volubility of the Yankee on the subject of the sloth, the wickedness, the general depravity of the South is simply the ordinary reaction of the second-rate criminal too feeble of soul to face the consequences of his own iniquity, which he must justify to himself by endless abuse of his victim. The murderer, in spirit, revisits the scene of his crime.

There is, of course, an apparent objection to the theory, namely, that that is precisely what the murderer, if he is sane, does not do. The objection, however, is only apparent, for the condition is not met. Yankeedom is lunatic, has been so for years, and appears to be growing wilder every hour. Dismiss its attitude toward the South entirely. Conduct the clinic along other lines. Examine its politics, religion, business, sport, manners and customs, social intercourse, speech, deportment in public. The stigmata of insanity are numerous, conspicuous and unmistakable.

Since we are now feeling the first tremors of that quadrennial epilepsy known as a campaign year, consideration of the subject in detail may as well begin with Northern politics. When the Southerner reflects upon the number of evidences of defective mentality that each succeeding Presidential campaign exhibits to a startled world, he ceases to regret, and even finds comfort in, the political *déclassement* of his native section. Since she was so misguided as to take the Constitution of the United States seriously in the sixties of the last century, even to the point of drawing the sword in its defense, the South has been rigidly debarred from effective participation in the conduct of the affairs of this Union except for a very brief period. *Passim* it is to be noted that during the year and a half that she did enjoy undisturbed control, in spite of sixty years' disuse of her powers, she ran this government with a vigor, intelligence and skill unprecedented in its history for two generations. But her fatal propensity for going to war involved her in a second row almost as disastrous in its political effects as the first. Now she is back in her old position, her vote already counted; and able therefore to observe dispassionately the cavortings of the North in its efforts to unearth two nonentities sufficiently free of the glimmerings of an idea to act as heads of the two tickets.

Now, politics in a democracy is not an edifying spectacle in any of its manifestations, but in the South it has some intelligibility, some traceable relation between cause and effect. The South elects a candidate to achieve certain results, and as a general thing they are achieved. The desirability of the end aimed at has nothing whatever to do with the reasonableness of the process. The election of Blease as governor of South Carolina, for example, was deplorable from the standpoint of literate Southerners; but there was reason in the process by which he arrived at the chief magistracy. The rapscallion element simply rose up and demanded the right to rule, and it had the votes to back the demand. Furthermore, it got what it demanded. Did Blease, immediately after his election, turn to the silk-stockings and repudiate his platform pledges to the woolhat boys? Not a bit of it. He stuck to his crowd; he released such of their friends and brethren as were in the penitentiary—many hundreds of them; he whooped for the lynching-parties; he gave South Carolina precisely the sort of government he had promised to give it, as an honest man should.

Is it remotely possible that a candidate with a program as plain, as candid, and as sincere as that of Blease would be regarded with favor by either of the two great national conventions, both dominated by Northerners? It is not. The qualifications of an ideal candidate for President, in Northern eyes, have nothing to do with lucidity, candor, or sincerity. On the contrary, political leaders would be more apt to regard them as hopeless disabilities. The ideal candidate would be absolutely devoid of them. This ideal candidate would be instantly nominated if he could be found. Fortunately, he does not exist. The fallibility of humanity renders impossible the production of so perfect a fraud. But he can be imagined better, perhaps, by a Southerner than by a Northerner, since the Southerner has no hand in prescribing his specifications. The Southerner's vote, I repeat, is already counted. If he is white, he is a Democrat by predestination; if he is black, he is a non-voter by request. In either case, his ideas are of no moment.

The business is thus determined by purely Northern standards, and the ideal candidate becomes a man able to make the New England manufacturer believe that his election will mean the issuance of letters of marque to all New England manufacturers to practice on the public the utmost piracy that their villainy can conceive; able to make the Northern labor leader believe that his election will mean unlimited license to walking delegates to black-jack employers and public and to strip them to their most intimate lingerie; and at the same time able to make the embattled Bedlamites of the wheat belt believe that his election will mean that Magnus Johnson[2] would be turned loose in the United States Treasury with shovel and pitchfork, to the end that no corn-fed peasant of the Middle West need ever do honest labor again. In short, the Northern idea of a fit person to grace the office once held by Lincoln, Taft and Chester A. Arthur, is simply that of a colossal liar.

The South submits that that is an insane notion.

From time to time a Northern critic rises to speak slightingly of Southern theological teachings. Many of them have gone so far as to cite the noticeable smell of sulphur that permeates religious practice below the Potomac as evidence of a certain irrationality in Dixie—"the Baptist and Methodist barbarism that reigns down there." It is, of course, no uncommon thing for a victim of hallucinations to insist that

2. Magnus Johnson, U.S. senator from Minnesota, 1923–25.

he is the only sane man in a raving world, so this peculiar attitude should, perhaps, excite no surprise; nevertheless, Southerners have not yet become so philosophical as to feel no shock at having cited as an eccentricity the most conclusive proof of the clearness of their thinking and the logic of their practice. If the South believes in hell, hanging and calomel, it is because all three have justified her faith by their works. Could there be a sounder or more rational basis of faith?

Souls not necessarily distraught but merely oversensitive revolt at the practice of Southern divines, particularly those of the more uproarious cults, in reclaiming the errant brother by dangling him over the fuming mouth of the Bottomless Pit and threatening to drop him in unless he "comes through." But sensitive souls revolt at vivisection, and at the execution of murderers, and at everything else that is unpleasant, no matter how necessary. Their revolt proves no more than that the Southern process of reclamation is somewhat ruthless. It is no indication whatever that it is illogical.

As a matter of fact, if the Southern assumption is right and Jonathan Edwards was correct in his belief that Sin involves moral turpitude on the part of the sinner, the logic of the brimstone treatment becomes inexorable. But it can be defended even if one accepts the contention of the modernists that Sin is a disease of the soul, a parasitic infection contracted from a morally insanitary environment. Where is there a better vermicide and disinfectant than the fumes of burning sulphur?

The proof of the pudding, in this case, is in the effect of religious exhortation and admonition on the masses of mankind in the two sections. Superior men may not be much impressed, North or South, but are they *ever* impressed by rites and ceremonials, religious or other? Superior men's premises do not require the attentions of the board of health, either, but that is no argument for the dismissal of sanitary inspectors. The man who will deny that religious admonition is the most powerful influence for public decency in the South simply does not know the South. Has it any perceptible influence in the North? Southerners venture to doubt it; and they ascribe that failure to the fact that Northern religious leaders have lost their understanding of their mission. They have gone in for thurification, whereas they should have stuck, like their Southern brethren, to fumigation.

They are a little mad.

When one begins to consider the matter even cursorily proofs of the mental incompetence of the North crowd to the mind in bewildering profusion. The appalling phase of the situation is the fact that certain forms of Northern aberration are infectious. The South, cut off from contact with the rest of the world by vast distances, is in the position of an ancient lady living in a remote farmhouse with a maniac sister. It would be miraculous if her own mind were not affected slightly, and it is. The South is distinctly off her balance in some respects.

For instance, the imbecile Northern idea that baseball, as the industry is operated in the United States, is a sport, has permeated the South so thoroughly that scarcely a hamlet large enough to dispense with a mail-crane fails to present the lamentable spectacle of grave citizens spending long summer afternoons watching eighteen manual laborers at their toil, and paying for the privilege of watching. This is surprising to an intelligent man, but when he realizes that the citizens aforesaid are under the delusion that they are indulging in sport it becomes staggering.

The Bokification[3] of America in respect to domestic architecture is another pernicious influence that has spread from the North to the South. The South half a century ago had developed the only American architects who built with an eye single to making their houses beautifully comfortable, and without the slightest desire to make them conform to the architectural standards of Wops, Greasers, Bohunks, Frogs or Squareheads. Then the *Ladies' Home Journal*, which, naturally, had found no reference to the South in its naturalization papers and therefore was unaware of its existence, proclaimed the dictatorship of the proletariat in the architectural world, and broad verandas, great windows, and high ceilings, exigently demanded by the Southern climate, were swept into the limbo of forgotten things. Mount Vernon and Monticello were despised and rejected of men, and the prosperous residential sections of Southern cities broke out in a loathsome rash of imitation Dutch, Spanish and Italian atrocities as perfectly adapted to the landscape and to the climate as an igloo in the heart of Senegal.

For the most part, however, this influence is confined to Southern cities. The bulk of the South, the countryside, is not much affected, but the great towns have gone over, lock, stock and barrel, to the invaders. In the rural South the arts may be derided, and learning held in low esteem, but at any rate a man is not measured by his bank account. The Southern rustic is sometimes held in villein socage by a man's reputation for carrying a wallop in either fist, or for having a nervous trigger-finger, or even for being on a footing of intimate familiarity with either God or Satan; but he is impressed faintly, or not at all, by a man's possession of a million dollars. The rural South has its zoölatry, but, like that of all uncontaminated peoples, it is explicable, if not reasonable. After all, the strength of the bull, the ferocity of the wild-cat, the

3. Edward W. Bok, editor of the *Ladies Home Journal*. 1889–1919.

cunning of the serpent, are worshipful attributes. One must go to such places as Atlanta or Birmingham to find as the dominant cult that inexplicable and reasonless new religion of the North, the apotheosis of the hog. But there one finds it developed to a degree of refinement hardly surpassed in Lowell, or Detroit, or Omaha, or even in San Francisco. There are cotton-mill sweaters who have learned and applied most of the devildoms practiced on their serfs by the cotton-mill sweaters of Massachusetts, just as their great-grandfathers learned and applied most of the atrocities invented for the benefit of Negroes by New England blackbirders, before the blackbirders begat Abolitionists and were gathered to Abraham's bosom. There are municipal politicians who have learned all that Tammany ever had to teach regarding public office as a private graft. There are statesmen who have sat at the feet of trans-Mississippi Gamaliels, and from their mouths, those great open spaces of the West, where men are wind, have heard as zealous disciples the proclamation of the political gospel of vacuity and fatuity. There are luncheon clubs of business men, tireless as any in the North when it comes to praising their own spirit of tolerance and equity, and equally with those of the North of the type that attained its dizziest height of fairness and liberality when Pontius Pilate washed his hands.

There are even—God save the mark!—city-bred men, born in the South, who carry their Yankee-mimicry to the point of altering, with prodigious and painful labor, their native speech into the frenzied goose-cackling of the North with its tormented r's, its whanging g's, the general cacophony of its consonants and the horrible mutilation of its vowels. They would actually change the soft and mellow English of the South, still faintly reminiscent of the stateliness and dignity of the Elizabethan age, into the current speech of the North, aptly described by an Elizabethan poet's line: "a tale told by an idiot, full of sound and fury, signifying nothing."

Fortunately, the South is still predominantly rural so the Yankeefication of its large cities has not deeply affected its life. In fact, even in the Southern townsman there seems to be still a flicker of the spirit of the old South. In one respect he has stoutly refused to yield to the insanity that otherwise has overwhelmed him almost entirely. As a rule, he refuses, with finality and strong language, to eat jelly with his meat.

But there is one respect in which the tables were turned, in which the lunatic was affected by her keeper, with results practically as terrific as when the mimicry went the other way. The North imitated the South in the adoption of Prohibition.

Yet here is perhaps the clearest proof of that lack of sanity characteristic of life north of the Potomac. The North, dragooned by Anti-Saloon League agents, cowering at every crack of the moralistic lash, apparently never thought of making intelligent inquiry into the real reason for the success of Prohibition in the South. Doubtless any such inquiry was beyond its intellectual powers in any case. Victimized by its own megalomania, it could hardly have been expected to realize that there existed a section superior to it in character and courage and therefore animated by different motives. Frightened out of its wits by professional reformers, and conceiving itself as the boldest of the bold, how could it imagine that in the South fear of those reformers played only a trifling part in the affair?

As a matter of fact, it was not the Anti-Saloon League that made Prohibition inevitable in the South, but the madness of the North. In its moment of wildest frenzy the North had written into the supreme law of the land that the Negro is only a sun-burnt white man, and must be treated accordingly. This lunatic provision the South had to accept to humor the maniac, who was then armed to the teeth and in a homicidal frenzy; but of course without the slightest illusion as to the hopelessness of attempting to make it true. Ever since, she has quietly ignored the provision where it might have come into jarring collision with reality; but there are times and occasions when it cannot be ignored, and then the South patiently accepts the handicap and does the best she can under it.

One of those occasions arose when the South could no longer evade the issue presented by the combination of the United States citizen of African descent and the stuff that Northern manufacturers were selling him under the name of gin. The sensible and right thing to do would have been to recognize the Negro's status as similar to that of the Indian, that is, the status of a ward of the nation, incapable of withstanding the blandishments of the rascals in the liquor trade and therefore to be protected against them by appropriate legislation. The Negro would have benefited in health and morals, the South would have benefited by the removal of a menace fifty per cent worse than a Moro *juramentado*, and the North would have benefited by having immense numbers of its liquor dealers hanged in lawful and orderly fashion.

But that was impossible. In dealing with the Negro the Southerner is

> a discontented gentleman
> Whose humble means match not his haughty spirit

and he must e'en do the best he can with what facilities the mad gods of the North provide. One thing was certain, namely, that the Negro and gin must be divorced permanently and effectively or life in the South, especially in the poorly policed rural sections, would become a night-mare fecund of unimaginable horrors. Prohibition was the only re-course. Prohibition, accordingly, was adopted. The South went dry because the North had first gone crazy.

It is to be feared that after the policy had been forced upon them some Southerners took a malicious delight in fomenting strife in the North over the liquor question. It is certain that some Southerners in Congress voted for submission of the Eighteenth Amendment with grim satisfac-tion, realizing that as boot-legging was already firmly established in the South they would suffer little personal inconvenience. Such a revenge-ful spirit is to be deprecated, but it is entirely natural.

There is one manifestation of Northern civilization that the South finds hard to forgive, even on the excuse of unbalanced mentality, and that is the North's abominable treatment of the Negro. We have our own methods of handling the Negro and they are sometimes rather too sum-mary; but we at least admit that he is a human being, and the cold ferocity with which the North oppresses, tortures, and not infrequently butchers him sickens the South. We know the Negro. We are honestly fond of him. We know that as a race he is incapable of exercising wisely all the functions of citizenship, but we also know that under firm, but just, control he makes an honest, peaceable and efficient workman; and to see him hounded like a dangerous beast and slaughtered for no other crime than being a Negro infuriates us.

It is not to be claimed for a moment that the South is guiltless of occasionally subjugating reason to passion in dealing with the Negro. On the contrary, Arkansas courts recently treated a group of Negroes almost as abominably as Northern courts treated Eugene Debs.[4] To be sure, the Negroes were suspected of having committed murder, whereas no suspicion of that sort ever attached to Debs; but the Arkansas case is indefensible, nevertheless. It is also true that in the course of the year 1922 the South lynched almost as many Negroes as the number of non-union workmen that the Herrin miners lynched in one day. But the Negroes were all suspected on strong evidence of having committed infamous crimes, and without doubt some of them were guilty; whereas no single victim at Herrin was even accused of anything except of trying to earn an honest living by his honest trade. There have been outbreaks of mob violence in Southern cities in which perfectly innocent Negroes perished; but every such outbreak was provoked by Negroes who were

4. Eugene Debs, labor organizer and Socialist party candidate for president in 1900, 1904, 1908, 1912, and 1920.

not innocent, and it never occurred to the wildest of the Southern mobs to butcher Negores as they were butchered at East St. Louis, simply in order that white men might have their jobs. None but an imbecile would deny that the South inflicts wrongs upon the Negro. But the point is that the wrongs that the South inflicts invariably have some reason, if a flimsy one, while the similar wrongs that the North inflicts have all the appearance of outbreaks of homicidal mania provoked by nothing but the sight of a black skin.

The stigmata of sanity and insanity likewise mark the treatment of the Negro in the two sections in the matter of his civil rights. The South assumes that if the Negro is protected in such rights as are essential bases of his continued existence and prosperity, he can easily sustain the loss of certain privileges of which it is necessary to deprive him. The North assumes that if he is permitted to enjoy those privileges, he can sustain the loss of the basic right to earn a livelihood in free competition with white labor. The comparative rationality of the two theories needs no comment.

The Southerner will not permit the Negro to sit beside him in a theatre or a public conveyance, but that refusal is based, not on any theory of racial superiority, but on two extremely practical considerations—his own protection and the Negro's. When a Southerner pays money for a railway or theatre ticket, he expects to enjoy his journey or the play in a reasonable degree of security and comfort. If a Negro occupies the adjoining seat, he is assured of neither. The reason is that most white Southerners have attained a standard of civilization at which a bath is a matter of routine of reasonably frequent occurrence, and most Negroes have not. That statement can be verified to his entire satisfaction by any Northerner who will, about thirty minutes after the curtain has gone up, thrust an inquisitive nose into the restricted section of a Southern theatre colloquially known as "nigger heaven." So much for comfort. As for security, well, there exist in the South, as in the North, certain elements of the population that can never be trusted to attain their ends by due process of law. When such a precipitate citizen's olfactory organs are assailed by the aroma of a Negro far gone he is practically certain to register his objections in a manner not consonant with the peace and dignity of the State. This was brought home forcibly to the South in the latter part of the last century, when the Negroes began to travel in considerable numbers, and coincidentally the railway rights of way began to be littered with erstwhile Negro passengers in bad order from being cast through the windows of moving trains by stifling and nauseated whites. There followed the enactment of Jim

Crow laws, and since whites and Negroes have traveled in comfort and security and the railway companies have saved vast sums formerly expended in replacing shattered window panes.

But the Northerner objects that while all that may apply to the common laborer, what about the exceptional Negro, educated, civilized, and as clean as any white? Should not the rule be relaxed in his favor? In theory, yes. But we are facing a condition, not a theory. In practice how shall we distinguish him—by smelling him? In that case, every Negro ticket-holder would have to be smelled, and what the Order of Railway Conductors would say, were any such duty imposed upon its members, I shudder to think. Furthermore, the South has the knowledge, born of bitter experience, that if it permits one educated, cleanly, and entirely inoffensive Negro to enjoy facilities provided for whites, a horde of the other kind will demand the same privilege with an insistence that will yield to nothing but shotguns. Why precipitate rioting and bloodshed upon an entire community simply for the convenience of an individual?

The North is not devoid of the maniac's cunning. It made the Negro a full-fledged citizen of the United States before he had been prepared for such citizenship but it had a good enough idea of what sort of citizen he would make to take care to keep him in the South, until circumstances forced it to permit him to cross the Potomac in numbers. When the war cut off European immigration altogether, and the post-war policy of restriction held the old flood to a trickle, scarcity of manual labor induced the North to begin offering work at high wages to Negroes at the very moment when the arrival of the boll weevil was making existence unprecedentedly difficult for him in the South.

This, however, is purely a concession wrung from the North by its own necessities, and is in no way indicative of a change of heart toward the Negro. Indeed, as early as last September the inevitable reaction was beginning to be felt. The mayor of a Pennsylvania town had felt impelled to solve the Negro problem in his own community by ordering the newcomers out, and rumblings were being heard in other cities, notably Chicago, where the Negroes had congregated in masses. Yet at that time only a small proportion, probably between five and ten per cent of the total Negro population of the South, had risen to the lure. From the beginning the South has known with absolute certainty what the movement portended—rioting in the streets of Northern cities, probably marked by frightful massacres of Negroes, followed by a stampede of the luckless blacks back to the section where they are treated with rigor, but with reason.

It could not well be otherwise, for on the Negro question the North is insane.

But the perfect evidence, clear, cogent and convincing, the final irrefutable proof that the North is mad, is its gait. The philosopher who could (metaphorically—only Civic Virtue can actually) stand in City Hall Park, New York, when the offices close and believe that the beings who pass him are guided by reason must be mad himself. The horrid scenes that are enacted daily in the subway stations I do not choose to review, even in imagination.

Certainly there are times and occasions when running is no indication of a mental defect, but rather the reverse. The imperious demand of Nature for exercise of his muscles accounts for the running of a child. The running of a man after a football, or along a cinder track is, I am assured by psychiatrists, susceptible of explanation on other grounds than the obvious one of insanity. There is ample reason for a man to run when his house is afire, or his train is due, or an irate householder is after him with a lethal weapon. But when men continually run not for exercise, nor for sport, nor to catch a train, nor to avoid peril or humiliation, nor for any other ascertainable reason except that all their neighbors are accustomed to run, how is one to avoid the conviction that such men are a little insane?

As if to render this melancholy conclusion entirely inescapable, the Northerner generally ascribes as a reason for his grotesque and fatuous haste the necessities of business; and his business usually turns out to be some picayune and inconsequential affair which, as often as not, had as well been left undone.

The extent to which this aberration has affected the Northern mind is mournfully apparent in the conduct of those Northerners who come South. Even after they are removed from the pernicious influence of the daft mob, and brought into an atmosphere of calmness and sanity, it requires some time to cure them of the obsession that they must tear through the streets at maniac speed in order to maintain their status as respectable business men. Even more striking is the fact that Southerners who have lived for years in the North become infected, and when they revisit their native places exhibit, unless restrained, a tendency to run like fools.

Now the very word "deliberation" expresses two ideas that are essentially indivisible—sanity and leisureliness. Idiotic Yankees are continually pointing out to the South that it is slow. So it is, and *D. v.*, slower it will become as the rest of the nation speeds up. *Somebody* must keep his head, if the rest of the world is not to be forced to com-

bine to put these United States under the restraints of gags and strait-
jackets; and how is the South to fulfill its great mission as the saving
remnant of sanity in a nation threatened mentally with total eclipse
unless it continues deliberate in order to deliberate?

We take no particular pride in the South in our lack of haste. We take
no particular pride in the fact that when it rains we are accustomed to
get under cover. But were a visitor to gibe because we showed sense
enough to come in out of the wet we should regard him with the same
mild surprise that we exhibit toward those Yankees who betray scorn
when they refer to the South as slow. To jeer at what are the most
obvious dictates of common sense is not the best evidence of one's own
rationality.

But why pursue the distressing inquiry further? After all, no one is
compelled by statute to live in the North. There are below the Potomac
vast areas only partially occupied—for instance, Georgia. As I write,
the evening paper lies before me. It carries a front page story announcing that since the Georgia Legislature has forbidden use of the lash in
state convict camps, the scrupulously law-abiding, but ingenious, convict guards in Georgia have substituted for whipping the method of
hanging obstreperous convicts by their thumbs for hours. The same
newspaper tells the fascinating story of Mr. Farrington, a citizen of my
own North Carolina town, who, when he was twenty-three, had measles
which "settled in his throat and left him with a hoarseness. 'Let your
beard grow long to protect your throat,' the doctor advised the convalescent and for forty years now Mr. Farrington has been obeying orders.
His beard is all hair and a yard long, coming below his waist."

A tractable people, a people amenable to reason, ready to listen to
and to be guided by competent authority. What more conclusive proof
of the fundamental rationality of a race could be offered than evidence
that it practices sadism only in strict conformity with the law and sinks
into imbecility only on medical advice?

# Southern Image-Breakers

"What are you offering to a pauperized section?" Johnson once asked DuBose Heyward of Charleston. "Jewels and silks and furs." Heyward responded that Johnson was expecting too much when he demanded the Charleston writers "*civilize* (to use an expression of Mencken's) an entire section of the country." But civilizing was expressly Johnson's purpose, and the Southern writers he preferred were those—chiefly his fellow journalists—who led in examining Southern shortcomings. Here, in the *Virginia Quarterly Review* (October 1928) he praises such Southern iconoclasts as Julian Harris of Columbus, Georgia, and Grover Hall of Montgomery.

Once upon a time I taught, or at least was a professor of, Journalism, and I suppose that for the rest of my life whenever my liver grows sluggish, reviving a latent faith in Predestination and Infant Damnation, I shall reflect miserably upon the terrible accounting I shall have to make at the Last Judgment for the mayhems I then committed upon the minds of quite decent college students. But in such moments of depression a small consolation remains to me. There is one outrage of the kind which I might have committed, and did not. At least I think I did not. I believe that I never told a class that personal journalism is a thing of the past.

Yet this statement has been made so often that it is accepted and repeated quite generally by men otherwise sane and intelligent. Even the South is coming to believe that it is axiomatic that personal journalism is gone forever. Nevertheless, the idea is a false one; it is applesauce, it is hooey, it is the sublime and ineffable boloney. In brief, there's nothing in it.

For we still have journalism, and as long as we have it at all we must have personal journalism, because there is no other kind. That is, there is no other kind that is worthy of the name. The newspaper world is filled with dreadful incompetents, to be sure. So is the world of business; ninety per cent of the men who set up in business for themselves cannot make the grade, and either go into bankruptcy or fail less spectacularly. The mortality in the law may not be as heavy, but it is tremendous. The rigorous training exacted of doctors eliminates most of the hopeless incompetents before they are permitted to begin to practice,

Copyright © 1928 by the *Virginia Quarterly Review* and reprinted with permission.

but happy is the man who has never in his life seen a physician who is no good. The sacred desk I hurriedly pass by to land with a crash upon the farmers. Farmers, as a class, are so notoriously incompetent that it was once thought that the present Presidential campaign might revolve around the question of whether or not they are to be supported out of the National Treasury, as Messrs. McNary and Haugen[1] demand.

Therefore, if the land is filled with bad newspapers, still it cannot be said that their worthlessness is a characteristic mark of the business. The swarms of bad business men, bad lawyers, bad doctors and bad farmers are sufficiently great to obscure the multiplicity of bad journalists. The point is that there remain numerous good newspapers, and in the South, especially, they tend to multiply. But every good newspaper indicates the existence of at least one good journalist; it is the personality of a competent man that makes a newspaper good—that, and nothing else under heaven.

Early this year a Southern newspaper—"The Enquirer-Sun," published at Columbus, Georgia—celebrated its hundredth anniversary, and not only the Georgia press, but half the metropolitan newspapers of America, as well, seized the occasion to fling editorial bouquets in that direction. Yet for ninety-two years the country had hardly heard of the place. I know five men who have been in Vladivostok, and three who have been in Tsinan-Fu, and two who have been in Bankok, but I have never, to my knowledge, seen but one man who had ever been in Columbus, Georgia, and he is the editor of "The Enquirer-Sun."

Why, then, did American newspaperdom get so excited over the birthday of this journal published in a remote Southern town? The answer is contained in two words—personal journalism. Eight years ago the editorship of "The Enquirer-Sun" was assumed by Julian Harris, a journalist who had learned his work thoroughly and who has the great courage which is as much the foundation of really fine newspaper work as a sense of rhythm is the foundation of good musicianship. Incidentally, he had prudently married Julia Collier, who is a good newspaper woman, and thereby doubled his effectiveness.

Julian Harris is not a "fine writer." His English is graceful enough to make pleasant reading, but he carefully eschews the ornamentation that obscures and weakens. His writing, however, depends for its effect on the matter, not the manner. Yet what he says is not bizarre, not unheard-of, not a plunge into unexplored realms of thought. Ordinarily it is just what any honest man of sense would say, under the same circumstances.

---

1. Charles L. McNary, U.S. senator from Oregon; Gilbert Haugen, U.S. representative from Iowa. Sponsors of bills in the 1920s to aid American farmers.

But unfortunately what any honest man of sense would say in private conversation is but rarely what the same man would write for publication in a newspaper. Therefore the effect was sensational when Harris began to print in "The Enquirer-Sun" just the sort of thing that intelligent men all over Georgia were saying in private about such developments as Ku Kluxism, and the pernicious activity of preachers in politics, and the ghastliness of Georgia penology. Not only was Georgia stirred, but newspaper men throughout the country took notice of the fact that here was a newspaper speaking sensibly, honestly, and candidly.

Most newspaper men desire to speak like that, but not all of them have the guts to do so. Harris has, and the fact has made the Columbus "Enquirer-Sun" one of the notable newspapers of the country. If this isn't personal journalism, what is it?

This story might be applied almost without changing a word to a newspaper man just across the State line from Harris. This man is Grover Hall, editor of "The Advertiser," of Montgomery, Alabama. Hall is apparently a more excitable type than Harris. He loves to put the language through its evolutions; he knows how to make it march, wheel, about-face, stand at attention and salute. He loves to make an editorial surge and thunder. When he gets in a weaving way on such a subject as, for example, the menace of Ku Klux government in Alabama his sentences, crowded, hurrying, almost leaping over one another, come crashing in like breakers with a Gulf hurricane behind them. But his rhetoric is effective because it is based on common sense. He has no preconceived notions which he is determined to sustain, even if he has to warp the facts all out of proportion to do it.

Both Harris and Hall have gathered able assistants around them, but they have none the less made their papers stand for the things in which they, personally, believe. Each paper represents a definitely individual point of view. And if this isn't personal journalism, I repeat, what is it?

The same thing is true of Charlton Wright, the South Carolina image-breaker of "The Columbia Record." Wright has laid violent hands on taboos that no South Carolinian had dared touch for generations. He does not, like Jurgen, content himself with doing what seems to be expected. He prefers rather, to do always what seems to be unexpected, at least in South Carolina. It is journalism as personal as a toothbrush.

On the other hand, personality need not necessarily be injected into a newspaper directly. Sometimes it is as well, or better, inculcated more subtly. A case in point is that of the Greensboro, North Carolina, "News," one of the sanest, steadiest, and withal most enlightened newspapers to be found in the South. Its editor, Earle Godbey, is one of those who hug the delusion that good journalism may be impersonal. He lays great stress on the impersonal character of his editorial page. His paper recognizes no pet enemies who must always be denounced, and no friends who must always be praised—in the language of the craft, no son-of-a-[Here the Editor used his blue pencil] list and no Sacred Cow. He lays no explicit inhibitions upon his men. He is the one editor of my acquaintance who has no assistants, but only associates.

But he has the knack of asking two questions in fifty-seven different ways, and they are perfectly appalling questions to a man who has just handed in an article which he knows is more ingenious than sound. One question is, "Are you certain of this?" The second, and even more destructive one is, "Is it fair?" These two queries inevitably force "The Greensboro News" into a certain, definite mould, which is the mould chosen by Earle Godbey, although others may actually fit the paper into it. Thus he stamps his personality not merely on his paper, but also on his men, which is surely carrying personal journalism to its ultimate extreme.

Robert Lathan, now of the same State as editor of "The Asheville Citizen," came into national prominence when, as editor of the Charleston, South Carolina, "News and Courier," he won the Pulitzer prize for the best editorial of the year. But his editorial was only an expression of what all intelligent Southerners were saying in private. No generalized policy, but Lathan's personal courage and common sense impelled him to put it into type.

As for North Carolina's most celebrated editor, Josephus Daniels, of "The Raleigh News and Observer," and President Wilson's Secretary of the Navy, nobody ever hinted that there is anything impersonal about his journalism. Mr. Daniels is full of romantic notions about the Democratic Party and the *ante-bellum* South which sometimes lead him to support what seem to me to be dubious men and more than dubious measures. But his newspaper is unquestionably a power, and what has made it powerful is the personality of its editor. He can't be bought and he can't be scared. Those two traits are the assets of "The News and Observer," and all the world knows it.

In the Old Dominion the prestige gained within the last few years by "The Norfolk Virginian-Pilot" is due largely to the sanity and courage of Louis I. Jaffé, another editor who has the nerve to draw the obvious conclusion and state it.

This list is not by any means exhaustive, but it includes a group sufficiently large to furnish an indication of the trend of modern journalism in the South. Anything that is true of all the newspapers here listed may fairly be regarded as true of the best Southern journalism; and I think that any careful observer of these newspapers will mark certain similarities among them.

The most conspicuous characteristic in which they are all alike is their common disinclination to accept traditional romanticism as established fact. Perhaps someone may rise here to point out a glaring exception to the rule. Josephus Daniels' conceptions of the Democratic Party and of the Old South are so romantic that by comparison with them the tale of Prince Charming and the Sleeping Beauty seems as prosaic and matter-of-fact as a statistical abstract. But these, after all, are generalizations. When it comes to modern instances the case is different. Mr. Daniels, after all, is in part a product of the old school. But when he turns his attention from Democracy and begins to discuss Democrats, he becomes a realist indeed. North Carolina has never hatched a Republican capable of flaying Democratic officeholders as dextrously and as ruthlessly as Daniels can and does flay them. And while he accepts all the fairy tales about the nobility and moral grandeur of the South, when it comes to the specific cases of the cotton-mill barons, the hydroelectric power interests, the railroads and other great corporations, he regards them with a cold and skeptical eye; and his refusal to fall down and worship the economic overlords of the South entitles him to a place among the followers of the new school as well.

These modern Southern newspapers differ somewhat in their economic theories, but there is nothing resembling true radicalism among them. They startle the conservatives often enough, but that is because the Southern conservative is the most easily startled man on earth. The Southern conservative has been on the defensive ever since 1831, when William Lloyd Garrison first began to hit his stride; and ninety-seven years of incessant defending and explaining have developed in the Southern conservative an inferiority complex so gigantic that it colors and flavors his whole life. He has established defense mechanisms which operate so perfectly that not only is he unaware of them, but it is next to impossible for him to be persuaded that they exist.

One of these defense mechanisms is the belief that the South is set apart from the rest of humanity so completely that the very laws of nature, not to mention statute law, do not operate in the region below the Potomac as they do elsewhere. Therefore the assertion that two and two make four in the South exactly as they do in darkest Yankeedom is enough to startle the true Southern conservative.

But the new Southern press seems to be completely devoid of the inferiority complex, hence under no compulsion to believe and to teach that the South is super-human lest the common enemy establish his doctrine that is it sub-human. Accepting the theory that the twelve Southern States are simply twelve States and not necessarily a peculiar spot set apart as the dwelling place of God's chosen people, the better Southern newspaper comments on events in the South precisely as it would comment on similar events in other regions.

The rise of the Ku Klux Klan therefore was regarded by this section of the press precisely as it regarded the activities of the Black Hundreds under the Russian czars, and the activities of the Mafia in Italy. A secret society which undertook to regulate the lives of non-members seemed to these newspapers as evil in the South as it would be anywhere else.

A Pogrom in Georgia or Mississippi was deplored by these newspapers precisely as they deplored race-riots in Kiev or Odessa.

Duels *à l'outrance* between Southern gentlemen have been regarded by these newspapers exactly as they regard fights between Chicago gunmen.

Peonage in the South they have seen as just the sort of disgrace to this country that peonage used to be to Mexico.

But in all this there is nothing even faintly reminiscent of red radicalism. It is merely the reaction to be expected of any intelligent man, decently educated, and candid enough to speak what he really believes. It is exactly the reaction that intelligent, educated Southerners exhibit in private conversation.

The new element that these newspapers have injected into Southern journalism is, in the last analysis, nothing but candor. But candor does not exist suspended in midair. It cannot exist except where it is based on a foundation of very solid courage. Now courage is an intensely personal quality. No corporation was ever *per se* courageous. No group was ever more courageous than its leader. And no newspaper ever possessed courage except as it was endowed with the personal courage of its directing executive. Therefore the new journalism that is reconstructing the South intellectually is primarily personal journalism.

To be sure, it is quite different from the personal journalism of the past. There is no Henry Watterson in the modern South, no Horace Greeley, no Charles A. Dana. There is not even a Henry Grady, nor an Edward W. Carmack.[2]

But who was Henry Watterson? Why, he was first and foremost the archetype of the Kentucky Colonel. He fought in the Confederate Army,

2. Henry Watterson, editor of the Louisville *Courier-Journal*, 1868–1919; Charles A. Dana, reporter and editor for the New York *Tribune*, 1846–65, editor of the New York *Sun*, 1868–97; Henry Grady, editor of the Atlanta *Constitution* and spokesman for the New South movement of the late nineteenth century; Edward W. Carmack, editor of the Memphis *Commercial* and other newspapers, and U.S. senator from Tennessee, 1901–7.

he presided over Democratic National Conventions, he served upon commissions, he advised Presidents, he made after-dinner speeches, he charmed the high-born and fascinated the lowly. Incidentally, he edited a newspaper. But if from his multitudinous activities he had omitted editing altogether, he would still have been a celebrated man.

To a lesser, but still important degree, this was true of Greeley, and it was conspicuously true of Grady and Carmack. All the old stars, except Dana, were not so much men who became great editors, as great men who became editors incidentally. Dana, alone, was an editor primarily and a great man incidentally. The rest found in their newspapers only one of many expressions of their personalities, and in some cases not the most important one. Their newspapers were appendages, not their whole lives. They wore their newspapers as a man wears a *boutonnière*. Men respected the papers on account of the editors, instead of respecting the editors on account of the papers.

But was this really personal journalism, or the reverse? Did it not, in fact, strip the journal of personality and convert it into a purely impersonal stage property, a mere background for the editor? It might be argued very plausibly that the great protagonist of real personal journalism is not Greeley nor Watterson, but the elder Joseph Pulitzer, who buried his personality in "The New York World" and thereby made it the greatest personal journal of his day. It is argued that this is impossible, because "The World" survived Pulitzer; but the most astonishing achievement of Pulitzer's career was his picking an editor as big as himself. Frank I. Cobb, indeed, made the paper glitter as it never did under J. P. himself. And Ralph Pulitzer inherited something of his father's genius, as well as his father's fortune. If "The World" survives Ralph, then the theory will begin to wabble.

"The London Times" remained the Thunderer under generation after generation of the Walter family; in the course of a century it had gained enough prestige to carry it forward for years after Northcliffe bought it. But it was plainly going to pieces when Northcliffe died, and the method adopted recently to restore it was to return it to the control of another Walter. This is stretching the theory of personality pretty far, but not too far. There are plenty of examples of an art being handed down from father to son through several generations. The violin makers of Cremona come to mind at once, as do certain painters, goldsmiths, potters and other artists. These families gave a distinctive stamp to all their work, and what shall we call it, if not personality?

The confusion of ideas that had led to the assumption that personal journalism is out has grown up since newspapers have become immensely profitable. When newspaper proprietors die leaving scores of millions—and this has come to be nothing at all uncommon—the public assumes that such men must have been engaged in a business, or a profession, with a sound scientific basis. Not only do laymen make this assumption, but newspaper men themselves do the same thing. Within the craft for years there has been a persistent and vigorous effort to persuade journalists that they are professional men.

This is arrant nonsense. The professions are, in theory at least, born of the sciences. The case of the medicos is obvious, but laywers maintain that jurisprudence is a science, and some day it may become true. So do clerics claim that theology is a science, while economists advance the same claim for economics, and historians for history. These claims may be pretty shadowy, but they exist, and on them is erected the claim of professors of these branches of knowledge to the status of professional men.

Newspaper men have no such claim, for their work is as unscientific as any activity in which men engage. There are rules, to be sure, but a man may observe every rule with scrupulous care and produce a bad newspaper, just as a man may observe all known rules of play-writing and produce a rotten play.

Newspaper work is not a science, but a craft, and its practitioners are craftsmen, that is to say, artisans or artificers. They fall naturally into the three grades of apprentice, journeyman and master-craftsman; and when one adds a touch of genius to superb competence, he is not a professional man, but an artist.

This concept is difficult because the world cannot be persuaded that art produces colossal fortunes. Yet what is so strange about that? After all, even in newspaper work it is not the artist who gets the fortune, but the impresario. Why should it be strange that a publisher should die a multi-millionaire, when it is well known that a theater-manager who knows an actor when he sees one can do the same thing? Yet no one seriously regards actors, or singers, or pianists as professional men.

Nor is producing plays, or operas, or managing concerts regarded as the same type of occupation as practicing medicine or law or preaching. The impresario may be something of an artist himself, but he is not a member of a learned profession. No more is a newspaper publisher.

There is, indeed, a sort of journalism that is almost completely impersonal, just as there is a sort of acting that is impersonal. There are scores and hundreds of newspapers as mechanical as the presses they are printed on, as mechanical as a performance by a troupe of ham actors. But which of the arts is not full of dull fellows who ought to be swinging a pick or carrying a hod? Which of the learned professions has no ignorant members? Which of the sciences is free of quacks?

It is not by the dull, machine-minded, uninspired hacks that journalism deserves to be judged, but by the best it can produce. And the best newspapers are being produced today, at least in the South, not by a corporation and not by a committee, but by individual men who stamp their personalities upon their papers. I do not mean that every good newspaper is a solo performance. On the contrary, no big newspaper can be anything of the sort. It is necessarily more in the nature of a symphony. But no symphony was ever played creditably without a conductor who made a personal matter of it.

Most competent newspaper editors seek advice constantly, but none worth his salt accepts dictation. An able staff, ably commanded, makes a great newspaper; but under incompetent command the abler the staff the more certain it is to fly to pieces, and probably to explode the newspaper too. A really fine newspaper never existed without the presence on its staff of at least one journalist who is better than a master-craftsman and approaches the rank of an artist.

Now the most curious fact about the intellectual life of the modern South is its sudden fecundity in literary artists. The last ten years have brought into national fame Paul Green, DuBose Heyward, Julia Peterkin, Frances Newman, James Boyd, Clement Wood, T. S. Stribling, Laurence Stallings and I know not how many more. What obscure forces are responsible for this sudden flowering I have no idea; but I do believe that the same forces that are responsible for these acknowledged artists are responsible for such men as Julian Harris, Grover Hall, Charlton Wright, Robert Lathan, Earle Godbey and Louis Jaffé. They are part of the renaissance. Their contribution to the life of the South affects its economics, its science, its mechanics; but in itself it is no more economic, scientific or mechanical than is the "Perseus" which Benvenuto Cellini contributed to the Florence of Lorenzo de' Medici.

# The Cadets of New Market
## A Reminder to the Critics of the South

---

After reading the following essay in the December 1929 *Harper's*, William Alexander Percy wrote Donald Davidson: "It left a lump in my throat." Such was hardly the usual response of a Southern conservative such as Percy to a Southern liberal such as Johnson. But in his tribute to the cadets who had fought and had been defeated in the Battle of New Market, Johnson honored an entire generation of Southerners who worked from 1870 to 1900 in an attempt to rebuild the civilization they had lost.

"I was born," said O. Henry, "in a somnolent little Southern town. . . ."

This statement is almost unique, because in it William Sydney Porter wasted no less than two words—a record for him. He was born in 1867, therefore "Southern" was the only adjective he needed; for in 1867 Southern towns were all little and all somnolent.

The town to which O. Henry referred is Greensboro, North Carolina, and it was still little and still somnolent when he left it, about the time its population was increased by the birth of the child who was to be his successor in the favor of the story-reading public; for Wilbur Daniel Steele also first saw the light in the same village.

But neither man wrote anything memorable in Greensboro. Steele was taken away by his parents when he was still a child; and in O. Henry's time Greensboro had no more use for a short-story writer than a hog has for a hip pocket. Will Porter was a drug clerk and drug clerk he remained until he went, first to Texas, then to jail, and finally to New York, where he became famous.

His most vivid memory of his birthplace, thirty years after he had left it, was of summer evenings spent on somebody's front porch with a crowd of boys and girls. Someone always had a guitar, and the group sang old ballads behind a lattice heavy with honeysuckle. So it happened that the name of the town was always associated in O. Henry's mind with soft summer nights whose air was drenched with the scent of honeysuckle and disturbed by no noise harsher than young voices singing "Ben Bolt" or the "Spanish Cavalier" to the twanging of a guitar.

The charm of this picture is due, of course, to the haze of memory;

Copyright © 1929 *Harper's* and reprinted with permission.

for in the years between, say, 1870 and 1900 Greensboro was desperately poor as well as small and quiet. The struggle for a bare existence was so stern that its citizens had no time to hearken to a spinner of yarns, even though he were gifted with the magic of an O. Henry. So he had to go away to obtain a hearing.

To-day this same town still calls its principal business thoroughfare Elm Street, although there has been no elm there for a generation; but that is almost the only feature of the place that fits O. Henry's description. There are half a dozen skyscrapers on Elm Street. There are traffic bells that jangle, and trolley cars whose wheels screech on curves. There are policemen's whistles, and thousands and thousands of automobile horns. There is, in short, the same devilish uproar that characterizes every lively American town. Somnolence is no more possible there than it is in the interior of a boiler factory.

Universal poverty has disappeared along with tranquillity. There are now a platoon of millionaires and a battalion of bootleggers in the town's sixty thousand population. The largest denim mill in the world and half a dozen giant insurance companies testify to the vigor and acumen of the businessmen; and a garland of colleges, two of them excellent schools for negroes, does credit to the intellectual activity of the place.

This transformation occurred since the turn of the century. It is merely a sample of what has taken place all over the South since the year 1900. It is the work of the new generation, whose youth was not poisoned by the aftermath of the Civil War. Within these latter years North Carolina cotton mills have acquired more spindles than those of Massachusetts. Southern tobacco has produced a group of millionaires with fortunes great enough to impress even Wall Street. Birmingham has become a gigantic steel manufacturing city. Norfolk threatens to dominate the shipbuilding industry. New Orleans claims the rank of the second greatest American port.

Nor is the new activity below the Potomac wholly, or most impressively, industrial. Broadway has blossomed with the names of Southerners, picked out in electric lights—DuBose Heyward, Laurence Stallings, Paul Green, others. Pulitzer prizes for writing folk stream South—to Green, to Julia Peterkin, to Robert Lathan, Julian Harris, Grover Hall, Louis Jaffé, Lamar Stringfield.[1] A South Carolinian takes

---

1. Paul Green, North Carolina playwright, author of *In Abraham's Bosom* (1926) and other folk dramas; Julia Peterkin, South Carolina novelist and short-story writer of 1920s and 1930s whose work focused on Negro life; Robert Lathan, editor of the Charleston *News and Courier*; Julian Harris, editor of the Columbus (Georgia) *Enquirer-Sun*; Louis Jaffé, editor of the Norfolk *Virginian-Pilot*, Lamar Stringfield, North Carolina composer.

the Prix de Rome in sculpture. With Heyward, Mrs. Peterkin, and James Boyd at work in the Carolinas, Ellen Glasgow no longer represents the farthest south of the fine novel. Poets, as distinguished from poetasters, pop up like crocuses in the spring; Addison Hibbard[2] compiles an anthology including thirty who have published each a volume of verse which is better than respectable. The Universities of Virginia and North Carolina publish in the *Virginia Quarterly Review* and *Social Forces* a literary quarterly and a learned journal which are viewed respectfully throughout the country.

Small wonder, then, that the world has decided the South at last is waking up, and is inclined to give young Southerners enormous credit for having shaken off the intellectual and moral drowsiness that afflicted their fathers.

The South has its glamorous traditions, to be sure, but they come down only as far as 1865. George Washington, Thomas Jefferson, John Marshall, James Madison were giants, as everyone admits; and the South in their day dominated the nation. Andrew Jackson, John C. Calhoun, and Henry Clay were no weaklings, either; such men do not spring from a degenerate race. In moral stature and military genius Robert E. Lee overtops George Washington himself, although Lee had not the statesmanship that secures Washington his primacy. And Stonewall Jackson, the two Johnstons, Longstreet, Beauregard, Stuart, Early, and Forrest were such soldiers as delight the heart of the romancer and flutter the maiden pride of any nation. Tardy justice now begins to admit that Jefferson Davis and Alexander Stephens also were men of genius.

Who was the next Southerner to fire the imagination of the nation in a way comparable to the least of these? Woodrow Wilson—but you have leaped a generation to come to him. Furthermore, his notable work was done outside of the South. What happened to the Southern boys just a little older than Wilson, who remained in the South? Were they really unworthy of the tradition of the South, incapable of greatness?

At New Market, in the Valley of Virginia, when the Confederates were hard pressed on one occasion they threw into the line of battle the cadets from the Virginia Military Institute. They were largely striplings of sixteen or so, too small to handle a heavy army rifle except by straining, far too young to have anything to do with the business of organized butchery. As they marched into battle the band of a veteran regiment played "Rock-a-by Baby." But they held their position and

2. Addison Hibbard, professor of English at the University of North Carolina and spokesman for a new realism in Southern literature.

actually captured a Federal battery. When the fight was over they buried their dead, gathered up their wounded, and the heroic, pitiful survivors marched back to their schoolbooks. What became of the New Market cadets after the war?

Theirs is the lost generation of the South. Remarque[3] has lately won the applause of the world with his eloquent threnody of the generation that Europe lost in the war of 1914–18; but no man has had a good word for the generation represented by the New Market cadets. It was during their maturity that the South lay as in a coma. Economically, intellectually, morally, Dixie, as the world believes, drowsed those years away; and now that the sons of that generation are bestirring themselves enough to make a noise in the world, men congratulate the South on the passing of the Rip Van Winkles—Walter H. Page called them Mummies. Of this generation the consensus of mankind seems to be that nothing in its life was so becoming as the quitting of it.

There is no arguing away a popular superstition, and it is much too late to attempt to retrieve the reputation of this generation if it were possible. The men and women who composed it are already in the graveyard, or so nearly there that another injustice, more or less, affects them but little. The world will doubtless go on believing that the new activity in the South, intellectual and industrial, was generated in a vacuum and that the young Southerners who are now commanding the admiration of the nation sprang from the head of Jove, or anywhere rather than from the loins of their putative forebears. Can the intellectually dead generate intelligence? Can mummies give birth to living offspring? Can any good thing come out of Nazareth?

But while this theory may be well enough for outsiders, to credit it would be shameful in a Southerner of the twentieth century. We cannot forget the pit whence we were digged, nor the crushing toil that went into the digging. What went on in the South between 1870 and 1900 was too completely tragic to furnish material for theatrical tragedy, far too high in spirit for written romance which crawls along the beaten paths of life, too stark for poetry. The New Market cadets went back to their schoolbooks for a little while after the battle; but a few years later they were flung into the line again, and this time they were never relieved, for the battle never ended. They went home from school to find the old civilization wrecked; and they spent the rest of their lives fighting hand to hand with intangible foes far more ruthless and far more dangerous than Federal infantrymen.

It is all but impossible now to present an adequate picture of the odds

3. Erich Maria Remarque, author of *All Quiet on the Western Front* (1928).

these men faced. The material destruction in the Southern states is relatively easy to compute. Most of us are under the impression that the United States fought quite a war ten years ago; but to survivors of the Confederacy it was a mere skirmish. The war ten years ago cost the country something like an eighth of its total wealth, and called into military service about one-sixth of the men of military age, that is, 4,000,000 out of 23,000,000 available. Suppose the war had taken all the money and all the men? Suppose we had put into the field 25,000,000 men? At that, we should have failed to equal the record of the Confederate State of North Carolina, which supplied 120,000 soldiers to the Confederacy when the State had only 105,000 voters, including all those too old and too infirm for military service.

This part of the situation can be put into figures. We are also able to construct a statistical representation of the damage caused by a policy of reconstruction of which one is at a loss to say whether its stupidity or its viciousness was the more conspicuous. For instance, this same State of North Carolina, already so completely bankrupt that Serbia, in 1919, was by comparison in a flourishing condition, was loaded with an additional debt of $32,000,000, nearly all of which was stolen outright by officials put in power, not by the votes of the people, but by the bayonets of the Federal army of occupation. Much the same sort of thing happened to all the other conquered States.

All this, also, can be represented to a certain extent to the modern world. What cannot be represented is not the outward difficulties under which this Southern generation labored, but its own inadequacy to the task which it had to perform. One can imagine the bombardment to which the cadets were subjected at New Market. One can find out the number of troops flung against them. One might calculate the intensity of the rifle-fire along their front. But there is still a factor in the equation not taken into account, and it is the most important factor of all. That is the weakness of the cadets themselves, due to their youth. Everyone who has been a soldier knows how a grown man's arms ache, how his shoulders turn to water, how his back bends and his head droops after he has handled a heavy army rifle in rapid fire for even a short while; but who can imagine the fatigue of a small boy subjected to the same inhuman strain for hour after hour? The sheer weariness of that child-regiment makes the heart ache, even after seventy years.

But the generation which had to fight its way out of the chaos that followed the Civil War in the South was hardly better prepared for the task than were the cadets for theirs. The great crime of the Old South was its neglect to exercise a larger measure of intelligence in its economic organization. The fact that it was involuntary, that it involved no malevolence, has no relation to the magnitude of the offense. The really great crimes are nearly always committed by stupid people rather than by bad people.

When the old order was overthrown by the Civil War, the rising generation found itself without either the equipment or the training to establish a new order in conformity with the altered environment. The lack of equipment was a handicap, but the lack of training was a well-nigh fatal handicap. France, after 1870, and Germany, after 1918, proved that lack of equipment cannot long keep a nation submerged if it has been bred to commerce and industrialism. But the economic system of the Old South was already falling into ruin before the war struck it; the war itself might be described as the last desperate expedient of a people exasperated beyond endurance by its own inability to devise any better economic order than a one-crop system and slave labor. But it was a suicidal expedient, for no such moribund system could possibly stand the strain of war. As a matter of historic fact, it collapsed so completely that not even the amazing military genius exhibited by Southern commanders could stave off ruin. The world is still unable to comprehend, not their defeat, but how they managed to last so long.

And there was no resilience in it, no rebound after the war. It was the deadest system ever killed by a disastrous campaign.

So the New Market cadets and all their generation were faced with a worse than Israelites' task. Not only were they required to make bricks without straw, but also without any adequate knowledge of how bricks are made even with straw. The old system was demolished, and, far from being trained in another, they were hardly aware of the existence of any other. Yet they were required to build a new civilization.

And in forty years they had built it. It is no Periclean Athens, or Augustan Rome, but it serves to produce scholars and artists. It begins to bring forth romancers, scientists, poets, playwrights, philosophers. It begins to excite the admiration of its contemporaries, who say that at last the South is undergoing an intellectual and moral regeneration.

But those of us whose memories are long enough to reach back twenty years have a different point of view. These members of the new generation are very fine fellows, but they did not draw their vigor, their stamina, their intellectual power out of the air. They got it from the hard-bitten old boys who sired them; and for my part, I cherish serious doubts that, with all their admitted brilliance, they are quite the men their fathers were. That is to say, if they were suddenly stripped, not merely of all they possess, but of all their traditions, all their habits of thought, all their manner of living, and compelled to build anew and in a different order of societal architecture, I doubt that they would build in forty years as high a civilization as the Southern States enjoyed in 1900.

As I write I recall the achievement of a certain Southerner who shall be nameless here for reasons which will presently appear. He was a schoolman. He was shockingly ill-educated, judged by modern standards and, to adopt the phrase of John Kendrick Bangs, if his mind had been a slot you couldn't have inserted a nickel in it. He was fat, oleaginous, and tawdry. He was never addicted to pineapple, or any other sort of rum, but otherwise he was a replica of the Reverend Anthony Humm encountered by the elder Mr. Weller at the Brick Lane Branch of the United Grand Junction Ebenezer Temperance Association. And his school was like him. In the light of 1929 it seems to have been everything connoted by the Southern word "tacky." It was a starveling institution in which famished professors half-educated gawky country girls. It was enormously long on piety, and short on good manners and good sense.

Nevertheless, this squat, dull, semi-illiterate almost single-handed pounded into the head of a bankrupt, starving, and distracted State the notion that it must educate its women at any cost. To this accomplishment he gave his whole life. For it he planned, he spoke, he intrigued, he toiled like a convict in a chain gang. To secure his scanty appropriations from the Legislature he had to resort to every known political device, from eloquence to blackmail. Again and again when the cause seemed lost he wept openly and unashamed on the floor of the House. He was laughed at, reviled, slandered, and kicked, but he stuck to it, and before he died, in his early fifties, he had committed the commonwealth to the principle of unlimited educational opportunities for every girl.

With a little less intensity, with a little more easeful living, he might have lasted another twenty or thirty years; but it is my profound conviction that he would have regarded the shortening of his own life by twenty years a small price to pay for the success of his idea.

But in this is no pettiness. Here is no smallness of soul, no cheapness, "nothing but good and fair." What, then, is the true measure of this man—the oddities, provincialisms, asininities so conspicuous in the eyes of outsiders? They are attributable, largely if not entirely, to the accidents of his environment. What education he had he scrambled for in the chaotic days immediately following the Civil War; no wonder it was a thing of shreds and patches. His experience of the world was that of a man desperately put to it to find enough to eat; no wonder it was narrow and acidulous. But the keen vision with which he pierced the future and saw the future need, and the intense, terrific devotion which made him pour his whole life into one purpose—these were no accidents. Perhaps he was a fool. Perhaps any martyr is a fool. In any case, he was worth more to his State than five gross of assorted cotton mill barons, plus three dozen Grade A poets, novelists, and dramatists, and a million run-of-the-mine statesmen. His State to-day spawns shoals of pedagogues who are better educated, handsomer, and far more gentlemanly fellows; but if it can find among them just one who is half as much of a man as was this pot-bellied little ignoramus, then well indeed may it thank God and take courage.

I have seen a farmer come in, dripping with sweat, from the fodder-field. He wore half a shirt, trousers tattered from the knee down, broken shoes without socks, and the ruin of a hat. He plunged his head into a basin of water, splashed vigorously for a moment, and then, looking at me quizzically over the towel as he dried his hands, recited in tones too mellifluous for sincerity, *"O fortunatos nimium, sua si bona norint, agricolas!"*

In 1859 they taught the classics thoroughly at the University of North Carolina, and as a freshman there he had learned his Georgics by heart; but before he could obtain a degree the curse fell upon the land, and he rode away from the campus to follow J. E. B. Stuart, instead of Virgil. "My heart was with the Oxford men who went abroad to die" reflects pretty faithfully the attitude of all England; but who ever gave a damn for the Carolina men who did the same thing? The Oxford men won, and the Carolina men lost, which makes all the difference. This man, for instance, when the fighting was over, came home to find the University looted and closed, and women and children of his own blood starving. He fed them by the labor of his hands; and in the sweat of his face did he and they eat bread for the rest of his life.

> God rest you, happy gentlemen,
>   Who aid your good lives down;
> Who took the khaki and the gun
>   Instead of cap and gown—
> God bring you to a fairer place
>   Than even Oxford town!

It brings tears to the eyes of Englishmen, but all it gives North Carolinians is a horse-laugh. "A fairer place than even Oxford town"— to wit, a fodderfield, where back-breaking labor is performed in a temperature of 115 degrees. "O too happy husbandmen, if only they knew their good fortune"—do you wonder at the sarcasm in his voice? The marvel is not that he was sarcastic, but that he was gaily sarcastic.

The man was designed by nature to wear the academician's robe. He was meant to be a citizen of the gentle and fair republic of letters, where he might have won renown; but the fortune of war made him a field-hand, and he could smile ironically over the ruin of his own aspirations. And to do this, surely, one must be a manful man.

I knew a doctor of brilliant attainments who died in the gutter, died like a dog. Liquor, said the neighbors, dolefully shaking their heads. But nobody ever thought to seek for any reason other than original sin for his drinking too much. He had come out of the Confederate army still a stripling, and how he contrived to get his medical education God only knows. But for forty years he carried on a practice so immense and so widely scattered that it would drive three modern medicos into nervous prostration in six months. The horses the man drove to death would have remounted a regiment of cavalry; and in the vast, poverty-smitten region over which he ranged, not one patient in five could ever pay him a cent. He could hardly buy a decent coat, not to mention expensive surgical equipment; yet I doubt that he slept a single night through for half a lifetime. Through sleet and snow on many a bitter night alcohol carried him through when he must otherwise have failed some suffering pauper in the remote wilderness. Alcohol got him at last. It was foolish of him to rely on it, of course. He should have guarded his own health and let the poor devils die in the backwoods. Then he might have had time to study, and to become famous in his own profession. Yet I am inconsistent enough to believe that the old doctor, drunk, was a more valuable citizen than is the soberest prohibition enforcement agent ever heard of.

I knew an editor whose paper, judged by every standard of modern journalism, was a lousy one, but who was, nevertheless, a great journalist—greater, I almost suspect, than the Lathans, the Harrises, the Jaffés, and the Halls, although these have won Pulitzer prizes, and the old fellow was hardly heard of across his own State line. He lacked the brilliance of a Watterson, and the technical training, as well as the mechanical equipment, which fortifies modern Southern newspapers. But in the late eighties and early nineties, when the South touched its nadir, when passion was most venomous and obscurantism loudest, this man was truthful and fair. Financially, socially, and politically, it was a disastrous policy; for truth and fairness in journalism, so far from being in demand, were regarded as damnable heresy; political office, prestige, and such money as was available were all reserved for the kept press. Yet, against every conceivable outside obstacle, and against the more formidable inner handicaps of poor education and narrow experience, he maintained his standard of decency and intelligence so well that his spirit slowly infected the press of his State and hauled it up from barbarism. He made no stir in the outside world, but he was decent when it was harder to be decent than it is now to be great. Yet he was of the generation which we are accustomed to regard as intellectually and morally sterile.

Even the textile industry, which now threatens conversion of the South into a region of brassy, loud, and curiously brutal go-getters, had, in its early days, its magnificent men. In the beginning many a man toiled at the business with no real liking for it, and not much hope of financial profit, because the creation of industry promised to drag his native land from the morass. These, indeed, had their reward, since climate, proximity to the raw material, and an almost limitless supply of pauper labor combined to make cotton manufacturing vastly profitable. None the less, the first venturers into this field were farseeing, bold and vigorous—certainly no slothful generation.

Any Southerner thirty-nine years of age or over can remember, if he will turn his mind to the past, such feats of valor, endurance, and resourcefulness as amaze him in retrospect. Money, of course, is a highly deceptive standard of value; probably most Americans would find it difficult to live on the sums which represented their fathers' total earnings. But in the South the disparity between this generation and its predecessor is greater than elsewhere. A dollar was bigger thirty years ago than it is now; but even then a man who supported and educated half a dozen children on a salary of seventy-five dollars a month was a financial wizard who need not stand abashed in the presence of Henry Ford or Andrew Mellon. Yet the South was full of them.

Nevertheless, the impression persists that this was a lethargic, drowsy, dull generation. The truth is, of course, that only those who were vibrantly alive, incredibly keen, superlatively wide-awake survived. The others went to Texas. In the South from the seventies to the end of the century one dared not go to sleep, on penalty of his life. Perhaps he might not actually be carried to the graveyard, but he found himself promptly a charge on the charity of his neighbors, and his children definitely went under—the boys usually departing for the West, and the girls winding up in the cotton-mill.

Art did not flourish, it is true, but when did art ever flourish on the frontier? The South after the Civil War was to all intents and purposes a frontier, except for the fact that its fields had been cleared. But this was an advantage more than compensated by the fact that if the fields had been cleared, they had also been sterilized by a ruinous cropping system. For the rest, the old order had been completely wrecked, and the inhabitants were compelled to build anew. Since their training, such as it was, had all been designed for the old order, they were compelled to proceed by the slow and expensive method of trial and error. They were surrounded by an economic and moral wilderness, much more difficult to subdue than the physical wilderness their forebears had entered.

In such circumstances, mere living is a triumph, and art would be a miracle. The Muses, indeed, are and have always been kept women. Artists may be poor, but art is for the rich, and it flourishes only in rich countries. A nation, like a man, may be crass, as well as rich and, therefore, devoid of art; but art cannot survive except where the country is rich enough to maintain a certain number of dreamers. In the years immediately following the Civil War to dream, in the South, was death. Every able-bodied man was desperately needed for the task of rebuilding material civilization, and he who abandoned that task, even if he survived physically, suffered the moral death of betraying his people. The least he could do was to take himself away, to do his dreaming in some region where the surplus was sufficient to enable some men to refrain from materially productive labor without inflicting appreciable injury upon society.

Perhaps the most tragic figures in the South are the men who might have been artists had not their obvious duty compelled them to throttle their dreams and turn their hands to material labor. Every Southerner knows them—wistful figures, a little apart from their fellows, even in old age, dimly aware that they have somehow lost, but not sure what, or why, or when. In his latest novel DuBose Heyward sketched one of them lightly; it is a pity he did not do a full-length study, for they are worthy of justification.

But the necessity for that sort of sacrifice is passing, if it has not altogether passed. Heyward himself, with nothing to offer the world but poems and plays and stories, not only survives in Charleston but is acclaimed as a great man there. Julia Peterkin was born late enough to be able, after long years devoted to the affairs of her house, to lay aside the broom and pick up the pen; and the State of South Carolina recognizes her as one of its ornaments. William Alexander Percy can sing in Mississippi, and John Crowe Ransom in Tennessee. Paul Green and James Boyd are honored in North Carolina. Indeed, the most ill-rewarded of all the arts begins to raise its head in Dixie; Lamar Stringfield, a Tar Heel composer, won the Pulitzer prize in 1928 for an orchestral suite based on folk music of the North Carolina mountaineers, and last summer he conducted a symphony orchestra in his home town, Asheville.

In all this Southerners can take legitimate pride. In so far as the individual artists are concerned, it is in every respect creditable. But I submit that as regards the whole generation which rules the South at this moment, it proves only the existence of money below the Potomac. That is to say, it substantiates what the existence of the cotton mills, the hydroelectric lines, the steel plants, the furniture and tobacco factories had first asserted, namely, that the material losses of the Civil War have been made good. The South now has leisure, therefore it can give some attention to other things than the struggle for existence.

But who gave it the money, and so the leisure to appreciate and encourage art? Who but the lost generation, which had no time to search after learning, or abstract beauty, or anything but the bare necessities of life? Who but the Rip Van Winkles, the Mummies, regarded by the world as having drowsed their lives away?

A life may be hard and bare and bitter without necessarily being degraded. Indeed, it is rare that true degradation sets in until some degree of softness, of fatness, has been attained. Consider the worst offenses charged against the generation in the South that has just passed, and compare them with the corresponding charges brought against the present generation. There was a Ku Klux Klan in the South immediately after the Civil War. But it was no preposterous group of addlepates striving to give themselves dignity by mysterious trappings. It was an organization of desperate men committed to desperate deeds. When the old Ku Klux Klan donned its robes and sallied out, it was not for child's play. Before it returned it was more than likely that somebody had died—far more often than is generally realized, one or more of the Klansmen. Harried by private detectives, Secret Service agents, organized bands of negroes, and the United States Army, the member of the old Klan rode with death on his crupper. How does that compare with the Klan which the modern generation has produced?

Far worse than the Klan, the older generation evolved tolerance of Judge Lynch. For this there are many reasons, but no adequate excuse, so let the reasons go. The modern generation has to its credit the reduction of lynchings from 255 in 1892 to 16 in 1927. But if we are to believe Walter White,[4] who has made a meticulous investigation of the subject, as the lynchings have decreased in number, they have increased in bestiality. The older generation hanged or shot its victims; it remained for the younger to invent and apply tortures that might appall a Chinese executioner. In the olden time there was no suspicion that there existed in the South a race of connoisseurs of lynchings—men who would race

4. Walter F. White, 1920s investigator of lynchings for the NAACP and Negro novelist, wrote a study of lynching, *Rope and Faggot*, in 1929 and later became executive secretary of the NAACP.

across country a hundred miles to attend an event of the kind, to offer their expert aid in dispatching the victim with the utmost possible cruelty.

The older generation, as most frontiersmen have done, developed a religious faith as hard, as gnarled and knotty, as were their own lives. Puritanism flourished then in its sternest and stiffest form. But Puritanism in Jonathan Edwards' day had dignity, at least. The Puritanism of the South's lost generation had dignity, and more. It was a bleak faith, if you please, but it was a powerful faith, with which nobody trifled. Its priests were frequently austere men, and not seldom terrible men, but they believed themselves to be servants of the Most High God. Nobody suspected them of selling their religion to cotton mill owners as a convenient narcotic with which to keep the wage-slaves quiescent. Nobody found them denouncing the carnalities of the poor white trash and discreetly glozing over the faults of the rich and influential. They did not convert their pulpits into sounding-boards of partisan politics. Their bishops did not invade Wall Street. They may have served God in ways sometimes not to His liking, but they served Mammon in no way whatsoever.

The South remains perhaps the most religious section of the country, but it finds it more and more necessary to rely on the strong arm of the police to sustain the faith. Comment is unnecessary.

The South may be waking up, as the optimists assert; but it might be plausibly argued that the reverse is the truth—that it is just now beginning to drowse, because only now has it dared sleep. At any rate, as it develops the graces of a rich civilization, it begins to develop the vices also; and it should take heed to these things before it congratulates itself on having produced a finer generation than those who, as children, fought at New Market, and, as men, cleared the way to greatness for their sons.

# No More Excuses
## A Southerner to Southerners

If the author of "The Cadets of New Market" in 1929 betrayed a certain fondness for the Southern past, one year later he was harshly critical of those he believed wanted to take refuge in that past. In November 1930, when the Southern Agrarians produced their manifesto, *I'll Take My Stand*, Johnson saw their indictment of an industrial society, and of Southern industrialism in particular, as a retreat from reality into romance. First, he responded to the Agrarians in "The South Faces Itself" in the *Virginia Quarterly Review* of January 1931; next he gathered all his ammunition and wrote a much longer essay, "No More Excuses," which appeared in *Harper's* the following month. One of Johnson's few angry utterances, the *Harper's* essay outlines better than any other his differences with the Agrarians. It drew a heated response from the Nashville group.

The appalling stenches that have come out of the cotton-mill towns of Dixie within the last year, distressing as they are to thoughtful natives of the region, may serve, in the end, a more useful purpose than all the essences of magnolia and cape jasmine that all the professional Southerners have scattered over things Southern since the Civil War. For these are frank, undisguised, forthright stinks, not, like many odors which have emanated from the South in the past, compounded of the breath of the honeysuckle with just a faint suspicion of putrescence.

There is this to be said for the pole cat: when he is abroad in the land, something has to be done. You can make excuses for the goat, you can apologize for the wet dog, without ever quitting your rocking-chair; but when the polecat makes his presence manifest, you must rise and get your shotgun.

The events of the last year or two centering in Gastonia and Marion, North Carolina,[1] were deplorable, but they have one singular merit—they can by no stretch of imagination be attributed to the institution of human slavery, to Appomattox, or to Reconstruction. In short, they

1. Gastonia and Marion, North Carolina, sites of violence involving textile workers and organizers, 1929.

Copyright © 1931 *Harper's* and reprinted with permission.

cannot come under the old excuses which we Southerners have been using for sixty years to explain all our derelictions. Here is one monstrous apparition which never was conjured up by the Damyankee; and if Dixie faces the fact, with all its implications, it may be the making of her.

Few things can contribute more to the moral ruin of a man than to give him a reasonable excuse for every sort of fault and frailty. The greatest misfortune that the Civil War and its aftermath brought to the South is the fact that it has provided her with such an excuse for sixty years and more. With her material resources wrecked by material force, and her moral resources gangrened by infection deliberately rubbed into her wounds during Reconstruction, she has had excuse enough, Heaven knows, for greater bestialities than she has ever committed. If I criticize her, it is not because I think her record dishonorable, but merely because it is less honorable than it might have been.

And one reason for this failure to measure up to the highest standard unquestionably is the fact that it has been so easy for thoughtful Southerners to salve their consciences by reference to the old, sorrowful past. It might so easily have been worse! Do we lynch Negroes occasionally? Well, everything possible has been done to incite us to a war of extermination against them. Do we regard the Constitution of the United States as a scrap of paper? Well, for sixty years it has been the instrument of our oppression, not the bulwark of our defense. Do we consistently manipulate the electorate to secure such ends as seem good to the ruling class, rather than to secure a numerical expression of the will of the populace? Well, we were merely the first to discover that democracy in a heterogeneous population is but another name for anarchy.

But at last we are faced with a question to which there is no such convenient answer. Do we permit murder to stalk unchecked the highways around Gastonia and Marion? Do we permit the courts of justice to be turned into farcical vaudeville shows? Do we permit, nay, approve, the suppression of freedom of opinion as ruthlessly as if North Carolina were Italy, or Russia, or even California? We do. And how was this villainy forced upon us by anything the Yankees did, or failed to do, during the Civil War or afterward?

To this there is no answer. All the crimes and all the follies of the Blue-bellies stopped short of this. Neither Sherman nor the carpetbaggers had anything whatever to do with Gastonia and Marion. They are Southern products, born in North Carolina and fostered by North Carolina conditions.

Furthermore, it is not merely the blood that has placed the deepest stain on the South in connection with these disturbances. After all, men die by violence every day in every State of the Union. It is not for any of her dripping sisters to point the finger of scorn at North Carolina merely because of the blood. But the total incapacity of the State to convict a single policeman for killing seven strikers, while she found it easy to convict seven strikers of killing a single policeman; the scorn of the very elements of justice and fair dealing exhibited, with the consent of the judges, by the State in its prosecution; and finally, the cynical decision of the State's Supreme Court that, while the injection of religious prejudice into a criminal prosecution is undoubtedly subversive of justice, still, in this case it would not be held sufficiently damaging to warrant granting a new trial—these are what have placed North Carolina on the defensive in the minds of decent men all over the world. And these things are not to be explained away by anything that has happened in the past.

However, the practice of sixty years has developed in the South a fertility in the making of excuses which is not to be daunted by any such combination of circumstances. The latest dodge is to lay it, not to the invasion of Northern armies, indeed, but to a Northern invasion, just the same—this time to the invasion of industrialism. The shootings, and the subsequent obscenities, arose from an industrial dispute. Had there been no cotton mills, there could have been no strikes. And there would have been no cotton mills had not Northern industrialism come South.

Waiving the fact that the textile manufacturing industry is peculiarly Southern, since only within the last ten or fifteen years has any considerable infiltration of Northern capital taken place, this thesis is fairly sound. Gastonia and Marion are products of industrialism. Certain ways of thinking which they revealed seem also to be characteristic of industrialism at its most brutal. Nor are these labor wars by any means the only evils that have come to the South in the train of industrialism. It is plain enough that industrialism is by no manner of means an unmixed blessing to Dixie.

These circumstances furnish the reason, although not an excuse, for the rise of the latest cult in Dixie, the cult of agrarianism. Certain of the intellectuals, especially the younger among them, have lately begun to exhort the South to go back to the land. As one group puts it, "The theory of agrarianism is that the culture of the soil is the best and most sensitive of vocations, and that therefore it should have the economic preference and enlist the maximum number of workers." This is from a large book lately off the press in which twelve Southerners, all of them men of respectable attainments, set forth with perfect seriousness the theory that the South must "throw off" industrialism on the ground that neither religion, the arts, nor the amenities of life can flourish in "an industrial age except by some local and unlikely suspension of the industrial drive."

At first blush it seems incredible that twelve men, all born and raised in the South, all literate, and all of legal age, could preach such doctrine without once thrusting the tongue in the cheek or winking the other eye. Not only have these done so, but here and there all over the South others are arising, usually—to do them justice—very young men, to assert that industrialism, because it created Gastonia and Marion, with all that they imply, has been the damnation of Dixie.

Of such a philosophy one can only say that it smells horribly of the lamp, that it was library-born and library-bred, and will perish miserably if it is ever exposed for ten minutes to the direct rays of the sun out in the daylight of reality. Perhaps the most delicious line in the solemn tome which I have been quoting is the assertion, "Opposed to the industrial society is the agrarian, *which does not stand in particular need of definition.*" The italics, it is hardly necessary to say, are mine.

Perhaps a philosopher could detect in this one line a great part of the tragedy of the South since the Civil War. We have never thought much of precise definitions, of precision of thought in any sense. Facts are so often inconvenient things; let us stick, rather, to emotions. A Democrat does not stand in particular need of definition, therefore we can send an Oscar W. Underwood and a J. Thomas Heflin to the Senate under the same party label. Civilization does not stand in particular need of definition, therefore we can tolerate lynching and at the same time claim to be civilized. Honor does not stand in particular need of definition, therefore we can conscientiously nullify the Fourteenth Amendment and at the same time roundly damn those who would nullify the Eighteenth. Religion does not stand in particular need of definition, therefore we can indulge in phrenetic orgies of hatred against Roman Catholics and still assert that we are the most Christian part of the Union.

So a considerable number of Southerners, feeling that agrarianism stands in no particular need of definition, joyously proceed to recommend it as the medicine for the South. Probably they will never get around to a definition of agrarianism, so it will never occur to them that what they would press to the lips of their ailing country is a draught compounded of the essences of civic disease, of communal madness, of moral and probably physical death.

If this seems to be soaring into the upper levels of gaseous rhetoric, let it be subjected to the test which our agrarians so blithely dismiss. Let it be compared with the known facts.

The principal fact by which it is to be checked is that the South did adopt agrarianism in the beginning and clung to it until about forty years ago. But in the beginning she had no choice, because the industrial revolution had not been dreamed of, and there was no other sort of civilization possible in the American colonies. It is only since 1830 that she has had a choice presented; but for nearly seventy years after 1830 her choice was agrarianism.

And what did she get out of it? The South of 1900 is your answer— a hookworm-infested, pellagra-smitten, poverty-stricken, demagogue-ridden "shotgun civilization," as Henry Cabot Lodge put it. One might, by diligent search, discover here and there families, even small communities, of rare excellence, like lilies growing upon the dung-heap. But the lot of what Walter H. Page called "The Forgotten Man" in the South of those days bore a remarkable resemblance to the lot of the Russian serf prior to the imperial ukase of 1861.

But here we run into the ancient excuse—the Civil War. It is a part of the Southern credo that before that war we possessed a civilization which was one of the ornaments of the world. This is, of course, sentimental tommyrot. Our civilization at that time was based on human slavery which is to say, it was economically rotten. It was so rotten, in fact, that it was swiftly crumbling into ruin long before the blast of war struck it. The enormous movement westward of slaveholders in the two decades prior to 1860 is eloquent of the impoverishment of the land due to a ruinous agricultural system. And when the war came, the fact that, although she had magnificent troops and the ablest military leadership ever known in America, the South lost the decision, is as eloquent of a feeble economic and social structure.

That, however, is neither here nor there. As a matter of fact there was a war, and it is with the country as the war left it that Southerners have had to deal. For a full generation after the close of the war the region clung to an agrarian civilization, and that policy brought it to the condition it was in at the close of the century. But about 1900 it began to take industrialism seriously, and for another generation it has been developing swiftly along the new line.

The fair comparison, therefore, is not between the South of, say, 1850 and the South of 1930, but between the South of 1900 and the South of 1930. For even if we accept at face value the romantic novelist's idea of the South of 1850, we must not ignore the fact that beautiful as this civilization may seem, it was plunging swiftly down to ruin; and to reproduce it as it was, we should have to reproduce the doom that hung over it.

What, then, has industrialism done to the South since 1900? Since it is in the State of North Carolina that industrialism has made the greatest strides and produced the beastliest incidents, North Carolina ought to furnish the most horrible example of the ruin industrialism brings to a commonwealth.

I should certainly be among the last to maintain that the mushroom growth of cotton, tobacco, and furniture factories has made a heaven on earth of Tarheelia. Gastonia and Marion, although they are the most startling, are far from being the only ugly things industrialism has produced there. Uglier than either is the horde of parvenus it has inflicted on the State. When the Steel Trust was formed about thirty years ago, the group of "Pittsburgh millionaires" suddenly brought into being gained national notoriety. They were regarded as setting a world record which would endure for a long time for loud and brassy vulgarity. But there are cotton and tobacco millionaires—and some people with less than a million—by comparison with whom a typical Pittsburgh millionaire would actually resemble the celebrated violet by a mossy stone. These persons are not in fact important, but they do constitute a ghastly nuisance, and they do decrease materially the desirability of residence in North Carolina.

Nor can it be truthfully denied that Southerners display the general human tendency to appreciate money more as they acquire more of it. Since North Carolina has begun to breed millionaires, her respect for them has advanced materially and disproportionately. But let us not forget that this has been true of every complex civilization since history began, not excluding the most brilliant. It was notably true of Elizabethan England, where Sir Walter Raleigh lost his head when his ability to pay tremendous dividends to his backers failed him, and where Shakespeare became *armiger* not in recognition of the fact that he had written "Hamlet," but in recognition of the fact that he owned property in Stratford.

Furthermore, industrialism tends to destroy the picturesque element in the countryside. The slave quarters on a big plantation offered so much more to the artist's eye than does a cotton mill village that the comparison is revolting. However, there was more typhoid in the quarters.

Nor is it to be denied that the factories have hastened the tempo of life; or if it isn't the factories, it is something else, for North Carolina moves much faster in 1930 than it did in 1900. Unfortunately the suspicion will not down that it is, in part at least, something else; for it was in 1902 that Charles Wardell Stiles began his really serious assault on hookworm disease in the Southern States. Perhaps the characteristic deliberation with which the Southerner moved before industrialism began was proof of mild manners and a philosophical mind; but perhaps it was merely a symptom of uncinariasis.

Let us assume, however, that the industrialism of the South and specifically that of North Carolina, its most advanced example, is productive of awful bounders, of money-lust, of architecture that amounts to a felony, and of nerve-racking haste, as well as of occasional butcheries, both of men and of the law, such as occurred at Gastonia and Marion. Is it, therefore, worthy of condemnation?

Certainly not until we have heard the case for the defense. And as the first item in that defense, I suggest the fact that if industrialism created Gastonia and Marion, it also created Chapel Hill and that neighboring hill on which Duke University is now rising.

The University of North Carolina, which does not include the women's college nor the agricultural college, both separate institutions, now receives from the State in direct appropriations about nine hundred thousand dollars a year. In 1900 the State's total expenditures for all educational purposes amounted to only about a million a year. Yet if the truth were known, North Carolina in 1900 was probably as generous as she is to-day. The million she spent then perhaps meant more to her than do the thirty-odd millions she spends now on schools. The difference is that now she has the money, and she has it because industrialism has put it in her pocket.

In 1900 Murphy, in the high mountains in the extreme western end of the State, knew less of Manteo, on the Atlantic Ocean, than either knows to-day of Boise, Idaho. Gasoline and asphalt have changed that, with the result that to-day, it is infinitely more difficult, if not impossible, for a demagogue to sow seeds of suspicion and reap a harvest of hatred between the two ends of the State. And the gasoline and asphalt, like the universities, are gifts of industrialism.

It took money to reduce the percentage of illiteracy by half in the single decade between 1910 and 1920. It took money to establish and maintain a State Health Department that won a conspicuous reputation for excellence not merely in the South, but among all the States. It took money to produce a State Board of Public Welfare that has battled so valiantly against politics that North Carolina prisons and chaingangs to-day are almost semi-civilized, that the school-attendance law is better than half-enforced, and that a cotton mill manager would rather meet

Raw-Head-'n'-Bloody-Bones on a lonely road at midnight than be trapped into employing a child under legal age. And the money has come from industrialism.

All this, however, is arguing an academic question. The condition, not the theory, is that industrialism has arrived. It will not be abolished, nor will its hands be set back out of respect to any theory whatever.

So the real point at issue involves, not industrialism, which is *hors concours*, but the attitude of intelligent Southerners toward it. This is, however, a real question, for it is easily possible for industrialism to replace the Civil War as a convenient excuse behind which Southerners may mask their intellectual indolence and incapacity.

It would be worse than foolish, it would be treacherous to the South, to attempt to minimize the evils which the growth of manufacturing has brought to the section or the dangers with which it threatens the South. To meet and abolish, or at any rate to alleviate these evils is a task which will tax the South's utmost resources of intelligence, of skill, of learning, and of character. If any considerable proportion of these resources is dissipated and lost in vain repining for a system which led the South into the disaster of 1865 and was steadily driving it toward cannibalism in 1900, the battle will be lost before it is fairly joined.

I am enough of a Southerner to be a little arrogant in my demands of the South. A civilization which I might regard as admirable in Kansas or in Ohio would seem to me woefully inadequate to Dixie. I am bound to admit that at the moment we seem, in some respects, even farther away from the ideal than Kansas and Ohio; but that simply means that our task is not merely to overtake them, but to surpass them. For those States were built originally from the wilderness, and make their own standards as they go. The South was cut out of the wilderness as far back as the seventeenth century. We have built one civilization and seen it collapse; but the standards we erected while building it still exist, and they are very high.

I have seen a little Negro driven into frantic denials, then into recrimination, and finally into furious tears by a rapscallion who sniffed at him suspiciously, made a wry face, and said in a disgusted tone, "Boy, I b'lieve you've got ancestors!"

But as a matter of fact, ancestors *are* in some circumstances a liability. Living up to them is frequently a painful and laborious task. Yet the task which the South must face is that of living up to her group of distinguished ancestors; and no merely material success, however brilliant, will accomplish it. George Washington was for his day a very rich man, and he would approve of the material progress the South is making; but his approval of its wealth would not appease his wrath with the South if it sent him as colleagues in the Federal City Senators Heflin and Blease.[2] Thomas Jefferson would approve of his own University today, and also of that which his Southern neighbors have raised; but his approval would soon curl up and char in the heat of his indignation could he read the reports of a certain trial at Dayton, Tennessee. John Marshall would find in modern Southern codes much to admire, but in his reading he would be certain to run across that decision of the North Carolina Supreme Court in the Gastonia cases. Robert E. Lee would find nothing discreditable in the incident of the Thirtieth Division and the Hindenburg Line, but what would he say to a lynching?

The job of the South is to take industrialism and with it fashion a civilization in which such men as these could live. And she will not accomplish it by seeking excuses, or by dismissing her ideal as not standing in particular need of definition. On the contrary, to accomplish it she must seek forever definitions and definitions of the sharpest kind. She must labor with facts. She must struggle drearily and through tons of statistics, through endless miles of dull reports and dry analyses. She must eschew guessing and *know*. She must learn more and more, and then more. She must, in brief, subject her intelligence to a discipline as harsh and as onerous as that to which the great men who are her chief ornament subjected theirs.

Of course I do not suggest this as the proper preparation for life of every Southern school child. I mean only that the handful of men who are the flower of each generation must do it.

But if they do, I believe they will erect a glittering civilization in the midst of industrialism. In any case, this is the only line open to them, for sniveling and excuse-hunting on the part of intelligent Southerners are a worse betrayal of their ancestors than are Gastonia, lynching, demagoguery, and religious fanaticism combined.

2. J. Thomas Heflin, U.S. senator from Alabama, 1920–30; Cole L. Blease, governor of South Carolina, 1911–15, and Democratic senator, 1925–31.

# Race and Southern Politics

# A Tilt with Southern Windmills

Writing in the *Virginia Quarterly Review* in July 1925, Johnson speaks as a Southerner and a Democrat, but he is not uncritical of his homeland or his party. The South, he asserts, by adopting one-party politics trades its national political clout for the assurance of retaining white-only government. A representative Southern liberal of the 1920s, Johnson insists that the Negro should receive equal treatment before the law but not social equality. He manifests a paternalism in race relations which he, to some extent, always retained.

Having been born of white parents in a county in the Black Belt of North Carolina, I, of course, supported Davis[1] in the last campaign. As it happened, I also wished that he might win. He seemed to me a good man for the job. That, however, is beside the point. Had William G. McAdoo been the candidate, I would have supported him, as many of my Ku Klux acquaintances did support Davis, sullenly but effectively. Had Alfred E. Smith been the candidate, without doubt the Protestant prohibitionist vote of the Solid South would have smothered opposition to his candidacy below the Potomac. Had Beelzebub been the Democratic nominee, the clergy would have been deprived automatically of the privilege of the franchise, and no doubt many of the laity also would have laid down the ballot unused; but I have a strong belief that the stalwarts would have rallied by tens of thousands and gallantly gone to hell.

It is of course, merely a matter of the payment of reparations. Two generations ago we bet on the wrong horse, as Germany did in 1914. Ever since, our political independence has been held in pawn by the winners. We retain it in theory, to be sure, much as the estimable M. Windsor in theory retains the sovereignty of the British Isles; but when the North and the West have finished their jousting we are no more free to reward the champion with a swift kick, instead of an accolade, than His Majesty is free to accord similar treatment to the man in whom the Commons have voted confidence. In the choosing of candidates, we do not count; and in the subsequent election we are already counted. With what delightful irony we claim to be followers of the man who had

1. John W. Davis of New York, Democratic candidate for president, 1924.

Copyright © 1925 by the *Virginia Quarterly Review* and reprinted with permission.

"sworn upon the altar of God eternal hostility to every form of tyranny over the mind of man!"

For proof of this, it is necessary to look back into history no further than June, 1924. The Democratic convention in New York that month developed into a furious battle between Catholic and Protestant, between Ku Klux and anti–Ku Klux, with McAdoo and Smith heading the contending factions. Where was the strength of the South while the battle raged? Alabama was voting for Oscar Underwood. Virginia was voting for Carter Glass. Arkansas was voting for Robinson.[2] North Carolina was wandering around, casting fragmentary votes for every candidate in the race, including the leaders of both the combatant parties. The Texas delegation was torn by the internecine strife that later resulted in a massacre of the Ku Klux at the polls. Whatever else the South might have been trying to do, she was not attempting to nominate John W. Davis. Yet in November the South, and the South alone, voted for Davis. The real fight of the campaign was in New York, and if Georgia be excepted, the South furnished no shock troops to either side. Her forces were about as important in that fight as the Portuguese battalions were in the fight in France.

In the end, she did perform a more or less important service for the Democracy. She furnished the organization's burial party, and accomplished the last sad rites over its mangled remains.

Naturally, we Southern Democrats prefer to blind ourselves to the real situation. Having no political principles, we set up the assertion that we are conspicuous for our extraordinary loyalty to our political principles. Do we not incessantly march through slaughter-houses to open graves behind the banner of the Democratic party? The trouble is that the Democratic party is hardly a more specific term now than the human race. The organization led by William J. Bryan, and the organization led by John W. Davis, were both termed "Democracy," but only an imbecile could believe that the election of William J. Bryan would have meant the adoption of the same political policy that would have followed the election of John W. Davis. Neither would have been likely to put into effect the policy that was put into effect by Woodrow Wilson. Yet we voted for Wilson, too. Our sole political principle is to vote for anything bearing the Democratic label. The North and West determine the bearer of the label. The South supplies his votes. The list of candidates for whom the South has voted in the last twenty-five years is, by its diversity, irrefutable proof that the section is politically unprincipled.

2. Joseph T. Robinson, U.S. senator from Arkansas, 1913–37, Democratic candidate for vice-president, 1928.

A section devoted to fixed beliefs and unswerving in its allegiance to those beliefs might vote for Parker[3] or it might vote for Wilson, but it could not possibly vote for both.

Of course, all Southerners know what has happened—we have traded in our political principles in return for the privilege of maintaining a white man's government, unmolested by attempts to enforce against us two constitutional amendments adopted in wrath and as irrational as the enactments of furious men always are. Under the circumstances, few Southerners are disposed to repudiate, or even to regret, the bargain. As long as there is even the remote danger that division of the South along party lines will mean the loss of white supremacy, no such division can be accomplished. That is why, in case Beelzebub were nominated by the Democrats, the vote of the Southern clergy would inevitably be lost. They would feel that to cast a ballot either way would be to vote for a Prince of the Powers of Darkness.

But are we to remain indefinitely in this state of bondage? Are we to await always the result of the quadrennial contest between the North and the West, slavishly voting as we are bid, for some minion of the Money Devil if the North wins, for some Mad Mullah of the prairies, if the West wins? Are North Carolina, which is rapidly becoming an industrial state, and Mississippi, which remains purely agricultural, to remain forever "unequally yoked together?"

Perhaps an answer may be supplied, in part at least, by the great migration of the negroes, whose presence in numbers in many Northern and Western cities is bringing a sudden and uncomfortably acute understanding of the Southern attitude. It is more likely that an answer will be supplied, in part, by the development of the Negro race itself in intelligence and in social and political capacity. But both these forces are in large measure beyond the control of the Southern whites. Is there nothing that we may do toward our own liberation from a position that is, to say the least of it, humiliating?

There is a great deal that we might do, but the project is so ambitious that one hesitates to outline it. It is, in brief, the ascent from Avernus. Our troubles, beginning with the Fourteenth and Fifteenth amendments, date from the Black Codes adopted by certain Southern states immediately after the war of the sixties. It is not of the slightest importance that unprejudiced modern investigators have found that the laws embodied in tbe Black Code were, in essence, intelligent, humane and honest. What is of importance is the fact that the North, still suffering horribly from its wounds, believed that they were an effort to cheat it of its

3. Alton B. Parker of New York, Democratic candidate for president, 1904.

victory and to reduce the negro to the slavery from which he had been so painfully freed. Then and there the South came under suspicion of the rest of the country. It gained the reputation of a people capable of trying to effect by fraud what it could not accomplish by force. That reputation still exists to some extent. The North is still afraid to give us an entirely free hand with the negro, and while it harbors that suspicion, while it is still under the spell of that fear, it cannot be expected to co-operate with us heartily and freely. It will always keep a gun behind the door if it can.

Obviously, the only way to dispel such fears and suspicion is to prove them groundless, and to prove it so thoroughly and so often that the most unscrupulous demagogue in all the country cannot revive them.

This is a task so terrific in its difficulties that its accomplishment is certain to be long postponed. But what more profitable form of self-searching can a Southerner indulge in than to ask himself seriously and soberly what the section is trying to do toward its accomplishment? It is easy to see what it is doing in the other direction. Every lynching in the South rivets our chains more firmly. Every nocturnal raid of the Ku Klux adds to the weight of our fetters. Every case of denial of a negro's rights under the civil law, every gratuitous insult flung at the race by the lower element among the whites, every needless brutality practiced ostensibly to enforce segregation, every repression of the negro's legiti-mate aspirations to education, to mental and spiritual self-development and to the right to a peaceable existence under decent standards of liv-ing—in short, every unnecessary hardship inflicted on the black South postpones the day when the white South can resume its full member-ship, political, moral and intellectual, in this union. That such just causes of offense have been fearfully numerous in the South, no honest and candid Southerner can deny. That they are becoming less numerous is all that the most optimistic among us dares to hope.

There is a discouraging significance in the fact that our accomplish-ments in the other direction are far less known, for we work at them much harder. It is infinitely more laborious to arrange and carry to a successful conclusion a conference on inter-racial relations than it is to perpetrate a lynching. But how many inter-racial conferences does it take to efface the impression made by a single lynching? More than one, I fear. How many schoolhouses for negroes must be built to win back that portion of the confidence of the country that the rise of the Ku Klux Klan has cost us? How many years of scrupulously just dealing are necessary to wipe out the memory of one race-riot?

Inter-racial conferences, schoolhouses, additional safeguards of civil rights represent the South's conscious program of race relations. The barbarities are convulsive reactions to local stimuli. This really does not help our case, since as long as we are unable to prevent the convulsions and adhere to our carefully reasoned and deliberately adopted policy, we cannot be regarded as trustworthy. Nevertheless, for the purpose of this argument, it is worthy of emphasis that this is the South's program. Without exception, every Southern leader of any genuine dignity and worth, and 99% of the leaders of any influence, long years ago subscribed to the theory that the South must afford to the negro equality of economic opportunity and equality before the law. If the negro has not as yet acquired either, he is in that on a par with most workingmen elsewhere. It does not affect the theory, any more than the fact that a newly-arrived immigrant in New York is at a disadvantage as compared with the descendant of the patroons affects the theory of New York justice. The fact remains that the white South, as represented by all its outstanding characters, does accept the theory, and does labor to put it into effect, albeit with the fitfulness and inefficiency which men exhibit everywhere when they are striving to live up to their ideals.

Of late years it has been the fashion, especially among negro writers, to speak with bitter scorn of this ideal. The theory of the white South, that its business is to do what it can to make an industrious, intelligent, socially competent citizen out of the negro, is spat upon by negro essayists and novelists. That, however, does not affect the truth that it is an ideal so high that its like is not to be found in history. Where else has the dominant race ever admitted its duty not merely to afford to the dominated race the advantages of the stronger's civilization, but to assist the weaker race to achieve competence in that civilization, which necessarily means to move toward its mastery? The point may be raised that this ideal was not originally the ideal of the South, but the ideal which the North imposed upon the South by force of arms. The answer is that the imposition of ideals by force is a grotesque contradiction in terms. The ideal of Northern abolitionists and the ideal of the white South are separated by the extent of the universe. The difference is the difference between my belief that you ought to be a noble fellow and your belief that you ought to be a noble fellow. Your belief is an ideal—mine an impertinence. The abolitionists' creed was that the South ought to treat the negro in a certain manner, but the abolitionists were not Southerners; and that fact made the imposition of their creed an impertinence so prodigious that, to find a greater, one must go back to Iscariot's kiss.

The ideal of the Southern white on the face of it involves the surrender by the dominant race of a considerable share of its present advantage. To educate the negro, to safeguard his rights in the courts, to encourage his spiritual development is unquestionably to make him more formidable and more resolute. None the less, the thoughtful leaders of the South have for years admitted the section's obligation to do just that, and little by little the individual states have been induced, in their political capacity, to discharge more and more of that obligation. It is conceivable that the Southern states, as political entities, may within a comparatively short time be discharging their duty to their negro inhabitants so conscientiously as to disarm every honest critic from the North and West.

But if and when that comes to pass, only the simpler and easier part of the problem will have been solved. After the political problem has been solved, there will remain the infinitely more perplexing social problem. The possibility of making the state live up to the high ideal of the South is already plain; but how are the people to be made to live up to that ideal in their individual contacts with the negro?

It is a rank impossibility. There is no more hope of its being done than there is hope of living a Christian life in this world—a task that has been attempted by hundreds of millions for two thousand years, and that has not yet been accomplished. Nevertheless, there are those who hold that the mere attempt to introduce Christianity has done more toward making the world habitable for civilized men than has been accomplished in that direction by all the successes since time began. Social justice for the negro is out of the question in this generation, but what of that? Social justice for anybody else seems to be equally beyond our grasp. None the less, the pursuit of social justice continues to be the behavioristic character of a civilized people. The more difficult that pursuit, the more it absorbs the energies of the people, the higher the grade of their civilization.

For the South this pursuit is more difficult than it is for any other section that has a race problem to contend with, because in every other case, if political justice be assured, the problem is more than half solved since the weaker race has some sort of culture of its own, frequently a culture far older and richer than that of the dominant race. The South alone is under the necessity of strengthening the dominated race with her own culture, as well as affording it the protection of her own institutions while it assimilates that culture. Thus it comes about that the Southerner must inevitably go to extremes. He must fail completely in his effort to solve his problem, and become a barbarian, or he must carry it to the level of success of, say, the Californian, by becoming not merely as decent a citizen as the Californian, but something a great deal higher, something far exceeding the Californian in tolerance, in sympathy for the weak, in intelligent dealing with the mentally limited, in higher aspiration, in clear vision, in unbreakable resolution, in generosity, in self-sacrifice. In brief, if he is not to become a barbarian, the Southerner must needs become something not readily distinguishable from the saints in glory.

Omitting the possible effects of negro migration, and omitting the certain effects of what the negro is doing for himself, this is the way out. This is the way to complete political freedom, to full and adequate functioning as American citizens. After all, it does not include anything that is altogether beyond reason. It does not contemplate anything so profoundly repulsive to a white Southerner that it seems worse than barbarism. No one expects or desires the white South to repudiate its racial integrity. No one, except a fanatic, expects or desires it to abandon reasonable police regulations, as, for instance, separation of the races, provided such regulations are enforced equally, which is not done now. It does not contemplate the abandonment of any Southern ideal. It contemplates merely living up to those ideals.

But even at that I dare say most of us will elect to remain Democrats.

# To Live and Die in Dixie

In an essay (*Atlantic*, July 1960) written thirty years after most of his writing on the South—and thirty-five years after he had left Dixie—Johnson perhaps best defines himself as Southerner. Adopting a more personal tone than was his custom, he explains that he feels both pride and shame in being Southern. He is indignant at the racial blindness of many Southerners but continues to "feel deeply" about the South. "I am a Southerner," he concludes, "and I wish the fact to be known; for the land of my birth is right now enduring the discipline that makes a nation great."

As the twentieth century swung toward its three-quarter post, the American who felt left furthest behind was probably the citizen of the late Confederacy who was unfortunate enough to be able not only to read the newspapers but to understand something of what was in them.

The ability is not universal, not even, as our semanticist would say, "coterminous" with literacy. All America, but the South especially, seems to be afflicted with great numbers of citizens who apparently do their reading through spectacles equipped with lenses having a special property of fluorescence that enables the reader to detect infrared and ultraviolet where nothing appears to the naked eye except prosaic black and white.

These persons are happily free of any feeling of retardation. On the contrary, they are convinced that they move in the van of civilization and are irate when their certainty is questioned. To me they appear to be insane, but they are not unhappy, and who knows? they may be the only sane people in a mad world. There is profound philosophical penetration in the sweet singer's immortal lines:

See the happy moron;
    He doesn't give a damn.
I wish I were a moron—
    My God, perhaps I am!

Nevertheless, irrevocably committed to the illusion that I am sane, I see in the antics of the region of my birth in recent years evidence of a cultural lag appreciably greater than that of the rest of the nation, and to

Copyright © 1960, 1961 by Gerald W. Johnson and reprinted with permission of William Morrow & Company.

say so is to accuse the South of being far behind indeed. When Eisenhower dispatched federal troops to occupy the city of Little Rock, Arkansas, he retreated behind the year 1877, when President Hayes withdrew the last of the army of occupation; but Eisenhower did so because the state of Arkansas had retreated behind the year 1833, when President Jackson embalmed, cremated, and buried the doctrine of nullification.

The genesis of this lag is easily detected. In 1868, the year of its ratification, the Fourteenth Amendment bore no more relation to the facts of human experience than the axioms of non-Euclidean geometries bear to them. The South, living of necessity in a factual world and under compulsion to adjust to nonfactual law, resorted to subterfuge as the only way out of the impasse, and the rest of the country, unable to devise any workable alternative, tolerated the subterfuge for many years.

But the departure from candor bore the fruit that it always bears. In the course of time, the South came to believe its own bunk. The grandfather clause was written into the constitutions of various Southern states by men who were perfectly aware of its disingenuousness. It provided that the literacy test might be ignored if the applicant for registration as a voter was a descendant of a citizen qualified to vote before 1867, and its purpose was to disqualify illiterate negroes—at that time, the great bulk of the negro population—while admitting illiterate whites to the suffrage.

It was frankly a device for defeating the purpose of the Fourteenth Amendment while apparently complying with the letter of the law. In some cases the quality of this device was kept in mind, and when white illiteracy had been sharply reduced, as in North Carolina in 1908, the grandfather clause, having served its purpose, was abrogated. But in other states it remained until it was struck down by the Supreme Court of the United States. By that time, its essential fraudulence had been forgotten and it was regarded by many not as a doubtful expedient to gain time until the negro could be prepared for full citizenship but as the embodiment of a sacred principle; to wit, the principle that the negro should not ever be admitted to full citizenship.

Acceptance of a fraud inevitably involves some deterioration of character. In that sentence is compressed the political history of the South since Reconstruction. Its exegesis is the whole corpus of William Faulkner's work, admittedly the greatest artistic achievement of the South in this century. The tale that Faulkner tells in many volumes is that the very section in which once the concept of honor was so highly esteemed that for even a fantastic idea of honor men did not hesitate to sacrifice life itself has now accepted fraud for three generations and has become, as one critic put it, "tricky and mean." It is a tragedy worthy of the novelist's genius, tragedy on a more than epic scale.

Yet I have never encountered a white Southerner without pride in his heritage. Some no doubt exist, but they are invisible, presumably because they conceal their Southern nativity. For the rest, the danger in which they stand is not that of losing their pride of birth but that of permitting it to swell into a foolish and offensive arrogance. Men whom ambition or economic or professional necessity drove out of the South decades ago still tend to proclaim, rather than to conceal, their origin. Even those who fled from the intellectual sterility of their early environment realize that its emotional wealth is prodigious; they may be able to think better almost anywhere else, but nowhere else can they feel as intensely, so they are aware that their voluntary exile is not all gain.

On the face of it this is a paradox, and to resolve it should be interesting and possibly instructive. That it can be done completely is incredible, but even a partial resolution may contribute somewhat to a clearer understanding of the continental confusion that is the United States of America today.

The greatest enemy of the late Confederacy was certainly not Ulysses S. Grant, or even William T. Sherman. They were, in fact, its political and economic liberators—a trifle rough in their methods, careless of life in Grant's case and of fire in Sherman's, but in the end highly effective. They had a job to do, and they did it; the modern South has no just cause to regard either with anything but a somewhat grim yet very real respect.

Far more lasting damage was done it by men whom the South adores: at the head of the list, Stephen Collins Foster, the Pennsylvania magician who betrayed the South into hugging the delusion that melody is all in all, in compete disregard of the tonic value—nay, the harsh necessity—of counterpoint. Deceivers of the same kind were orators of Henry Grady's school and a long procession of literary gents, beginning with John Pendleton Kennedy and culminating in Thomas Nelson Page.[1]

They meant no harm and, to do them justice, they told no lies. But a lie does not have to be told; by what they did not tell, these fictioneers propagated the titanic lie that Keats has preserved in the amber of great poetry:

---

1. John Pendleton Kennedy, nineteenth-century Southern novelist, author of *Swallow Barn* (1832) and other romances; Thomas Nelson Page, Virginia novelist and Southern apologist, author of *Red Rock* (1898) and other romances.

Beauty is truth, truth beauty,—that is all
Ye know on earth, and all ye need to know.

The South believed it, and since the South is beautiful, it developed a
complacency that has wreaked more permanent devastation upon it than
Sherman perpetrated all the way from Atlanta to Savannah and thence
up to Durham Station, where Johnston surrendered. Atlanta was soon
rebuilt on a greater and finer scale, and before they died, such great
ladies as my old friend Mrs. MacMaster, of Columbia, had acquired
other spoons. That damage was temporary. But to this day there remain
far too many otherwise intelligent Southerners with an implicit faith that
the beauty of the South compensates for all else that it lacks.

Precisionists will promptly argue that when these Southerners say
"beautiful," what they mean is "pretty." There is some force in the
objection, but not much. Even the geographical South defeats it; to call
pretty the Valley of Virginia, or the view from Mitchell, highest peak
east of the Mississippi, or old Charleston, or the enclosed gardens of
New Orleans would be to perpetrate a semantic crime. The magnificence of Daytona Beach, the sullen menace of Hatteras, the Potomac
before Mount Vernon, and Old Man River himself command reverence,
not delight. Even the magnolia, which cynics have made almost a term
of disdain, is superb—somewhat spectral, perhaps, but far beyond mere
prettiness.

It is beauty of a different type, however, that worked the ensorcelling
of the modern South and, like Vivian's spell upon Merlin, put its strong
magic to sleep. It is the beauty of the legend, informing and irradiating
the landscape but distorting the vision and paralyzing the will. It is the
fashion of the moment to denigrate that beauty, calling it sickly senti-
mentalism; but beauty it was, and is, and ever will be—Circean, indeed, but real.

From Kennedy's *Swallow Barn* to Mitchell's *Gone with the Wind*,
just a hundred years apart, it has enchanted men of every section and
undoubtedly will continue to enchant them as long as the telling of tales
delights the human heart. It is, in fact, a recrudescence of the Arthurian
legend, of loyalty, love, and derring-do all compact—in short, romance.
Tara and Red Rock were never built of brick and stone but of the same
dream stuff that composed the walls and towers of Camelot; yet when
all is said and done, it is the only building material that is utterly
indestructible.

A man from Iowa or Maine can read this legendry with no sense of
personal involvement, therefore with no more damage than he sustains
from reading the exploits of the Round Table. Who in his right mind

would seriously claim blood kinship with Gareth or Pelleas? But in the South, all this is told as of grandfather's day; it is close, it is intimate: hence, the Southerner is moved by a dangerously strong impulse to maintain the legend, and "that way madness lies."

Nevertheless, the beauty is there, it is real, and it is imbued with potent sorcery. It involves the three great verities, poverty and love and war, whose acquaintance every man must make if he is to be completely educated; and no amount of abuse by the mawkish and the maudlin can destroy it. The calamity of the modern Southerner is that of Don Quixote—his wits were already lost before the curate arrived to sort out the meretricious from the sound.

But the South is in fact beautiful, whether you construe the South as meaning the land or the legend, and the memory of its beauty grips the emotions of its sons, no matter how long they may have been away. The misfortune is that all too many Southerners believe Keats not only when he says truthfully "that is all ye know," but also when he lies by adding "and all ye need to know."

However, nothing absolute can be said of forty million people, not even that they all exist; for within the time that it takes to make the statement some will die and others will be born. Not all Southerners have succumbed to Vivian's spell, and relatively few have succumbed entirely. O. Henry's former Confederate colonel turned editor of *The Rose of Dixie* is a recognizable type that survives to this day, but even fifty years ago his obsession with the legendary South was recognized as an oddity which was not to be taken seriously.

As recently as the spring 1960, the British critic D. W. Brogan considered it worthy of note that, although when he began reading American history as a boy in Scotland he sided with the South, after he became a mature man he realized that "the right side won" the Civil War. As I am some years older than Mr. Brogan, it may interest him to learn that, as a boy in North Carolina, I heard and heeded an uncle who had served the Confederacy faithfully and well but who told me, "Yes, they had more men, and more artillery, and more rations, and more everything else, but, boy, don't you ever believe that was what whipped us. We lost that war because God Almighty had decreed that slavery had to go."

Mr. Brogan is quite right in noting that, although the legalists, citing Abraham Lincoln as their chief witness, have proved conclusively that slavery was not the issue, the fact remains that the war was about slavery because the legal issue, secession, arose out of slavery. But Mr. Brogan is quite wrong in assuming that the South had not realized that as early as fifty years ago. It was known in North Carolina that the right side won, even when boys in Scotland were still siding with the South.

The argument against the South that would be conclusive, if it were sustained by fact, is that having appealed to the arbitrament of the sword, the South refused to abide by the judgment it had invited, and so was forsworn. But the argument is only doubtfully sustained by the fact. The undisputed fact is that the judgment was that slavery had to go, and it went. Even the furiously reviled Black Codes of Mississippi and Louisiana did not attempt to reestablish legal slavery and were less rigorous than the apartheid legislation of South Africa ninety years later. If the North, victorious but stung by grievous wounds, imposed, after hostilities had ceased, new conditions not nominated in the bond, who was then forsworn? It is a pretty question, one that has given Southern casuists their opportunity.

After so many years, however, even to admit the argument to debate is casuistry in the pejorative sense. Attempts at the attribution of blame hinder, do not help, the search for a solution of current problems, most of them arising from the refusal of the South to grant the negro all the rights and privileges appertaining to the status of first-class citizenship.

Note well the phraseology: "to grant him the rights"—not "to recognize his status"; for the latter is a refusal based on the simple and solid fact that, taken in the mass, the negro is not a first-class citizen. There is no convincing evidence that he is biologically inferior, but even Gunnar Myrdal[2] admits that there is every evidence that he is culturally inferior. Two hundred and fifty years of bondage have left their mark, which ninety-five years of freedom have not erased.

The casuists of the South contend that this is in itself evidence of the negro's irremovable inferiority. Those of the North contend as fiercely that it is evidence only of the irremediable wickedness of the white South. Both contentions are empty gabble, innocent of logical consistency or historical perspective. Logically, the existence of this republic can be justified only on the assumption that the status of a freeman is favorable to the development of political competence; were it not so, we should have done better to adhere to some other system. Historically, Runnymede, starting point of the English-speaking peoples' struggle for political liberty, is nearly seven hundred and fifty years in the past; yet he who thinks that we have perfected our competence is an optimist indeed. Shall we then brand the negro as inferior because he has not accomplished in ninety-five years what the white man has not completed in more than seven centuries? Or shall we brand the white South as

---

2. Gunnar Myrdal, Swedish sociologist, author of *An American Dilemma* (1944), a study of American race relations.

wicked because it has not performed the miracle of endowing another race with qualities it is still struggling to develop in its own character?

Citing individual exceptions is no rebuttal. Certainly to call Ralph Bunche a second-class citizen would be as preposterous as to call King Arthur a second-class Briton. Thurgood Marshall is a first-rate lawyer, Marian Anderson a first-rate artist, and so it goes down a long and scintillant roster. But these are examples of what the negro is capable of becoming, not of what he presently is; and what he presently is determines his influence upon the situation existing here and now.

The difficulty of the South is that, although it sees clearly enough what is directly before it, its distant vision is blurred. It is weak in applying the logic of its own experience to test the hypothesis now presented. It is beyond belief that many Southerners will concede that their political history since 1776 has been so complete a failure that they have made no advance in the art of self-government. It may be admitted that they have produced no masters of the theory of government superior to Jefferson, Madison, Marshall, Clay, and Calhoun, but the masses certainly know more about the management of public affairs than their great-great-grandfathers knew, and the development of their skill they owe to long practice under political freedom.

The hypothesis now presented is that the same conditions will produce in negroes the same effect. The method of testing it is, of course, to proceed as if it were true. The objection to applying that method is the necessity of risking the whole social structure upon the outcome. For this a courage is requisite that to many Southerners seems temerity, not to say foolhardiness. Their opinion is perfectly honest and could be correct. The sole answer to their objection is Danton's advice to the Convention, that audacity is the only way out.

Above and beyond all this, there is a psychological, or perhaps a biological, block, ignored by the thoughtless, but formidable nevertheless. It is the primeval impulse, not monopolized by man but shared by bird and beast and creeping thing, to equate "alien" and "enemy." Jeremiah, who antedates the Confederacy by a very considerable time, took note of the speckled bird that "the birds round about are against her." Whatever is not of our kind is *ipso facto* objectionable, and a definite exercise of the intelligence is required to neutralize the repugnance. The negro merely by his coloration is, of all other races, the one most completely alien to the white man, hence the one surest to arouse—and to reciprocate—this ancient hostility. The primitive, or in ordinary parlance, the natural relation of black and white is one of dislike.

This is no defense, but it is a partial explanation of such policies as segregation. Morality may be defined as the conscious suppression of destructive biological urges, and the advance of civilization is measured by the success of that suppression, so the appearance of any instinctive reaction is a slip backward toward Neanderthal man. But that such reactions do appear constantly is attested by trials everywhere and every day for homicide, theft, rape, and abduction. It will be a very long time before they are eliminated. Race prejudice will not be eliminated soon; the hope is not to eliminate it but to prevent its expression in race injustice, at least as far as the forms of law are concerned.

The theory cherished by idealists that race prejudice is exclusively the product of miseducation and bad environment is only about 90 per cent true. There is a residue that can be traced back certainly into prehistory, and the attitude of the animals toward a variant strongly suggests that it can be traced back into prehumanity. However well suppressed, the thing exists, in Detroit as certainly as in New Orleans, in Massachusetts as in South Carolina. Latent everywhere, it needs only a certain combination of evil chances to become manifest. And its existence is one more complication added to the other troubles of the South.

This adds up to a dismal sum. The odds are plainly against the South, and if the region survives as more than a mere Boeotia, as an effective participant in American civilization, it will be only by dint of bitter travail, for it contends against itself as well as against adverse outward circumstance. The passions and frailties common to all humanity are doubly dangerous to the South, made so by the peculiar course of its history; while it must also contend with all the dangers and difficulties that bring woe to other regions, because they are inherent in the democratic process.

What, then, is the reason, if there is a rational reason, for a Southerner's pride in his birthplace? Why, its difficulties, of course.

"I," said Saint Paul when they taunted him with being a nobody from nowhere, "am a citizen of no mean city." Every Southerner knows how he felt. We are the sons of a land that has paid its way. For a century, in fact, it has been paying not only its own debt but that of the whole nation, first incurred in 1619 when that Dutch ship of evil omen cast anchor off Jamestown and, among other items, sold the Virginia colonists "twenty negurs"; and that was augmented for the next hundred years by the middle passage of New England shipmasters, running rum to Africa, bringing slaves to Southern ports, and thence carrying molasses to Medford to make more rum.

For their part in that crime the North and the West were let off at the price of four years of blood and agony a century ago. But the South paid that price, and in addition to it, ten years of military occupation, thirty years of poverty and grinding toil, ninety years of harassment, anxiety, frustration, and moral deterioration. The South has been granted no favors. The South has paid in full.

Every historian is aware that, up to about the year 1900, it labored in economic thralldom under a fiscal system that exploited it ruthlessly for the profit of the industrialized sections, but that loss was merely monetary. Far more galling to intelligent Southerners has been the inevitable result of the acceptance of fraud as a legitimate device in politics. Heaven knows fraud is no stranger to the politics of any part of the country, but elsewhere it enters furtively and is killed by exposure. It is a vice that pays to virtue the tribute of hypocrisy. But in the South the grandfather clause and, later, innumerable tricky registration laws were adopted for the open and avowed purpose of doing indirectly what the Constitution forbade being done directly. Political leaders otherwise of good repute publicly justified this course, and in order to sustain it did not hesitate to appeal to every villainous prejudice and passion in the lowest elements of society.

The inevitable result was the reduction of the political process to a level so ruffianly that it became a national scandal, and this in the very region that in the early days had produced more brilliant thinkers on the art of government than came from any other part of the country. The South that had once graced the halls of Congress with Pinckneys, Randolphs, Clays, and Calhouns now sent Heflins, Bleases, Bilbos, and Eastlands. The South that had given to the presidency the Virginia dynasty—Washington, Jefferson, Madison, and Monroe—could furnish only one President in ninety-five years, and that one by first having him processed by twenty years' residence in New Jersey.

The South has paid in money. It has paid in toil and trouble and anxiety and humiliation. But it has paid in full, and it still survives. More than that, even as it staggered under its backbreaking load, it has accomplished a feat unparalleled in the history of the white race. In less than a century, it has brought a formerly illiterate and servile population numbering many millions from tutelage to a point so close to the van of civilization that they are now ready to assume the most difficult citizenship in the world, that of responsible members of a self-governing nation that is also a great power.

In this, the white South did indeed have assistance, but not from the victors of the Civil War. It was the assistance of the Southern negro himself, who wrought the major part of his own transformation and therefore is entitled to the major part of the credit. But not to all. The ignorance, prejudice, and stupidity that would have blocked the negro's advance have always been combated valiantly and not without success by Southern whites.

The very Alabama that produced Tom-Tom Heflin also produced, and in the same generation, Edgar Gardner Murphy. The same Georgia that is in socage to the Talmadges also tolerates Ralph McGill. "Our Bob" Reynolds flourished in North Carolina, but so did Howard W. Odum, and so do Frank P. Graham and Jonathan Daniels.[3] If it can ever pay off its debt to the past, the South still has the germ plasm to produce great men, and they will be tempered and toughened by the tribulation through which they have come.

With the eyes of a child I once saw the process at work, although it was many years before I understood what I had seen. At the age of perhaps ten, I was one midsummer noon at the house of a kinsman when he came in to dinner from the cornfield where he had been stripping fodder, one of the nastiest jobs attached to farming in those days. This man had taken his degree at the University of North Carolina just in time to spend the ensuing four years as a trooper in Wheeler's Cavalry, C.S.A. But as he stepped up on the back porch that day there was nothing about him suggestive of either the scholar or the soldier. The oven heat of the cornfield had had sweat rolling off him all morning, and the black soil's powdery dust had settled and caked until he was inky except for his teeth and the whites of his eyes. On the shady porch I pumped, and he held his head and then his arms under the spout for a long time before it became evident that he was actually a white man.

But his comment on his own state has rung in my ears ever since. When he had mopped his face and was toweling his hands and arms, he looked at me with a sardonic grin and broke into the thundering strophes of one of the *Georgics* of Virgil: *O fortunatos nimium, sua si bona norint, agricolas*—O most happy farmers, if only they knew their good fortune!

The small boy was merely startled by the rolling Latin measures, but an aging man knows now that he had there before his eyes the South triumphant. The soldier had returned from the war ruined, like everybody else. Like everybody else, he had moiled through thirty years of a depression that made the episode in Hoover's time a trifle by comparison. Not for his own fault, but by the ruin of his country, he had been sentenced to hard labor for the term of his natural life, with small hope

---

3. Robert R. Reynolds, U.S. senator from North Carolina, 1933–45; Jonathan Daniels, editor of the Raleigh *News and Observer*.

of ever achieving ease, none of achieving luxury. Yet in the stifling heat of the cornfield, in a land of poverty and defeat, so far was he from broken that the ear of his mind could hear a great poet singing and his stout heart could laugh at the absurdity of human fate.

The small boy gaped, but the aging man remembers how Desdemona found "'twas strange . . . 'twas pitiful, 'twas wondrous pitiful. She wish'd she had not heard it . . . yet she wish'd that heaven had made her such a man." I, too, Desdemona, would to God I were such a man!

But he was my kinsman. However far I may fall short of his strength, we are of the same blood, of the same origin, we are of the South. Therefore, I would be ashamed to fall into despair because the rising generation in our land is hard put to it to cope with the same problem, unchanged except in the degree of its urgency. Time is running out, and the South must not only lift itself by its own bootstraps, but lift suddenly. The problem is what it has always been—to raise 30 per cent of the population, now handicapped, to the level of the rest, politically, economically, and culturally; the change is that it must be done more quickly than most of us had believed was imperatively necessary.

But to accomplish the feat, the white South must first lift itself to a moral and intellectual level higher than it has ever attained, or than has been attained by any dominant race anywhere in the world. It is a formidable task. It is so formidable that the Southern lower classes— lower, even though some have millions and pedigrees of enormous length—have shrunk back and renounced it. But the lower classes have always failed in every great emergency, so Faubus and Eastland and Talmadge are not of any great significance. The men who will count are the saving minority, unbroken and unbreakable, men who can respond to a challenge after the fashion of sturdy old Pierre-Samuel, the original Du Pont de Nemours.[4] In 1816, when a swarm of troubles seemed about to overwhelm the new republic, he wrote to his old friend Jefferson: "We are but snails, and we have to climb the Andes. By God, we must climb!"

The South will climb. A romantic illusion? Possibly, but a living faith at this moment, nevertheless, and one not destroyed by reports from Little Rock, or even Poplarville, not shaken when presumably sane men talk of interposition, of concurrent majorities, of the compact theory of the Constitution. For it is precisely by wrestling and overthrowing the giants of madness and despair that the thews and sinews of the South will regain their old-time power, endowing it with the moral and intel-

---

4. Pierre-Samuel Du Pont de Nemours, pioneer French-American industrialist of early nineteenth century.

lectual vigor to become again the great instructor in political philosophy that it was when our history as a nation began.

I am a Southerner, and I wish the fact to be known; for the land of my birth is right now enduring the discipline that makes a nation great. So, in the midst of its current tribulation, I can think of it as my toilworn kinsman did, and can echo his chant: *O fortunatos nimium*, O most happy, land!

# After Forty Years—Dixi

On the fortieth anniversary of his earlier essay, "A Tilt with Southern Windmills," Johnson again writes on Southern politics and race relations for the *Virginia Quarterly Review* (Spring 1965). In the earlier essay he asked whether the white Southerner was to be a "barbarian" or not in his treatment of the Negro. Here he responds that the South is now more "civilized," that the Negro revolution indeed has the support of some white Southerners. Johnson is cautiously optimistic about the South's racial future. The "Dixi" of the title comes from the Latin verb "dicere," and the title can be roughly translated as "After Forty Years—I Have Spoken."

"In brief, if he is not to become a barbarian the Southerner must become something not readily distinguishable from the saints in glory."

That dictum appeared under my by-line in the Virginia Quarterly Review for July, 1925. It was the conclusion of my first contribution to the Review, a consideration of the state of civilization at that time in the region below the Potomac. When I was informed that the fortieth anniversary number was in preparation I dug that article out of the files and re-read it, with the intention of offering to the editors such corrections and emendations as might seem appropriate after the lapse of forty years.

I have none to offer.

There are, to be sure, some passing references to then current events that time has rendered obsolete. For instance, there was a remark that abandonment of the policy of separation of the races was unthinkable. It is thinkable now and it is immaterial that the abandonment was involuntary on the part of the white South.

The article was colored, also, by the disastrous political campaign of the preceding year. In 1924 Alfred E. Smith and William G. McAdoo, calamitously abetted by Father Duffy and William J. Bryan, had wrecked the Democratic party over an issue that had no legitimate place in American politics, the quarrel of the Ku Klux and the Catholics; the result being that the colorless nominee, Davis, lost everything but the then still Solid South. This inspired the observation that the late Confederacy had performed one final service for the Democracy—"she furnished the organization's burial party and accomplished the last sad

Copyright © 1965 by the *Virginia Quarterly Review* and reprinted with permission.

rites over its mangled remains." It was premature, but at the time no other soothsayer foresaw the coming, eight years later, of Roosevelt, the fabulous Resurrection Man, under whose incantations the party, like John Barleycorn, "Got up again, And sore surprised them all."

Today, it seems more likely that the party will bear the South to its last resting place, rather than the other way about.

The substance of the article, however, and the conclusion I believe still sound forty years after its writing. I am aware that this position will be challenged by observers who can cite impressive evidence that the moment of decision has gone by and that the Southerner, or at least the white Southerner, has become a barbarian. Disregarding a multitude of minor incidents, they may be expected to mention these undeniable facts, all dated within the past year and a half:

Item: In the South a President of the United States has been assassinated by a Southerner.

Item: Even before the assassination the United States Ambassador to the United Nations was assaulted and spat upon, an incident less heinous but more vulgar than murder.

Item: In the South four little girls were blasted to death in a Sunday-school room, undoubtedly by white Southerners.

Item: A reserve officer of the United States Army, who had gone to the South in obedience to military orders, was murdered for no known reason except that he was a Negro.

Item: Three young idealists, exercising their legal right of American citizens to travel, were murdered in the South and not even allowed civilized burial, but concealed in a pile of clay.

Item: An agent of the National Association for the Advancement of Colored People, going about his lawful occasions, was murdered from ambush.

Disregard an uncounted number of beatings, jailings, maimings, and tortures, most of them without even a pale shadow of legality, and consider these six items alone. They constitute a fearful indictment. Standing alone they are enough to persuade a fair-minded observer that the society in which such things are tolerated more closely resembles that of the headhunters of Borneo than that of the heavenly host; but they do not stand alone. They are merely the most spectacular incidents in a reign of terror that has flailed the South ever since the Southern Negro began to make a serious claim to the rights guaranteed him by the Constitution of the United States.

In the circumstances the burden of proof rests upon one who asserts, or implies, that freedom of choice rests with the Southerner; for not cynics only but all superficial observers are persuaded that he has definitely, if not irrevocably, chosen barbarism. They may be right, but the case is not closed. There is a formidable mass of evidence on the other side. Hitherto it has been obscured by the dust and smoke of controversy, but it is there, and it must be weighed before a just judgment can be reached.

To begin with, nearly one-third of all Southerners are black. This immediately acquits a large Southern minority of the charge of regression; for the Southern Negro has given, especially in the years 1963 and 1964, a demonstration of political maturity that is among the most impressive in all history. Having decided upon a policy of non-violent protest he has adhered to that policy through years of intense provocation, resorting to violent retaliation only in sporadic and isolated instances.

That record is written. Such is the speed of the historical process today that before these lines come under the reader's eye the record may have been blotted by black men whose nerves could no longer stand the strain, but it cannot be blotted out. Two years of steadfast adherence to a considered policy of quietism cannot be ignored by any honest historian. Adherence under fearful pressure to any kind of policy is a notable achievement for a democracy; and when the policy is one of non-violent protest, it is an amazing achievement, indicative of a degree of political maturity that Periclean Athens never reached.

Furthermore, the feat was accomplished by the Southern Negro under Southern leadership. Of course he was stimulated, encouraged, and assisted by Northerners, white and black; but when he rose *en masse* it was at the call of his own kind. It has always been so. The Northerners, Frederick Douglass and W. E. B. DuBois, are Negro heroes and deservedly so; but the men who really shook the race in the South were Booker T. Washington and Martin Luther King, both from Alabama [sic]. It is the fashion now to look scornfully on Booker Washington, and it is becoming fashionable to sneer at King, because both were to some extent quietists. But Gandhi also was despised and at last was murdered by a Hindu. Nevertheless, it was his policy that succeeded.

In addition to that, these people led off. The so-called "Negro revolution" had been in progress for many months before Harlem, Rochester, Jersey City, Chicago, and Chester, Pennsylvania, exploded. It is generally assumed that the Northern Negro's educational and economic position is distinctly superior to that of his Southern brother. Nevertheless, it was the Northern Negro who was guilty of the folly of aimless and self-defeating violence. The first sit-ins were staged, mostly by college students, in Greensboro, North Carolina. The first streetcar boycott occurred in Montgomery, Alabama. The first economic boycott was organized in Albany, Georgia, by Negro citizens of Albany, without even the participation of Martin Luther King until the movement had been under way for a month or two. But the first great riots broke north of the Potomac; and it was the riots that provoked the "white back-lash."

On the face of these facts it is evident that nearly one-third of the South, the black third, far from regressing has been rapidly advancing toward a level of civilization rarely attained by any race. If one-third of the remainder, that is, a third of all white Southerners, are as mature politically as the mass of the Negroes, we have a numerical majority of the whole population against a reversion to barbarism. Statistical proof is impossible, but there is evidence that more than one-third, indeed, more than one-half and possibly sixty per cent of white Southerners are civilized.

In witness whereof I cite another passage from the essay of 1925. It reads: "to educate the Negro, to safeguard his rights in the courts, to encourage his spiritual development is unquestionably to make him more formidable and more resolute." This statement evoked no comment whatever at the time. In the South of forty years ago it was regarded as so trite that nobody thought of questioning it.

There is no manner of doubt that the Southern Negro of 1965 is more formidable and more resolute than any of his ancestors were; and most competent observers agree that this is the case because he is in fact a new man—better educated, less intimidated, more spirited by far than was the Southern Negro of forty years ago. I have designedly repeated the word "Southern" not only because this development occurred in the South, but because white Southerners in 1925 knew that it was bound to occur unless they took vigorous and effective measures to prevent it. They took no such measures. On the contrary, such measures as they did take were designed to assist, not to retard, the cultural advance of the black South. Nor were these measures as halfhearted as critics of the white South assert; the notorious Tom-Toms, such as Watson and Heflin, were much louder but less effective than such Southern leaders as Edgar Gardner Murphy in the earlier days, and Howard W. Odum in the latter.

The adoption of this policy can have but one explanation. It is that an effective, which is not necessarily a numerical, majority of white Southerners, although they realized that the cultural and economic advance of the black Southerners would make them more formidable and resolute, realized that it would at the same time make them more valuable cultural and economic assets; and they estimated that the increase in value would be greater than the increase in danger.

But this is a highly civilized view. Indeed, it is so highly civilized that it is difficult to maintain consistently. If passion and prejudice have oc-

casionally obscured the white South's vision of its ideal, it is certainly
not unique in that respect; and to glimpse the ideal at all is not characteristic of a people sinking into barbarism.

In sum, the theory of reversion is flatly and obviously contradicted as
regards the black South and is not sustained by the record as regards the
white.

It must be admitted, however, that this estimate imposes upon optimists an embarrassing obligation—that of explaining why an essentially
civilized people submit to being misrepresented and traduced by yahoos
whose public careers reflect the intelligence of a chimpanzee and the
ethics of a gorilla. There, at last, we come upon a failure that no white
Southern apologist can evade or avoid; but it is an intellectual, rather
than a moral lapse, inability to grasp the implications of an unprecedented situation.

The fact seems to be that the dimensions of the problem that intelligent Southerners of both races face has been but dimly appreciated by
themselves and hardly at all by others. The problem, as it is generally
conceived, is that of assimilating into a culture derived from western
Europe many millions of people drawn originally from the completely
alien culture of Africa. But it may be plausibly argued that that problem
was solved two hundred years ago. The Negro arrived in what is now
the United States in 1619, a full year ahead of the Pilgrim Fathers;
chronologically, at least, he is as fully American as any descendant of
the *Mayflower's* company.

The unsolved problem is not that, but the one posed by the Emancipa-
tion Proclamation, just over a hundred years ago. It is the problem of
the incorporation of the Negro in our political system, and the central
difficulty there arises from the fact that the white man himself has never
fully mastered the management of that system. The Negro, after his
long exclusion, has every right to expect from the white man competent
instruction in the management of the system, which is to say, in the art
of being free. But how shall we teach him what we have not yet learned,
except fragmentarily and uncertainly?

Specifically, the Southern white man lies under another inhibition,
imposed upon him by two really great Southerners, John C. Calhoun
and Roger B. Taney. Both were men with powerful minds; their fault,
indeed, was that they were too intelligent. Both fell into the characteristic folly of the intellectual, that of identifying intellectuality with reason, ignoring the fact that reason includes both cogitation and emotion,
both thinking and feeling.

Biographers mention, but without stressing the fact, that the young
Calhoun indited a poem to his lady-love each line of which began with

the word "whereas." But, surely, it is highly significant. Such a mind would naturally fall into the error of believing that the binding force holding the Union together was the Constitution, not a deep emotional attachment to the ideal of the Founding Fathers.

Taney, in his turn, unquestionably believed that in blasting the Union he was saving it. Like Calhoun, he conceived of law as more powerful than love, and therefore assumed that animosities adjudicated by law were thereby abolished. He persuaded himself that the quarrel between the sections, if brought within the field of law, could be juridically composed; ignoring the fact that logic applied to emotion is equivalent to the very best butter applied to the works of the Mad Hatter's watch.

Calhoun and Taney are long gone, but their misconception still clouds Southern political thinking. The heresy that equates legality with morality is far from being confined to the South, as the rise and fall of prohibition proved; but its evil effects have been conspicuous in the South because it affects the immense social problem of race relations there; and that very fact is illustrative of the immensity of the problem.

The arguments of the more fanatical segregationists may be dismissed; they are not based on thinking, but are simply repetitive of the exploded theories of Calhoun. But some Southerners who are anything but fanatical are hard put to it to distinguish the basic philosophy of *Brown v. Board of Education*, the school integration decision in 1954, and that of *Dred Scott*. They are uneasy lest the Supreme Court should be repeating the error of applying strictly juristic thinking to the solution of strictly political, which is to say, largely emotional, problems.

But if the Supreme Court has, in fact, made that error, it was in *Plessy*, the "separate but equal" decision of 1896. In *Brown* it was trapped. There, after long and sometimes tortuous evasions, it was confronted squarely with the question, "Is or is not the Fourteenth Amendment part of the supreme law of the land?" I do not see how any nine rational men, to say nothing of nine learned Justices, could have given any other answer than, "It is." Yet inescapable though it was, *Brown*, like "the gallant Hood of Texas" in the Confederate infantrymen's doleful lament, "played hell in Tennessee."

The grim fact is that the South is trapped in a worse predicament than that of the Supreme Court. After a hundred years of evasion, avoidance, and intricate sophistry, it has learned that such a course leads only to what James W. Silver euphemistically terms "The Closed Society,"[1] although it is actually the anteroom to barbarism. That string has run out. The hideous events in Dallas, in Birmingham, and in the Missis-

---

1. James W. Silver, author of *Mississippi: The Closed Society* (1964).

sippi hell-hole ironically named Philadelphia prove that the next step is into a state of savagery that the civilized part of the nation, including the civilized South, will have to extirpate, with tanks and machine guns if necessary. The issue is squarely before us and must be met.

But the South is less fortunate than the Court in that the answer cannot be yes or no. For the question does not involve the Constitution or the statutes. It is not legal; it is political. It is, by what procedure may some ten million members of a formerly dominated race be inducted into full participation in a self-governing society without subjecting the whole social and political fabric to a strain that it cannot withstand?

That is the question, and it has never been answered yet. On rare occasions it has been answered as regards a class, or a caste, and it doesn't even arise as regards a minuscule minority. But when it applies to many millions, sharply distinguished by physical characteristics, that is, to a race, human wisdom has not yet been able to supply even a reasonably adequate answer.

But Southerners, black and white inclusive, must supply an answer because the alternative is to descend below the lowest level of civilization that the United States of America can afford to tolerate. The Negro, once a slave, is now a freedman; and the problem is how to convert him into a freeman, with all that the word implies. Scoffers may say that the answer is easy: through the same process by which the white man was made a freeman with all that the word implies. But if the scoffer is asked, "And how was that? And when and where was that?" he has no reply—not if he is an honest man. We won our independence nearly two hundred years ago, and therefore call ourselves freemen. But if the word implies the enjoyment of equal justice under law, he is an optimist indeed who would claim the status for every American—in grim truth, for any American.

The historical significance of this republic is simply that it affords men an opportunity to learn how to be free, unhampered by the bonds that Church and State have laid upon the generations of the past; but every rational man knows that the heaviest bonds of Church and State were not as weighty as the gyves locked upon our wrists by passion, prejudice, ignorance, and superstition. Then to expect the white South to teach the black, or the black the white, how to strike these off is to expect it to rise to a state of wisdom and grace that only the sanctified have attained, and they but rarely.

The fact that we have not attained it in the past forty years is insignificant; the pertinent question is, have we moved, if only by an inch, in that direction? The conclusive answer is supplied by the "Negro revolution" itself. The utterly hopeless do not rebel, but these have rebelled, proof positive that they have seen a gleam of hope not apparent to an earlier generation. They do not yet know how to be free, but they are trying harder to learn than they ever tried before.

There, no doubt, is the answer, so far as there is an answer this side of the New Jerusalem. The endeavor to learn how to be free is an activity not characteristic of a people reverting to barbarism, but of one struggling upward on the scale of civilization; and it is through that struggle that some men have developed such moral and intellectual power that their names are inscribed in the calendar of the saints.

This is why, after forty years, I have nothing to add to, or subtract from what I wrote in 1925. Without complacence, but equally without cynicism and without despair, I repeat: "If he is not to become a barbarian, the Southerner must become something not readily distinguishable from the saints in glory."

# Tar Heel Portraits

# Chase of North Carolina

Despite his criticism of the South, Johnson found many individual Southerners, native and naturalized, to admire. In one essay written for the *American Mercury* (July 1929) he praises Harry Woodburn Chase, the Massachusetts-born president of the University of North Carolina, for his courage in fighting religious fundamentalists, his support of Howard W. Odum and the controversial *Journal of Social Forces*, and his leadership in preventing the passage of an antievolution law in North Carolina.

The Hon. Harry Woodburn Chase, A.M., Ph.D., and four times LL.D., has lately scandalized all his hard-boiled friends by refusing the directorship of one of the big foundations at a salary twice as large as the one he gets as president of the University of North Carolina. Not that the money was the sole consideration—after all, it is worth something, indeed, it is worth much, to be privileged to live in Chapel Hill, N.C. It wasn't so much the money as the principle of the thing. It was as if a bishop had refused the red hat, or a lawyer an appointment to the Supreme Bench. Directors of foundations are the shiniest officials in all the pedagogical world; yet rather than be one, Chase preferred to continue as president of a State university in the South—to continue, that is to say, as the target for all the bricks, bottles and dead cats which the enemies of intelligence and civilization are able to hurl.

It is not as if he were a young enthusiast, just starting in on the job. Although he is only forty-six years old, he has been president of the university now for ten years, and his acquaintance with politicians, Fundamentalists and cotton-mill barons is as intimate as it is mournful. Nor is it as if he were another Dr. Redfield, that fraudulent Man of Learning delineated by Nelson Antrim Crawford so lovingly that half the reviewers thought he was true. Chase's school today is at once among the most active and the least idiotic of all the State universities; which is to say that all the natural foes of enlightenment are aflame with a passionate yearning to put it down.

Nor is it as if Chase were such an intellectual two-gun man as, for example, Clarence Darrow, snuffing the battle afar off and saying among the trumpets, ha, ha. He is of another type. Physically, he resembles nothing so much as a particularly holy saint done by a Thir-

Copyright © 1929 by the *American Mercury* and reprinted with permission.

teenth Century sculptor—long, narrow and immensely pious. His prematurely silvery hair gives him the effect of a halo, and his soft voice seems admirably adapted to preaching to the birds. One would expect as soon to find Francis of Assisi emitting blood-curdling yells and leaping among the spears, as this gentle scholar. As a matter of fact, he did omit the yells, but he certainly took a header into the spears when he chose to remain at Carolina.

But, as another matter of fact, President Chase's sanctity is largely on the surface. Oh, no, there is nothing in the least Rabelaisian about him; he is a Congregationalist in regular standing, and irreproachable in all his personal activities. But it is impossible to believe that in years to come images of him will be used as charms to cure ring-worm. It isn't holiness that enables a man to survive ten years as president of an American State university. When one considers the brand of politics that perpetually boils around such an office, it is evident that in this environment the children of earth are wiser than the children of light. Nor is it by holiness, but by shrewd manipulation, that a man builds a respectable institution of learning in the presence of Fundamentalism and Ku Kluxism and at the moment when they are coming to full flower. These things Chase has achieved; and his achievements are in themselves sufficient proof that he is not a fit subject for hagiology.

After all, an ascetic appearance is not always proof of ethereal mildness. "Yond Cassius," remarked an authority who was no mean judge of men, "has a lean and hungry look; such men are dangerous."

Certain facts in the recent history of the University of North Carolina are obvious enough to be common knowledge in the educational world. The institution has undergone a complete regeneration since the war. Although it opened for business in 1795, and is therefore the oldest State university in America, up to 1917 it had hardly made a dent in the consciousness of the country. It was a pretty good school for undergraduates, and its A. B. was regarded as respectable, but there was no reason known to man why anyone should come from beyond the borders of the State to seek instruction there. Today, however, it is recognized as the most aggressive and vigorous university in the South, and among the most aggressive and vigorous in the country. It is particularly strong in the social sciences, and its research work in that field now commands respectful attention everywhere. In addition, it has gradually collected a group of literary gents—essayists, poets, dramatists, critics and similar addicts to beautiful letters—whose average level of ability is as high, to say the least, as that of any group of similar size to be found in the

South. In brief, the school at Chapel Hill has become a genuine university, and a very good one.

So much is plain, and it stands to reason that the man who has been at the head of things must have had a good deal to do with it; but that is all that is known even to the majority of North Carolinians. There is a great deal behind the obvious facts, however, and the story has dramatic elements enough to be well worth knowing.

It started with the appearance on the scene of President Chase's predecessor, who was unquestionably a genius. This man, Edward Kidder Graham, stands aside from all categories. Technically, he was a schoolmaster, but in reality he was a flame. He conceived the idea of making the University of North Carolina a genuine servant, or rather, tool, of the State, not merely a pleasant place for gentlemen's sons to spend four years of elegant idleness. Being white-hot himself, he succeeded in igniting the State at large, while the alumni he raised to incandescence. Graham had everything. He was scholarly but not pedantic, he was strong but not rigid, he was gentle but not effeminate, and when he stood up before an audience he spoke with the tongue of men and of angels.

His faculty idolized him, his under-graduates adored him, the alumni regarded him as Joshua who made the sun stand still. He smote the Legislature with the hand of a Moses or of an Alexander Hamilton, and streams of revenue gushed forth. The war interrupted his programme but even during the fighting he organized public opinion in readiness for a great expansion of the university as soon as hostilities should cease.

Then the influenza epidemic of 1918 came along and killed him.

The chairman of the faculty automatically became acting president of the university, and he appointed in his place as chairman of the faculty a young professor of psychology who had been hanging around for several years. He was admittedly a good professor of psychology, one of G. Stanley Hall's pupils, but he had never attracted attention in the State at large. He came from Massachusetts; therefore he had no relatives among the prominent people in North Carolina. It was not even certain that he was a Democrat; therefore he had no supporters among the politicians. His name was Chase.

But within a few months the acting president also died, and one morning the Tarheels awoke to find it the amazing fact that their State university was headed by a Damyankee, a genuine, blown-in-the-bottle, Massachusetts Bluebelly. It was astounding, it was incredible, but it was true, and there seemed to be nothing in particular to be done about it. After all, he was president by chance, not by election; so the State assumed that as soon as the trustees met he would be replaced by a regularly elected Native Son, hence there was no excuse for excitement. The wise lads therefore dismissed Chase from their minds, and began to lay their bets on various Tarheels prominently mentioned for the place.

Now what followed may be interpreted two ways. The official account is this: after deliberating upon the merits of various candidates for a matter of eighteen months, the trustees in their wisdom perceived that none other was as well equipped in intellectual endowment, character and training as Dr. Chase, and therefore proceeded to make him permanent president.

But the unofficial account of the skeptical and ribald is this: there are one hundred trustees of the University of North Carolina, one from each county, elected by the Legislature. Therefore men who are politicians first, last, and all the time comprise a large proportion of the whole body. When one hundred men, largely politicians, get together for the purpose of handing out a large and ornamental job, a terrific battle always ensues. It did in this case. There were many candidates, some of them men of learning and dignity, but others broken-down political hacks, whose sole qualification was long and loyal party service. The hacks, however, were supported as ardently as were the scholars, and as month after month saw the deadlock continue, it became evident that years might pass before an agreement could be reached.

Then, according to the ribald, one of that group of trustees who had from the beginning favored Chase proved himself a political genius. He approached, one by one, supporters of Candidate A and Candidate B, and spoke to them in this wise: "Your man is undoubtedly noble, and all that, but it is plain we cannot elect him now. But it is equally plain that if we elect one of the other North Carolinians he will be elected practically for life, and your man never will have a chance. Yet we must elect a President of some sort some time. Now suppose we put in this Blue-belly—after all, he seems to be a pretty good man who certainly can hold things together for a year or two. Yet he has no friends with a political pull, so when we finally do get together on the Tarheel we want permanently, we can throw out this fellow without raising an uproar."

The skeptics aver that this seemed the summation of political wisdom to the supporters of A and B, so they came over to Chase, not because they regarded him as a first-rate president, but because they had no idea how good he really was. Had they suspected that he would make a great success, they would have voted against him until doomsday.

Perhaps this is all the base imaginings of low fellows, and the official account of Chase's selection is strictly accurate; but in any event he came into office under the most difficult circumstances imaginable. Not only was he a stranger in a strange land, but he was the successor of the magnetic and magnificent Graham; and he had to make good on the tremendous promise that Graham had held out to the State. It was a large order for any man and a tremendous order for an unemotional Yankee.

But within six years he had so far delivered the goods that when he received an offer from the West and was tempted to accept, the State, instead of seizing this opportunity to replace the Yankee with a true and tried Tarheel, howled its protest until the welkin rang. It was no perfunctory protest, either; North Carolina really stood aghast at the prospect of losing Chase, and the public relief when he declined the offer was not at all pretended.

This strong position in the State he gained by his organization of the university. Credit for the building programme, although it was executed under his administration, perhaps belongs less to Chase than to Graham. It was Graham, not Chase, who aroused the enthusiasm which drove the initial appropriations through the North Carolina Legislature. It was Graham, too, who outlined the general policy which the new institution was to follow; but death stopped him when his ideas were still all on paper. To Chase fell the infinitely difficult task of realizing what Graham had conceived.

It was he who had to face the universal human objection to intelligent action, which is as prevalent in North Carolina as it is everywhere else. In the beginning he did North Carolina the compliment of assuming that what the State desired in its university was value, rather than size. He calmly ignored that defeatist psychology which had cursed the Commonwealth ever since the Civil War, and proceeded to administer his office as if he had never heard that the South was bankrupt, backward and bitter. And the amazing fact is that he got away with it.

Of course, he promptly ran into trouble, and in trouble he has remained so long and so constantly that by now it must seem to him to be his natural element. But his technique has been superb, and none of his countless assailants has ever been able to hang anything on him.

For his play in every case has been to bet his shirt that North Carolina, in the long run, would react favorably to courage, commonsense and calmness. Only in one instance, which will be related presently, has he imitated the Highland Soldier by tucking up his kilts and going down the road looking for trouble. For the rest, he has simply filled his faculty with aggressive men, many of them young in years, and practically all of them young in spirit, and let nature take its course. Thereafter he did not have to look for trouble. It poured in upon him in great masses. The better the man, the more certain he was to do something which some-body in North Carolina would dislike intensely; and an astonishing number of Chase's men are very good indeed.

But when hell popped, and it was popping pretty much all the time through the first few years, President Chase invariably rose up himself and took the war. If the cause of the disturbance was the legitimate expression of an opinion, or a legitimate piece of research on the part of a faculty member, the professor involved frequently never was aware that he had started a row. The president would settle the disturbance somehow, quite commonly without thinking it worth while to mention it to anyone on the campus. I dare say there were years in which Dr. Chase did not open one mail in five without finding himself the target of a volley of abuse from some quarter. He has been denounced by the clergy, he has been raked fore and aft by editors, he has been bawled out by Governors and legislators for things with which he had not the remotest connection; but he has never salved his wounded pride by taking it out on his subordinates. No man has been fired from the faculty of the University of North Carolina for expression of unpopular opinion, or for telling unpalatable truth. And this, of course, has contributed enormous internal strength to the institution.

But it has contributed external strength, as well. If memory serves, the first really notable uproar of the Chase administration started miles away from the campus. It was shortly after the war, when smelling out witches was still the main occupation of professional patriots. A soldier made a speech at an Open Forum meeting. Incidentally, the warrior was a very decent fellow at bottom, but, like most members of his profession, completely devoid of political sense. One of the early organizers of the Ku Klux Klan apparently had gotten hold of him and had scared him out of seven years' growth; so his speech was a typical raw-head-and-bloody-bones deliverance. The country was living on the crust of a volcano. There was a Bolshevik under every bed. Thousands of spies swarmed through the land, and hell and damnation were just around the corner.

A pair of young instructors in the university happened to be in the audience, and when the soldier had finished, one of them took the floor. He said, in effect, Hooey! Immediately the soldier denounced him as a dubious American, whereupon the other instructor rose and bawled the officer in such terms as he had not heard applied to him since he was a second lieutenant and his colonel caught him with a pocket-flap un-bottoned.

Of course the university had nothing to do with this, but the King's coat had been insulted by a mere civilian, and the civilian belonged to the university. Therefore numerous people, ordinarily sane enough, were persuaded that the institution was filled with ravening pacifists burning with desire to bite the gentle American Legionnaires. Chase was thunderously ordered to clean house and to do it instantly. Then and there he laid his first bet. He wagered his official head that the people of North Carolina at heart did not care two hoots if a soldier had been bawled out by an instructor. He issued an unexcited statement to the effect that it was manifestly impossible for the university to undertake to control the personal opinions of faculty members, and never mentioned the matter again.

But he won his bet. After a clamorous week or two the common sense of the State resumed control and decreed that Chase was right. By exhibiting a little courage, a little calmness, and a little common decency, he rode the storm triumphantly. Incidentally, he made no martyrs.

In the meantime, Odum, the sociologist, had founded his quarterly, at first called the *Journal of Social Forces*, and had begun to afford in it a medium of expression for everyone who had anything worth while to say. From the very beginning the journal, whose title has since been reduced to *Social Forces*, was filled with dynamite, but for a long time nobody in North Carolina paid any attention to it. This was not strange, since it appeared in a drab cover, contained articles written in technical jargon, and was so ponderous that with a single copy, clubbed, you could stun a policeman. But one morning flaming headlines appeared in all the newspapers over an article describing how the Presbyterian ministers of Charlotte, one of the principal towns of the State, had assembled in convention and denounced the University luridly.

"What I long have feared at last has happened," said one sardonic Tarheel editor that morning. "Somebody has read the *Journal of Social Forces!*"

It was even so. By evil chance one of the clerics had dipped into a couple of articles, one by Bernard of Wisconsin, the other by Barnes of Smith.[1] Bernard had spoken of the American country church without much enthusiasm, and Barnes has spoken of God without any. The fact that neither writer was a member of the faculty of the university, or even a resident of the State, of course counted for nothing. The indignant clergymen assumed that the articles betrayed a secret design on Odum's part to abolish religion; and they demanded of Chase instant repudiation of Odum and all his works, the *Journal* in chief.

As it happened, Odum had done time in a sectarian college in Geor-

---

1. L. L. Bernard and Harry Elmer Barnes, both social scientists and frequent contributors to the *Journal of Social Forces*.

gia, therefore he knew by bitter experience what it means for a college president, especially in the South, to incur the wrath of the Church Militant. He was certain of Chase's sympathy, and all that, but he realized Chase's position. He would not have been surprised, and, indeed, would have borne no grudge had he been thrown out of the university so fast that he would have first hit the ground three counties away. But when he went to Chase with his resignation in his pocket, he was promptly advised to go back and attend to his own department. As for his resignation, when that was wanted it would be called for. It hasn't been called for yet.

This storm, however, was far worse than the assault upon the pacifists. It was in literal truth a *jehad*, a Holy War, and it continued for years. Fortunately, the only shock troops that could be brought to the assault were the Presbyterians, and they are not numerous in North Carolina. The Methodists could not be worked into a real frenzy, because they had no church college in competition with the university. Their school, Trinity, had long ago been taken over by the Duke family, who have since endowed it heavily as Duke University. As for the Baptists, they had a college, Wake Forest, but they did not have the gall to say anything against the State university, because for twenty years Satan had been president of Wake Forest. Of course Auld Hornie did not appear on the campus in red tights, with a flesh-fork, cloven hoofs and arrow-head tail. He assumed the appearance of a benevolent, scholarly, and exceedingly astute old gentleman who had been educated as a biologist by the Huns. This man, William Louis Poteat by name, first as professor of biology, and later as president of the college, had been brazenly teaching the hellish doctrine of evolution for more than a generation; and he had taught it to such effect that nearly every Baptist preacher in the State—or those of them who could read—was steadfastly opposed to burning evolutionists alive in the courthouse square, while many of them were opposed even to putting them in jail. Therefore the Baptists could get up no steam for an attack on the university.

However the Presbyterians, unsupported, did pretty well. Their ministers, practically to a man, could read, and they did read *Social Forces* with immense assiduity. One of them, Brother William P. McCorkle of Burlington, must have gone through every copy since the first issue, for he presently issued a pamphlet attacking the university. He indicted it, jointly and severally, on thirty-one separate counts, all based on statements he had dredged out of *Social Forces*. For instance, some reviewer had spoken well of a book which referred to auto-eroticism as being by no means the bugaboo it was once considered, and probably not as bad as some other practices less heartily condemned. Upon this evidence

Brother McCorkle wrote as the headline of the twenty-second count of his indictment, "Masturbation Advised." He had a thirty-second charge, but this one was too awful for him to take the responsibility of uttering it without reservation; therefore he advanced it as his belief, at the same time carefully stating that he could not prove it, that the university maintained a tolerant attitude toward Socialism!

Throughout this ungodly mess President Chase stood steadfast, and apparently not even agitated. The faculty, the trustees, the undergraduates, and the alumni raved, laughed and shuddered, as their several temperaments dictated, but the president did nothing. He issued one of his usual mild statements, explaining that Odum's magazine was not a text-book used in the university, but a medium for the exchange of information among scholars. For the rest, he relied on the common sense of the State to pull him through; and, foolhardy as that policy seemed at first, for the second time it worked.

However, he was forced into action at last. While the assault of the moralists was at its height, in the early part of 1925, an anti-evolution bill was introduced in the North Carolina Legislature. Representative D. Scott Poole, a country editor and a stout Presbyterian, was its author, and there was a dreadful moment when it seemed likely to be enacted, for the Fundamentalist tide was at its crest, and the Scopes trial had not yet come along to make monkey bills the laughing-stock of the civilized world. Chase had asked this Legislature for a substantial increase in the appropriation for the university, and the appropriation bill was still in committee; every consideration of political prudence therefore commanded him to avoid incurring the wrath of Fundamentalist members. The presidents of the other State universities, confronted with this menace, had unanimously crawled into their holes; but Chase went before the legislative committee and spoke against the bill.

The next morning a group of his faculty members were standing on the street, the morning newspaper in their hands, their minds torn between pride in the university and terror of Fundamentalist reprisals, when the president came up and joined them. Nobody had much to say—nobody knew what to say. But at last someone wondered what the effect would be on the appropriation.

"I don't know," said Chase, "I hope that it will have no effect. But if this university doesn't stand for anything but appropriations, I, for one, don't care to be connected with it."

The statement was matter-of-fact, but it was a burr under the university's tail nevertheless. Here was a president who would risk an appropriation in defense of a principle! The faculty was first stunned, then electrified; so were the students; and so, finally but most importantly, were the alumni. There was a heavy *bloc* of them in the Legislature, and when they found they had a president who would actually fight, after they had recovered from their astonishment they went into action with the reckless fury of janissaries. Representative Poole found his bill suddenly subjected to drum-fire by all the heavy artillery of the Legislature, for the Carolina alumni were ably assisted by the Poteat-trained Baptists, and the monkey-bill was incontinently thrown downstairs. Next Summer came the Scopes trial; and North Carolina, seeing the spectacle which it made of her neighbor State, began to realize what she had escaped.

His fight against the anti-evolution bill unquestionably made Chase, as far as public opinion was concerned. It did not sharpen the rancor of the fanatical Fundamentalists against the university, for that was already razor-edged; and it did arouse tremendous enthusiasm for the institution among the intelligent. The Poole bill, in fact, was beaten partly by the votes of legislators who were themselves Fundamentalists in religion, but who were fair-minded, and who admired courage, even in a college president. And the appropriation went through.

There has not since been serious assault upon the administration of the university, although there is always a certain amount of sniping, as there is against every institution of the kind which has the breath of life in it. The Fundamentalists still mutter darkly, and whenever a student is betrayed by tricky Orange county corn into sallying out on the street and fighting a policeman, the incident is held up as proof of the total depravity of the president and all his satellites. Whenever a research worker of the social science department discovers some unusually hellish mode of torture practiced in a county convict camp, there is a howl from the county affected against the "theorists" down at Chapel Hill. Whenever the economics department says anything, good, bad, or indifferent, about the textile industry, there is a growl from the cotton-mill barons who rule, or think they rule, the State. And whenever the education department, or the librarian, produces figures to prove that vast numbers of North Carolinians can't read, or that practically all North Carolinians don't read, the professional patriots get on their hind legs and roar about the Damyankee, oblivious of the fact that both the head of the education department and the librarian are, as the college song has it, Tarheel born and Tarheel bred and when they die they'll be Tarheel dead.

But these are minor irritations. The main point is that the university itself has been working hard and happily for ten years. Nobody is afraid of being thrown out of his job for doing honest work, or telling unpalatable truth; and under such conditions an occasional uproar merely adds interest to existence. To assert that there are no bickerings among the professors at Chapel Hill would be to give the truth a pretty severe wrench; and to assert that nobody there criticizes the president would be to drag it away from its footings altogether. But it is absolutely true that there is no anti-administration faction among the faculty members, and no real faction of any sort. The language men regard the social scientists with a jaundiced eye, to be sure, and the natural scientists sniff at both, but that is pure normalcy, with no relation to local conditions.

And the president is so well satisfied with conditions in North Carolina that he has refused the red hat! No Fundamentalists can get at a director of a big foundation. No bilious Governor can bawl him out for a remark made by some temporary assistant instructor in the Summer school. No group of cotton-mill barons can threaten his appropriation if his department of economics makes a competent investigation of the prevalent wage scale in the textile industry. No group of ebullient undergraduates can ruin his reputation by getting unanimously and gloriously drunk at the Thanksgiving football game. The director of a great foundation is bedeviled by none of the harassments that urge a State university president on down the road that leads to the foolish-house. And directors are well paid, with a comfortable pension awaiting them when they grow old.

But then directors of foundations seldom have opportunity to evolve a sociological theory and work it out on a grand scale. Chase has evolved the theory that the president of a State university need not necessarily be a rabbit. He has tried it out in a State that, when he came to it, was widely regarded as down and out financially, educationally, intellectually and every other way—that is to say, he has tried it out under the worst imaginable conditions.

And it has worked. Without the magic of a highly magnetic personality, without the aid of Bryanesque eloquence, without strong political, or social, or financial backing, with nothing in the world save courage, a level head and common decency he has won the confidence of his State to an extent that is matched by few of his colleagues in the country. I omit reference to the organizing ability which built up the university from within, for that would never have saved him against assaults from without.

In other words, Chase has built himself into that curious anomaly, a State university president who is neither the servant nor the master of politicians, clerical or lay. It is an achievement of such magnitude that perhaps, after all, even the educational cardinalate is a minor thing by comparison.

He gambled on the good sense of the people of North Carolina and he won. Whether that reflects more credit on him or on the State, I am not prepared to say, but doubtless there is glory enough for all.

# Graham of Carolina

In another essay on a president of the University of North Carolina, Johnson praises his fellow Carolina Scotsman Frank Porter Graham. In *Survey Graphic* (April 1942) he applauds Graham's courage, his penchant for attracting friends and enemies, and—most of all—his moral integrity, an inheritance from his Calvinist ancestors.

It is a truism that if you pin enough honorary degrees on a man, some of them will stick; but five institutions of learning at various times have appended various collections of capital letters to the name of Frank Porter Graham, president of the University of North Carolina and Libertarian-in-Chief to the late Confederacy, and none of them has stuck. To this day in the imperial commonwealth of Tarheelia he remains either plain "Frank Graham" spoken with a lilt in the voice, or "that damned Frank Graham," spoken through gritted teeth. That he is the best-loved man in the state admits of no more doubt than that he is the best-hated man there, too; and both emotions he has richly earned. But the suggestion that he is a learned doctor most North Carolinians hear with incredulity and, having considered it, dismiss as irrelevant.

It is a fact, though, that he started life as a historian and labored for years at a *magnum opus* relating to power, in the sense of mechanical force not derived from the strength of animals, and its effect on Western civilization. I am inclined to believe with the Tarheels, though, that this is a fact that may be dismissed with bare mention. If Frank Graham is a historian, then Kelly is a Chinaman. He makes history for others to write, which means that he is a man equipped with qualities far different from those of a good chronicler.

The man is a bundle of paradoxes. Leaving out of consideration Nicholas Murray Butler of Columbia, unprecedented and unparalleled, Graham is the most publicized university president in America, yet in his personal relations he is painfully modest. He is reputed to be the friendliest soul in the three and a half millions between Murphy and Manteo; yet he has started more fights than ever were precipitated by Blackbeard, the pirate, who, I suppose, was the unfriendliest of all North Carolinians. In private life he is a merry companion, an excellent story-teller—keenly appreciative of a jest told by another; yet when

Copyright © 1942 by the *Survey Graphic* and reprinted with permission.

engaged in controversy over what he considers a principle he exhibits just about as much sense of humor as was shown by the late Tomas de Torquemada. He has energized, inspired, and glorified the University of North Carolina—but if the institution were afflicted with two Frank Grahams it would certainly explode.

Beyond the confines of North Carolina, Graham is known chiefly as President Roosevelt's representative, or the public representative, on various boards and councils. Last December, then a member of the National Defense Mediation Board, he startled his friends and confounded his enemies by voting against the closed shop in the captive coal mines. There are those in North Carolina who had asserted loudly that Graham's vote could be counted in advance for anything that labor wanted; yet these same men will admit that he is, and always has been, his own man, taking orders from nobody, not even his own board of trustees. It is quite true that he has frequently cast his vote and his influence in favor of the cause of labor, not in the NDMB only, but in other situations that affected him much more closely; and in these cases it has been conspicuously true that he consulted his own conscience and no other authority whatever. Why anyone should argue from that record that he was likely to accept the dictation of John L. Lewis[1] is not clear; but it is clear enough that the anti-Graham faction in North Carolina was amazed and disconcerted when he voted against Lewis.

Subsequently he was appointed to the new War Labor Board as one of the public representatives on that body. This much the ordinary newspaper reader knows of him, but all this means little. Only those who have been in position to know what went on in the meetings of these various agencies have any appreciation of how important have been his contributions, sometimes to the untangling of knotted relations between labor and capital, sometimes to the framing of important legislation such as the Social Security Act (he was chairman of the President's Advisory Committee at that stage), and always to the support of government by the consent of the governed and only by their consent.

It is of the essence of this sort of work that it shall be unspectacular. The successful arbiter sedulously avoids drawing attention to himself. When Tom Girdler[2] and John Lewis fall out—no, let us avoid personalities, and say that when there is a dispute between Agamemnon and Achilles, it behooves Nestor to walk softly and speak quietly if he hopes to compose the quarrel. Frank Graham has done this so consistently that

1. John L. Lewis, president of the United Mine Workers of America.
2. Tom Girdler, chairman of the board of Republic Steel Corporation.

few people have any idea how often his unaffected friendliness and obvious eagerness to do the right thing have disarmed belligerent contestants and smoothed the way to agreement in cases in which there seemed at first no possibility of pacific settlement. But among the few who know the facts is the President of the United States; and that explains why Graham has been called away from Chapel Hill so often to handle some of the thorniest economic and social problems with which the administration has been confronted. His is the rare quality of being amenable to reason without being pliable. Perhaps only the rulers of the earth have an adequate appreciation of the scarcity of such men and the value of those that are to be found.

In the narrower world of educators he is known as a man who has been remarkably successful in maintaining a vital connection between his university and the people of the state that support it. He is known, also, as a sturdy defender of the principle of academic freedom. But the thing that has caused other university presidents, more especially presidents of state universities, to regard him with a sort of stupefaction is the fact that he has had the incredible nerve to outrage, not merely the trustees, not merely the legislature, and not merely the industrial barons of his state, but the very alumni themselves, and that with relative impunity. The so-called "Graham plan" that set the southern collegiate world by the ears a few years ago, was, as a matter of fact, not the invention of Frank Graham, but the recommendation of a committee of educators representing the most reputable southern schools. It was the forthright and uncompromising support given it by the president of the University of North Carolina that caused his name to be affixed to it, and gave most newspaper readers the idea that he had devised it without any other human being.

The Graham plan was radical, indeed, in its implications, although simple enough in essence. It was embodied in a formidable document but, stripped of academic phraseology, its meaning was that the signatory colleges agreed that on and after its effective date every man representing any of them on a football team should be at least semi-literate. The radicalism of the scheme lay, of course, in its setting education above athletics by assuming that the men on the football squad had come to college to learn something in the classroom.

To no theorist will this seem radical, for in theory all colleges are committed to support of that doctrine. But theorists commonly overlook the progress of the football mania that, originating in the East, swept across the Middlewest to the Pacific Coast, and is now swirling back through the South. Forty years ago Harvard and Yale, twenty years ago

Michigan and Wisconsin, were as insane over football as Oregon and Southern California, Duke and Alabama are today. The southern institutions that, in adopting the Graham plan, attempted to lay upon athletes the scholastic standards required of other students were taking a fearful chance—indeed, a fatal chance—for the fury of the attack precipitated by the action drove most of them to cover. The Graham plan was soon vitiated in all but a few schools.

The business gave President Graham a tremendous reputation in academic circles, but not exactly the reputation of a great educator in the apostolic succession of Mark Hopkins, Gilman, and Eliot.[3] It is probable that other college presidents, if they would abandon discretion for candor, might confess that they regard him as the spiritual successor, not of Witherspoon and Dwight,[4] but rather of such daredevils as Charles Blondin, who crossed Niagara Falls on a tightrope, and of Steve Brodie, who dived off Brooklyn Bridge. A university president who dares outrage the alumni is phenomenal, but as a hero, rather than as a pedagogue.

Nevertheless, I have heard a shrewd, hardheaded Tarheel lawyer, not an alumnus of the University of North Carolina and not connected with it in any way, describe Frank P. Graham as "without doubt the most influential citizen in the state." He did not say "private" citizen. He included officials from the governor down and the whole delegation in Congress.

The program that has made him a storm center for the last eleven years seems on examination rather innocuous. The educational policy of the University of North Carolina is, of course, not the creation of any one man, but Graham's contributions to it have been distinctly on the conservative side. As far as the public is aware he has never suggested, much less insisted on, any pedagogical experimentation. He is interested in original investigation in the graduate school, and much has been carried on, especially in the social sciences; but research is certainly not to be described as educational experimentation.

His social and his economic ideas are, on their surface at least, equally conventional. In spite of the loud asseverations of his enemies to the contrary, he is no more Marxian than was the late Andrew Mellon. He accepts the theory of free enterprise under the capitalistic system

3. Mark Hopkins, president of Williams College, 1836–72; Daniel Coit Gilman, first president of the Johns Hopkins University; Charles William Eliot, president of Harvard University, 1869–1909.

4. John Witherspoon, early president of the College of New Jersey (Princeton), 1768–76; Timothy Dwight, president of Yale College, 1795–1817.

without question, and if he cherishes many doubts as to the efficient working of that system, who doesn't?

With this in mind people sometimes take the view that the man's conspicuous position as a liberal is purely a geographical accident; if he lived anywhere except in the South, they say, none would dream of accusing him of radicalism. There is certainly some truth in this. Graham's defense of the right of labor to organize, for example, is no longer convincing proof of radicalism even in the least progressive parts of the South; and the fact that he put up bail for a former student arrested on a picket line would hardly be esteemed in the North an assault upon the foundations of society.

The hatred that he has aroused is based on his championship of unpopular people, rather than upon his advocacy of subversive ideas. Again and again he has fought doggedly to protect the civil rights of labor agitators and sharecroppers and people who believe in things as repulsive to North Carolina as agnosticism, pacifism, and the political, economic, and even social equality of Negroes. "The trouble with Frank Graham," said one of his non-admirers, wonderingly, "is that the damn fool will fight just as hard for the rights of a man he knows is an s.o.b. as he will for those of a decent citizen." Surely, it is not in the South alone that a man who, by insisting that they be given their full legal rights, throws the mantle of respectability over unpopular persons, draws upon himself some of their unpopularity. Surely, it is not a North Carolina industrialist only who, when balked in a scheme to dispose of a too successful union organizer by framing him on a trumped-up charge, turns furiously on the balker and denounces him as a Red. Yet it is upon such activities that most of the Tarheel hatred of Graham as a radical is based.

But this is not the whole truth. Frank Porter Graham does harbor one idea that is radical in the extreme, so radical that it would make him conspicuous in Moscow, not to mention North Carolina. This is the idea that the Sermon on the Mount is sound social and economic doctrine.

It is hopeless to try to explain the man on the basis of his intellectual, political or economic concepts, because all these are based on and shaped by his ethical concepts. It is a rarity in these days to find a man in a conspicuous position the whole foundation of whose manner of thought and action is so profoundly ethical, as distinguished from pragmatic. The fact that his system of ethics is strongly tinged with the Calvinism of his Highland Scottish forebears is, I think, fortuitous; if Graham had been born into a Catholic, or a Jewish, or a Mohammedan family, his point of view might have been different on matters of faith and doctrine, but his concept of the conduct of life as primarily an ethical problem would have been the same.

This characteristic contributes, of course, both to his strength and to his weakness. He is the administrative head of a tripartite university, with its technical schools at Raleigh, its college of liberal arts and graduate schools at Chapel Hill, and its women's college at Greensboro. The distance from Raleigh to Greensboro is eighty-one miles. The schools include some 10,000 students, several hundred faculty members, and several thousand non-academic employees ranging from scrub-women to architects. The management of such an institution is a matter of extreme complexity, and even with the aid of brilliant assistants in key positions, the president must get through an enormous amount of routine work to keep the machine running smoothly.

It is characteristic of Graham that he is usually much less exercised over a grave blunder in policy than he is over a wrong that affects only one person and him but slightly. Let him get wind of an injustice being perpetrated upon a student, a faculty member, or the lowliest employee of the institution, and he is instantly on the warpath, nor will he rest until the man's rights have been vindicated. Every soul connected with the university in any capacity is confident that he can always get justice from the president; and this makes for a loyalty that has built up an immense solidarity—the solidarity that withstood the battering of the depression years.

On the other hand, it is indubitably true that the most serious discussion of the most perplexing question of policy may be summarily adjourned if, in the midst of it, the president hears that some garrulous fool by talking too much has gotten himself locked up, or beaten up, or otherwise maltreated by the Philistines. That is a wrong, and nothing else is important until steps have been taken toward righting it. So, while every freshman is certain that he can get justice, no department head is certain that he can get attention from the president; and this makes for a measure of pessimism among the higher ranks, who have sometimes been provoked into wondering not if Graham is a good president, but if he is any president at all.

Such doubts, however, are the progeny of momentary exasperation. Disregarding hypothetical situations, the question of whether Graham has been a good president for this particular university at this particular time is answered definitely and completely by the existence of the university. Prosperity began to ebb in North Carolina, not in 1929, but in 1923, when the cotton textile industry got into trouble, and ten years later it reached a nadir far below that touched in many other parts of the country. If the wrong man had been at the head of the university then, there would be no university now. Oh, doubtless there would have been something that bore the name, but it would not have been a university. It would have been another of those woeful spectacles with which the country is all too familiar—an appalling pseudo-college, with a faculty of broken down political hacks, no equipment, no money, and no standing among respectable educational institutions. The United States has had many and still has some "universities" that in collecting their tuition charges are obtaining money under false pretenses, for they afford no education worth having. Had the wrong man been at its head, the depression might well enough have made the University of North Carolina another of that type.

Nothing of the sort happened; therein is the great justification of Frank Graham's existence. One is tempted to believe that Carolina must enjoy some special favor in Heaven, for three times in succession Fate has given it a president perfectly adapted by character and temperament for the task that came to his hand. The first was Edward Kidder Graham, a kinsman of the incumbent; he is the man of whom Thomas Wolfe wrote with a pen dipped in nitric acid instead of ink, the messianic college president in "The Web and the Rock." E. K. Graham's emotionalism revolted the satiric—the sophomoric—Wolfe, but it matched, mastered and directed the terrific burst of emotionalism that shook the state at the time of the first World War, adeptly turning that enormous force to support of the state university. Graham's tragic death in the influenza epidemic perhaps did more than his eloquence to insure the triumph of the cause for which it was commonly believed that he had sacrificed his life. At any rate, the first huge appropriation for a modern plant—some five or six million dollars—was made then.

His successor, who spent the money, was a man of a diametrically opposite type, H. W. Chase, now chancellor of New York University. A Massachusetts Yankee, austere in appearance, and not in his predecessor's class as an orator, Chase had a keen eye for a scholar and was one of the smoothest administrators ever heard of. He could never have won the money from a reluctant legislature; but having it supplied through the impetus of E. K. Graham's movement, he spent it with a skill that Graham probably never could have matched, and in ten years built up such a university as the South had never seen before.

Just before the grand crash of the '30s he moved on, and Frank Graham succeeded him. Perhaps the second Graham could never have initiated such a movement as the first one did; perhaps he could never have built such an organization as Chase built; but it is a safe assertion that neither the earlier Graham nor Chase could have taken the beating that the depression inflicted upon the university and emerged with as much salvage as this present-day Graham brought out.

What Carolina needed most in 1930 was neither a great administrator, nor a great educator, but a champion who could plead its cause effectively with people distracted by a fearful catastrophe. This Frank Graham did with an effectiveness that grows more remarkable in retrospect. He had the temperament that drove him inevitably to exactly the right approach. He told the people, not that it would be unwise, not that it would be imprudent, but that it would be wrong to let the university go down—an insult to the past, an injury to the present, a betrayal of the future. It was the one appeal that could catch their attention in the midst of their myriad troubles; and it was made by the one man whom they could not choose but believe—for all North Carolinians are agreed that if Frank Graham is an authority on anything, it is on questions of right and wrong. His tremendous preoccupation with the ethical may be a handicap in some circumstances, but it was his salvation when he pleaded with the people.

A stranger, giving him a casual glance, might easily fall into the error of underrating this man as an advocate for he is, physically, the very antithesis of everything Websterian. He was barely tall enough to get into the Marines during the war of 1917–18, and he is slightly built. His head is fairly large, but by no means leonine, and the hair is getting pretty thin on top. It never was a mane. His voice is clear and carries well, but has no such organ tones as Webster's. His coloring is neutral, his features passably regular, but no movie scout ever looked at him with a speculative eye. In short, the unsuspecting stranger, told to pick the orator out of two people present, would almost inevitably choose Frank Graham second. Yet I have seen tears running down the cheeks of some pretty hard-boiled alumni when he had been talking to them for twenty minutes, using almost no gestures and absolutely no flights of rhetoric, speaking hesitantly, almost stumblingly.

What did it? I do not know. Certainly it was not the voice, not the language, not the gestures, for all were simple and plain. But in the crisis, when there was real danger that a harried and bewildered legislature might throttle the university, whenever Graham rose to plead its cause a sort of white flame seemed to light up in him, and he became for the moment not a man at all, but the embodiment of a cause, the conductor through which shot the current of a passion of enormous potential, the filament blazing with a power not of himself but pouring through him and in transfiguring him driving night and its shadows away. If oratory is grandiloquence, music and thunder, Graham at the top of his form is no orator at all; but if it is the power that enables a man to melt a refractory crowd and mould it into whatever frame of mind he pleases, then he is one of the best. He can use rhetoric, but in his most powerful speeches he has depended on something beyond and above it.

The friendliness of Frank Graham is one of the natural wonders of North Carolina, comparable to the height of Mt. Mitchell and the sweep of the hundred-mile beaches on the coast. He is a friendly man, without a doubt, but it is possible that what makes him such a marvel is the fact that his genuine liking for people is backed by a prodigious memory for names and faces. If you are a person of no great importance in the world, if you have met the president of the university only once and have not seen him for a year, or maybe five years, and then if he jumps up when you come into his office, calls you by your first name and asks if your Aunt Sue recovered satisfactorily from that fracture of the hip she had suffered just before he talked to you last, well, you are going to be impressed. You would be more, or less, than human if you weren't impressed. You will probably be somewhat elated, too, and will make comments on the incident that in turn will impress your friends and relations; and so the legend grows.

One point about this hypothetical meeting deserves special emphasis; cannot, indeed, be overemphasized. It is the fact that "duke's son and cook's son" get precisely the same sort of greeting. This is not because Dr. Graham is studiedly and carefully democratic, but because he is quite literally unable to perceive any validity in distinctions as between man and man; all men interest him, and in some respects the bad and the mad are more interesting than the good. Every man offers him an opportunity to broaden his experience; the most ignorant can teach him something. He is genuinely glad to talk to anybody, and he is serenely confident of the Scriptural dictum that no man is contaminated by what he hears, but only by what he utters. That is to say, he is so sure of his own position that he doesn't have to fend off others to protect it. But this attitude is characteristic of very great aristocrats, and for this reason I am sometimes half inclined to believe that Frank Graham is the greatest aristocrat of my acquaintance.

However, no manner of doubt that the deepest of his convictions is that every man has a God-given right to order his own life within the boundaries that are marked by the rights of others; and that no man, prince, potentate, or even priest, has any right to proceed the fraction of an inch beyond those bounds, except as authority to do so may be conferred upon him by common consent in the common interest. This he calls democracy. Whether this definition can be justified etymologically, I do not know; but I do know that it is a strong philosophy at this moment. It has fortified this leader in the confidence of his people; and a leader strong with the people is unquestionably an asset to pretty much any institution in these chaotic days, and especially to one dependent upon public support for its very existence.

Nor is there any convincing reason to suppose that such leadership will grow less valuable in the predictable future. Whatever else may come out of the war, it is already clear that one effect will be a searching scrutiny of every institution, educational, political, social, or religious, that lays claim to special consideration. The right of inheritance, for example, is no longer sacred, nor is the time far distant when the abolition of perpetual endowments will be demanded with a louder clamor than ever before in our history.

Whatever is, will be called on to show cause why it should be tolerated; and the only sufficient cause will be a clear demonstration of value, not to a clique or a class, but to society at large. At that time a university that is already strong in the affections of men who never saw the inside of a college will be in a highly advantageous position; and among those universities Frank Porter Graham, more than any other individual, has placed the University of North Carolina.

# Billy with the Red Necktie

H. L. Mencken had asked Johnson in 1924 to write an essay for the *American Mercury* on William Louis Poteat, liberal president of Wake Forest College. Johnson had refused at that time because if he lauded Poteat's methods for placating his critics among conservative North Carolina Baptists, he explained to Mencken, "the brethren" at the next Baptist convention "would take the simple precaution of not letting Poteat speak" and would then proceed to fire him. After Poteat's death, however, Johnson was moved to write such an article. In the *Virginia Quarterly Review* (Autumn 1943)— not the *Mercury*—he pays tribute to the educator who had inspired thousands of Wake Forest graduates, including the author himself.

The President of the College was a short man and somewhat rotund. His massive head was bare on top, and his features would have been heavy and formidable had it not been for an irrepressible twinkle in his eyes that usually defeated his best effort to look solemn. On the day the college opened he made the customary address of welcome attired in a suit of dark gray smartly cut, carefully pressed, and accented with a wine-colored bow standing out sharply against immaculate linen.

Two hundred uncurried freshmen, drawn from the remotest fastnesses of North Carolina, regarded him doubtfully. Could this be the great Dr. Poteat, that William Louis Poteat whom most of them had heard discussed all their lives? He did not fit their preconceptions. They had heard him lauded to the skies, and they had heard him denounced with the bitterest invective, but they had never heard him discussed in any mood but one of the utmost seriousness. This man looked—well, "worldly" was probably the word that occurred to most of them, for they were products of pious homes. It is a word now fallen into disuse, but current among all the godly at the time—you can guess the year closely enough by the fact that the popular song hit of the moment was concerned with the whereabouts of one Kelly, alleged to be from the Emerald Isle.

The freshmen left the hall puzzled, and a few hours later most of them were scandalized; for upper classmen had attended the assembly, too, noting the President's habiliments, and shortly after darkness had

Copyright © 1943 by the *Virginia Quarterly Review* and reprinted with permission.

fallen upon the campus, the freshmen, immured by tradition in their rooms, heard the night made hideous with a roaring chorus that ended,

> Sure, his head is bald and his eyes are blue
> And he's a Dutchman through and through—
> Has anybody here seen Billy?
> Billy with the red necktie?

Of course, he wasn't a Netherlander; he was an American of English extraction, but at that time and in that locality "Dutchman" had a special significance. It was a generic term for one regarded with mingled amusement and amazement, comparable to the "dabster" of New England, and the "buster" of the Middle West. Thus the ditty was thoroughly ribald and added to the confusion of young gentlemen newly arrived at the seat of learning known as Wake Forest College, located seventeen miles from Raleigh, the capital of North Carolina. We were simple youths who swarmed over the lovely old campus, with its great oaks and innumerable magnolias, in the early days of the century. We were little given to scrutiny and analysis; we sang with tremendous emotion,

> Oh, here's to Wake Forest,
> A glass of the finest,
> Red, ruddy Rhenish filled up to the brim,

all untroubled by the fact that the finest Rhenish is invariably white; doubtless half of us thought it was something like mead, or hydromel, anyhow. But the least introspective, the least reflective youth could not accept Dr. Billy Poteat merely as part of the established order, therefore not to be questioned. He was always questioned, for he was always unexpected, always surprising, usually troubling. On the very first day of the term freshmen found him loudly and publicly jeered by upper classmen who privately adored him and swore fervently that he was the greatest man in the State. It was upsetting.

Nor did that condition alter with the passage of time. Through the four years that followed, Dr. Poteat continued to be upsetting, never quite what one expected, always adopting an astonishing point of view. In the class-room—for throughout his presidency of the college he continued to teach a class in general biology—he was not merely polite, he was courtly; but he had developed the ability to make, with the most deferential air, the most shattering observations. "But I have a right to my opinion," cried a rash and argumentative youth. "No man has any right to an opinion, Mr. Blank,'' returned Dr. Billy, blandly, "until he has first made himself acquainted with the facts.''

That this, the first principle of the scientific method, should have astonished us may reveal the abysmal depth of our ignorance; but before you smile too broadly, stop to consider how many men in high places—say, on the floor of the United States Senate—consistently accept and abide by it. If no Senator in this year of grace ever expressed an opinion until after he had familiarized himself with the facts, it is probable that debate in that august assemblage would be sharply restricted.

When we were a little older, and a little more accustomed to scholastic terminology, it was easy for us to classify Dr. Poteat as a master of the Socratic method. But that explained nothing but his technique. The man himself remained a question, uncatalogued and unclassified, a little troubling. Even on the great day when he welcomed us, in one of those polished, gem-like, baccalaureate addresses which he delivered annually for twenty-two years, into the fellowship of men of letters as Bachelors of Arts, he was still unexplained; and even now, thirty years later, when Poteat has been dead five years and retired from his college presidency for fifteen, at least one of his old students, thinking of him, still feels a trace of the confusion that filled the mind of a freshman when sophomores were making the night resound with inquiries for "Billy with the red necktie.''

Certain of his colleagues, wise and learned men with great names in the scientific world, have explained to me that he was a man who threw his life away. I can follow their argument without difficulty, even though I do not accept it fully. In 1883 William Louis Poteat, twenty-seven years old, returned to this country with glowing testimonials from his instructors in the Zoölogical Institute of the University of Berlin, where he had been doing graduate work in biology. It was a golden moment for a brisk young American scholar with German training. Only seven years earlier the famous Daniel Coit Gilman had begun, in Baltimore, an enterprise that was already revolutionizing the academic standards of the country. With what was, for the time, an immense endowment, Dr. Gilman had organized the Johns Hopkins University, not on the English philosophical model, thitherto followed by American schools, but on the German scientific model. The time was ripe for the innovation, and the new school was such an immense success that by 1883 all the universities in the country were reorganizing their curricula to conform more or less closely to the new pattern. The demand for young American scholars with German training suddenly became immense. Into this situation young Poteat stepped, with credentials good enough to be virtually a passport to any sort of academic position. Naturally, the scholarly world was open to him. I know that he received an offer from Yale, and I think he had others from rich and powerful universities in the North and West.

It was then, his colleagues declare, that he threw his life away. He refused the flattering offers from the great schools, and accepted, instead, the professorship of biology in the obscure and starveling college where he had taken his B. A. degree. He returned to Wake Forest, and remained there until his death, fifty-four years later.

The sacrifice involved in this is obvious. It is the other side of the ledger that bothers me. William L. Poteat was a highly intelligent man and anything but a fanatic; therefore he must have balanced his life's accounts in some fashion. But what were the items on the credit side? They must have been of considerable importance, at least in his eyes, for what he gave up was certainly important. We may dismiss the monetary consideration at once, for that was not important to him. I do not think his salary ever exceeded five thousand dollars a year, and I am not sure it was that large. Today a first-rate man in a big university may be paid two, or three, or four times as much; but this factor, I am sure, is literally irrelevant to the problem for the reason that the man, once he was assured of a frugal living, simply was not interested in making any more money. The financial consideration did not operate, either to keep him at Wake Forest or to draw him away.

Yet he did make a sacrifice that even in his eyes was tremendous. It was the sacrifice of a career. There were three elements in this sacrifice, the lowest of which is honorable, yet comprehensible even to people whose eyes are never lifted high. It was the sacrifice of that good name, which the Wisest Man regarded as rather to be chosen than great riches. It takes no very elevated spirit to understand that fame is desirable, sometimes, perhaps, even more desirable than riches. The hope of fame went when Poteat made his choice. The second sacrifice was on a loftier plane, but to men of a certain type it is worse than the surrender of fame. This was the loss of constant, daily association with his intellectual superiors. He was not deprived of intellectual companionship, for there were cultivated men around him; but rarely, indeed, did he encounter a finer mind than his own, yet intellectual swordplay with a fencer who is just a shade better than you are is certainly one of the supreme delights attainable by an intelligent man. Finally—and this is one that can never be fully understood by those of us who have felt no inclination toward scientific research—he yielded his opportunity to extend the boundaries of knowledge. This was probably by far the worst of all, for the man who feels within him the ability "to pick a little path of light into the surrounding darkness"—Poteat's own phrase—can turn his back upon that work only at the cost of a throe that is akin to the pains of death.

Wake Forest had once held a reasonably good position among American colleges, and seemed on the way to bettering it. But catastrophe had intervened. Endowment, books and equipment, students and faculty had all been swallowed up in the maelstrom of the Civil War. The very buildings had been converted into military hospitals, and at the end of four years were almost completely wrecked. In the ensuing eighteen years the college had been able to re-open its doors and to keep them open only by dint of the most heart-breaking struggle in a state that was as completely wrecked, economically, socially, politically, as Wake Forest itself.

All this was well known to the young scholar in 1883. Had he not spent his undergraduate days there and seen with his own eyes how poor was the equipment, how meagre were the opportunities, how desperate was the struggle? But nevertheless he turned down the brilliant opportunities, and chose that place. There is a type of man to whom the most powerful appeal that can be made is the appeal of bitter need. All the academic world was open to Yale; failing Poteat, she could, and did, call in whole platoons of scientists as able, or abler. But if Wake Forest had missed him, what had she to offer a stranger? She must have gone indefinitely with no adequate instruction in modern biological science. Daniel Webster gave to the name of Dartmouth a lustre that a hundred years have not rubbed away when he declared, "It is, sir, as I have said, a small college. And yet there are those who love it." But did not this man's act endow the little Southern school with something of the same glory?

It was not poverty alone that Poteat faced when he decided to return to the South. He knew he would encounter active opposition, as well. But on which side of the ledger should this item be entered? A fight is not always a misfortune. Poteat did battle for forty years, almost without cessation. There were times, no doubt, when he wearied of the fight, finding it onerous and painful; but it is impossible to believe that this was always the case. On the contrary, there were undoubtedly times when he gloried in it, for he had no doubt at all that he was fighting for the release of the human spirit from the thralldom of superstition and falsehood. This is certainly not a misfortune, and it is my belief that in the ledger of his life the man set down the opportunity to fight a good fight for many years as one of the compensations for the sacrifices he made.

But it was a bitter fight. It was part of the long contest that men commonly referred to as the combat between religion and science. This description always irritated Poteat. He asserted that neither science nor religion was in reality involved, and that the fight was between dogmatic theologians and arrogant scientists, each presuming to lay unhallowed hands on things not belonging to his sphere of life. Nevertheless, the fact that he deprecated the strife never prevented him from laying about him right heartily whenever the theologians undertook to dictate what he should say in his class-room.

In the early years he had plenty of opportunity. Wake Forest College is a denominational school belonging to the Baptists. It is true, as Allan Nevins has pointed out, that from Roger Williams to Harry Emerson Fosdick the Baptist clergy has always included some men of extraordinary intellectual distinction, perhaps as many as any other sect has furnished the country. But it is also true that, on account of the non-episcopal organization of the denomination, its most distinguished men have no power over their less capable brethren other than that of moral suasion. A Cornelius Woelfkin, a William Herbert Perry Faunce[1] has no more authority in matters of faith and doctrine than is possessed by the semi-literate pastor of some Little Bethel in the remote backwoods.

In North Carolina, Poteat had no great difficulty with the abler men in the denomination that controlled the college. Even when they cherished personal doubts as to the intrinsic value of that man Darwin and his novel ideas, they conceded the right of a scholar to search for truth, no matter where the search might lead him. But hardly a year passed without the organization of a sort of *jehad* among the shallower minds among the Baptist clergy. They would come to the Baptist State Convention, year after year, with resolutions denouncing the man and demanding his instant removal from the college.

Poteat's method of meeting these attacks was an interesting one. North Carolina, always prolific of orators, has produced few more eloquent than he was, when he chose to be. Warned in advance that an attack was coming, he would take the floor shortly before it was to be launched, ostensibly to speak on education; but education was for him on these occasions merely a springboard, which he hit once in the beginning and never touched again. It merely gave him impetus in diving into his real subject, and within the first five minutes his address would develop into a gospel sermon, so gorgeous in its imagery, so musical in its phrasing, so charged with passionate conviction that when

---

1. Cornelius Woelfkin, Baptist minister and author, pastor of the Park Avenue Church, New York City; William Herbert Perry Faunce, clergyman, author, and president of Brown University.

he sat down at the end of an hour even his adversaries would be weeping and anyone who dared attack Dr. Poteat would have been howled down. Then he would return to Wake Forest and resume the teaching of the hypothesis of organic evolution as before.

In the course of time the personal attacks dwindled and almost stopped. As the years passed, and class after class was graduated from Wake Forest, most of the better Baptist pulpits in the State came to be filled by Wake Forest men; so, at length, the charge that the college was being converted into a hot-bed of atheism began to be absurd on its face. Then came 1910 and the convention, not of Baptists, but of Episcopalians, not in North Carolina, but in New York, that launched upon the world the Fundamentalist manifesto, and the old battle was suddenly resumed, but this time in the political field. Within a few years the Fundamentalists were gunning, not for mere college presidents, but for whole Legislatures, and seeking to establish their doctrine, not by canon, but by statute law.

When the fight was transferred from a religious convention to the State Legislature, Poteat was no longer the principal victim. The man pilloried now was the president of the University of North Carolina, at that time Harry Woodburn Chase, at present Chancellor of New York University. The fainthearted begged Dr. Chase to follow the example of the presidents of other State universities where the same fight had come up and crawl into the storm-cellar until the tornado had passed. Already half a dozen States, including Tennessee, next-door neighbor to North Carolina, had passed laws forbidding the teaching of the hypothesis of organic evolution in tax-supported schools. A similar measure—the so-called "monkey bill"—was pending in the Legislature of North Carolina, and if Chase opposed the bill publicly, they told him, the Fundamentalists in the Legislature would pass it anyhow, and would take their revenge by cutting the university's appropriation. "If this university stands for nothing but appropriations," was Chase's reply, "I no longer want to be connected with it." He went down to Raleigh and at the committee hearing made a resounding speech against the bill, more than half expecting to lose his position as a result.

But then the life of William Louis Poteat suddenly counted. Chase felt that he could rely on the university graduates in the Legislature, but they were not enough, and he did not know where he could get the rest of the necessary votes. What he overlooked was the fact that, since there are half a million Baptists in North Carolina, the Legislature was studded with Wake Forest men, all former pupils of Poteat; when the test came, they rallied to Chase and the university. The "monkey bill" was knocked cold. There was no Scopes trial in North Carolina, with

William J. Bryan and Clarence Darrow fighting each other, but uniting to make a buffoon of the State; and one of the main reasons for that deliverance was the fact that a young scholar had "thrown his life away" by coming back to the State in 1883.

Not long ago the college collected Dr. Poteat's baccalaureate addresses and published them in a volume with the title, "Youth and Culture." I have been looking over that volume recently with growing amazement at the fact that certain persons once charged this man with being irreligious. He was a scientist who rejoiced in each new penetration of the microscope and of the telescope because, as he told his students, "we have to thank them for a greater universe and a greater God." He was a teacher who dismissed what most of the students regarded as progress with the withering comment, "A small man may make big money." To the taunt that science is forever repudiating its own beliefs of yesterday he made the superb reply, "The discovery of a mistake is not ignorance, however wholesome a restraint it may prove upon our pride. It is discovery, an item of new knowledge. The moment between the discovery of a mistake and its correction may be a moment of darkness, but it is a prophecy of light." He was a believer who said, when the Fundamentalists were raging against him: "If A or B or C or D intervene and protest, 'Who are you to ignore the succession of the rabbis and set aside the ancient formula?', I shall answer, 'Only a lover of the Truth, bent upon lighting my taper at the Master light, only a limping follower trying to keep in sight of Him, only a happy slave responsible to his Master alone and not another.' " That phrase, "a happy slave," is of the sort that sticks to a college boy's memory; and even a middle-aged man finds it curiously moving.

In the late twenties, as Poteat was reaching the end of his active career, disorder reigned in the scientific world. Bohr and Rutherford and Einstein had dive-bombed the science of physics until it was as complete a wreck as the city of Rotterdam when the Nazis were through; the old distinction between matter and energy was dissolving. The idea of emergent evolution, which nobody understood, was shaking not biology, only, but also the logical proposition that the whole is equal to the sum of its parts. Chemistry was spinning deliriously back toward something strangely like the alchemical theory of the transmutation of metals. In every field of science the foremost men were acknowledging that in the moment when they seemed to be approaching an end they had only uncovered another mystery, deeper and more obscure than any they had penetrated.

But in this confusion Poteat found, not disappointment, but justification of his faith; thus he was able to make to the class of 1926, his last but one, the serene declaration, "So I think of science as walking to and fro in God's garden, busying itself with its forms of beauty, its fruits and flowers, its beast and bird and creeping thing, the crystals shut in its stones and the gold grains of its sands, and coming now at length in the cool of the long day upon God himself, walking in His garden."

Thus he threw his life away, sacrificing not wealth and ease only, but also reputation and that greater thing, the joy of extending the boundaries of knowledge in his own field. For what? Only to introduce a little gleam of light into some thousands of young minds that went darkling. Only to arrest the progress of materialism in certain young men and to make it forever impossible for them to reject utterly the things of the spirit. Only to lift somewhat the level of intelligence and to reduce somewhat the prevalence of bigotry in the most powerful sect in his commonwealth. Only to contribute to saving the intellectual honor of his State. For these, his life was thrown away—perhaps. But I was one of those who profited by the sacrifice, and so I cannot repine. Nor am I prepared to deny the possibility that, for all his apparent folly, he ended by coming at length in the cool of the long day upon God Himself walking in His garden.

# Old Slick

Benjamin Sledd, Johnson's English professor at Wake Forest between 1907 and 1911, was the kind of teacher, Johnson believed, who was almost extinct. This late essay (*Virginia Quarterly Review*, Spring 1960), along with the tribute to Poteat, shows a different side of Johnson than that seen by the Southern Agrarians. Hardly the iconoclast here, he captures an earlier South in which he obviously finds much to admire.

"Rest assured, gentlemen," said Old Slick to his class in third-year English, "there is no form of human endeavor less profitable than skinning a jackass. The jackass will not thank you, and nobody else gives a damn."

The century was young when I heard that. The century is half gone now, but I remember it; for not a year has passed without bringing fresh, strong evidence that it is an important, perhaps the most important, canon of sound literary criticism.

Reading Mencken's "Chrestomathy," published in 1949,[1] set me to leafing through a volume of Poe's literary criticism and some of Hazlitt's reviews. All three were notable jackass-skinners. All three were such superb craftsmen that anything they wrote has a certain interest, if only for the workmanship. But their blasting arouses no emotion today save a mild wonder that such splendid ammunition was wasted on such piffling targets. When they discovered a solid piece of work and set themselves to explain why it is solid, their wisdom and perception remain as impressive as ever. There was profit in that—so much profit that they survive as notable critics. But the skinning is now as tedious as a joke about the venality of Federal prohibition enforcement agents.

Old Slick knew that, which is not remarkable, because every man realizes it as he comes to maturity; what is remarkable is that he also knew how to convey the idea to immature minds in such form that it would stick, as David Harum said, "like a burr to a cow's tail." That, I submit, is teaching. I know little about methods, and less about projects, and nothing at all about learning situations; but I know that when

1. *A Mencken Chrestomathy* (1949), a collection of H. L. Mencken's essays on religion, democracy, women, the South, and other subjects.

Copyright © 1960 by the *Virginia Quarterly Review* and reprinted with permission.

Old Slick desired members of the junior class in Wake Forest College to apprehend a certain notion, he caused them to apprehend it, and if that isn't teaching, then Socrates was an acrobat and Abelard was a tinker.

I grant that it was not good teaching in the narrower sense of the transmission of factual information. Old Slick was never strong on that sort of thing, largely, I believe, because he wasn't interested in it himself. I spent three years in his classroom and emerged still uncertain of the precise meaning of "caesura" and confused as to what Milton did—if he did anything—with the feminine ending. But I did come away with a firm conviction that John Milton was a great poet, not because he was clever at manipulating the language, but because he had the intelligence to grasp tremendous concepts and the boldness to proclaim them in the teeth of powerful opposition and in spite of poverty and affliction. In fact, said Old Slick, when Milton became most learned he ceased to be a poet; great masses of "Samson Agonistes," said Slick, are pedantic tripe worth the consideration of nobody except Doctors of Literature and other damn fools.

Since Slick, by grace of Washington and Lee, was a Doctor of Literature himself, this seemed to be authoritative, and the effect was to lift a burden off the shoulders of the class. We did not have to read "Samson Agonistes," and that being the case some of us promptly started to read it out of sheer perversity; but when we got far enough to realize that Slick knew what he was talking about, we quit without guilt. No pupil of his has gone through life with a sense of inferiority because he has never read "Samson Agonistes." To most of us it was a new and tremendously liberating experience to learn that because a book is signed with a great name it is not necessarily worth reading. It meant release from one form of tyranny over the mind of man.

What the Bureau of Vital Statistics accounts a full generation has passed since I left Old Slick's classroom for the last time, and I know now that what I learned there was trifling by comparison with the vast importance of what I unlearned. Perhaps a university, dealing primarily with graduate students, is justified in adhering strictly to the ideal of being an institution of learning; but a college, dealing with undergraduates, is not well equipped unless its faculty includes at least one member, and a conspicuously able one, who is not an educator, but a de-educator. Old Slick would have said that I mean a skinner of jackasses, and would have admitted dolefully that he spent his life in that unprofitable trade. But that is not exact. I mean, rather, a groom, a wielder of currycomb and bristle brush, who goes after the cockleburrs, the chaff, and the dried mud that the creatures bring into the corral with them, and who turns them out, at least looking civilized, and perhaps sleek and shiny. It is not what the groom adds that works the transformation; it is what he takes away. At most he can add only a bit of oil on the hooves, and a ribbon plaited in the mane, trifles that never made a show animal; and he can omit both, yet still turn out a new creature.

To compare a Professor of English Literature to a groom may be invidious, but the objection is irrelevant in this case, because the flat truth is that Benjamin Sledd was never primarily a Professor of English Literature anyhow. "If we turn out an occasional scholar, that will do no harm," he said to me once, "but the real business of this place is to turn out men. If we fail in that, an army of Doctors of Philosophy will not save us."

His surname, of course, accounted for half of his campus nickname, but the addition of "old" was a subtler matter. When I first knew him he was forty-four, and a number of other members of the faculty were obviously his seniors. The saintly professor of Greek, for example, was well up in the seventies, with hair and full beard both pure silver: a more venerable figure could not be imagined, yet he was merely "Dr. Royal," never "Old Dr. Royal." A bald and dignified President Emeritus of the college with nearly as many years was "Charlie," never "Old Charlie." But Sledd was "Old Slick" almost from the day of his first appearance on the campus at the age of twenty-five.

The collegians did not think it through, of course, but undergraduate instinct was accurate, as it frequently is. In one sense Benjamin Sledd was a broken man before he came to the college. A young Virginian with boundless ambition and a fine poetic imagination, he had taken his Master's degree at Washington and Lee and proceeded to the Johns Hopkins, then at the height of its fame as the first graduate school to combine German thoroughness with American energy. In those days, a Ph.D. from the Hopkins was a passport to almost any position in the academic world; but it was not for Sledd. In less than two years the light failed. The doctors told him that with care he might preserve his sight to a certain extent, but the close application required of a candidate for the Ph.D. was out of the question.

A distinguished career in one of the great universities being closed, he withdrew to the small Southern college, which readily accepted a Johns Hopkins man even without the doctorate. Within a few years his hearing began to fail, eliminating any hope that might have remained of a high place in the academic world. To suffer two heavy defeats at the hands of Destiny before the battle of life is well begun is enough to age any man. The college boys spoke better than they knew; he was Old Slick long before he had reached the half-century mark.

But "the Lord taketh no pleasure in the legs of a man." Consider

Roosevelt. Consider blind Milton. Consider Old Slick. I do not hesitate to mention him in the same breath with those great lords of the realm of the mind and spirit, because the true measure of a man is not how much he does, but how much he makes of what he has available. In Scripture the two-talent servant who doubled his money was on the same level with the ten-talent man who started with five. Old Slick, whose eyes were bad and whose ears were worse, went to work in the post-Reconstruction South, that is to say, in a region denuded not of material wealth only, but also very nearly stripped of faith and hope and charity. He had to work with practically nothing.

Wake Forest College, for instance, in 1859 had been relatively rich; but within the next five years its students were swept into the Confederate army, its funds were swept into the Confederate treasury, its buildings were converted into military hospitals, its equipment was broken or lost, its library was scattered, its faculty died or drifted away, its friends were bankrupt to a man. Its task became that of cultivating the spirit in a land in which it was bitterly hard for men to get enough to eat.

In 1888 Old Slick took his place among those engaged in that struggle and spent the rest of his life in it. The heroism of the Confederate army is the pride of the South to this day, and with reason, for it was a good army, one of the best the world has seen. Nobody pays much attention to those teachers in the South who struggled to piece together its shattered civilization after the military catastrophe, not even though General Lee became one of them; yet for sheer gallantry against hopeless odds the men who followed Lee after 1865 compare very favorably with those who followed him before.

More than that, they won. It is the fashion now to belittle their efforts by attributing every cultural lag that afflicts the South to incompetent teaching; but that is very much like belittling the Hon. Harry S. Truman because he plays Chopin less beautifully than Robert Casadesus does. Mr. Truman plays Chopin, after a fashion; but of late he has had several other things to attend to, and if he attends to them he will not be accounted a failure, even if his music leaves something to be desired.

The teachers in the post-Reconstruction South—other leaders, too, but the teachers especially—had their orders directly from Robert E. Lee, who said to the woman who explained that she was trying to make her sons good Virginians, "Not Virginians, madam. Make them Americans." To make good Americans out of a population that had suffered invasion, conquest, and ten years' military government by an army of occupation was a task of no small dimensions. If you doubt it, ask any of those Americans who are trying to make good Europeans out of German youth; and when you get the answer, which will certainly be heated if not profane, remember that those Southerners undertook their task with far less equipment, in most cases without even enough textbooks of the simplest kind, not to mention more expensive educational material.

But they did it. It they had failed, the United States would have had below the Potomac a bigger and bitterer Alsace-Lorraine, Poland, Ireland. Nothing of the sort exists, so they did not fail. Certainly they had assistance; nobody would claim that the teachers did it all; but they did a large part of the job of re-knitting the raveled country and it was the best repair job that has ever been done on a rent of such proportions.

Old Slick was, in my estimation, a particularly fine specimen of a group of men who earned far more honor and praise than they have ever received. He was memorable even in his physical appearance. Tall, but stooped, his thin frame carried a massive head that had been crowned with fiery red hair before time and trouble wore it off except for a fringe above his ears, and after that he maintained a pointed beard that must have been terrific in his prime, for even after its original fire had been thickly sprinkled with snow it remained aggressive, nay, fierce, truculent! Glasses of enormous thickness enlarged his pale blue eyes, but did not, as such glasses often do, give an effect of futility; for the pallor of his eyes was not that of skimmed milk, but that of a gas flame as it jets from a perfectly-adjusted Bunsen burner, almost colorless, but God help the blockhead who thinks it is mild!

His task, as he saw it, as his generation saw it, and as I see it, was not to create grammarians but to make reasonably competent American citizens out of boys whose experience and environment combined to thrust them in another direction and to make them embittered irredentists, fit tools for the hand of some Georgia Casement, some Alabama D'Annunzio, some South Carolina Aguinaldo.[2] To accomplish this, his first step must be to knock out of their heads the nonsense with which romantic idolaters of the Lost Cause had stuffed them, and then to extract from their hearts some of the venom injected by a blind and stupid postwar policy followed by the conqueror. The Southern boys who came to him in the closing decade of the last and the first of this century did not lack information. The trouble was that they knew too much of the wrong sort of knowledge. Old Slick had to de-educate them before he could re-educate them for responsible American citizenship.

What a ghastly job for a poet! Perhaps the picture of the young

---

2. Roger David Casement, Irish nationalist of the early twentieth century; Gabriele D'Annunzio, Italian novelist, poet, and soldier in World War I; Emilio Aguinaldo, Filipino insurrectionary leader of the 1890s.

Brahms playing the piano in a bawdy-house is the world's most appalling example of the waste of genius, but it is none too far beyond the spectacle of scholars and gentlemen trying to reconstruct the Republic of Letters with no building material other than rubble and cinders. Yet they were sustained by an abiding faith that the effort, not the event, is the measure of the workman. Sledd, stirred by some unfair criticism of Britain, once wrote:

> And yet, has she once stayed her hands to know
>> What blessing to her toil the years would send?
> Or taken thought save in her strength to sow?—
>> And this one glory let old England keep,
>> Though craven hands should of her harvest reap,—
> Her best she gave, howe'er might fall the end.

Like old England, let Old Slick this one glory keep—he and his colleagues gave their best, and if what they built seems crude and bare to the sophisticated eye, nevertheless it was strong enough to withstand the shock of the terrible twentieth century. It stands today, sturdy and foursquare, a strong foundation on which workers in lazuli and goldleaf may display their utmost art.

In the early days of the century most Southern colleges, especially those with a denominational connection, were what would now be considered puritanical in the extreme. The Demon Rum, in particular, was regarded with a horror that made it a necessity for every high-spirited student to cultivate his acquaintance to some extent, if only as a gesture of self-respect; but expulsion was mandatory for any student caught by a faculty member in a flirtation with J. Barleycorn. Old Slick never caught any. If he happened to be present when unfortunate incidents occurred, he blandly explained that he was too blind to see and too deaf to hear the evidence; therefore he could not testify.

On a certain occasion he was compelled to visit one of the dormitories, which he usually avoided. It was the end of the year; examinations were over for most of the students, which meant a good deal of celebrating. In the afternoon Old Slick received a telegram announcing the award of three top prizes to three of his favorite students, and he felt obliged to convey the news to them instantly. In the first room he visited, he found all three, all magnificently tight. He made his announcement without comment and withdrew, leaving three of the soberest and most appalled young gentlemen on the campus.

The second day thereafter brought them a summons to Old Slick's residence, where he met them in the library. "The faculty has its regulations," he began, "but I let the faculty enforce 'em. I have my own regulations, though, and if I ever catch you three again—'' and he gave them hell. But they weren't expelled, with the result that Wake Forest now has at least three alumni who are not, strictly speaking, entitled to a degree—or not entitled to the A.B., for each has since been doctored *honoris causa*, one as the high court of appeal for a great national industry, one as a Worshipful Master among the learned doctors of a famous university, one for adding to the woes of Freshman English by writing innumerable books.

Old Slick took no shame to himself for his part in this transaction. "I would rather have them as they are," he asserted without a blush, "than have three of the soberest prohibition lecturers ever seen."

Nevertheless, the three were keenly aware that the outcome would probably have been very different had Old Slick known them for shirkers and cheats in the classroom. The lesson he taught was that it is the right you do, not the wrong you avoid, that will save you in the estimation of this world, no matter how the Recording Angel looks at it. It wasn't English, but it was education; which is the basis of my assertion that the man was primarily a fashioner of men and only secondarily a Professor of English.

Yet his students would be unworthy of the effort he expended on them if they utterly forgot its cost. The new South will be unworthy if it forgets the pit whence it was digged. The broken men who rebuilt the broken state in the long agony of the Forty Years' Depression deserve to be remembered with reverence for their fine work, but they should also be remembered with more than a touch of terror for their bleeding hands and aching bones. They worked in an immense loneliness, almost cut off from communication with their own kind, rarely permitted the supreme delight of the intellectual, the rapier-play of ideas between strong and equal minds. It was a deprivation far outweighing financial poverty or even the burden of an unconscionable teaching load. In some lines in a group of poems entitled "To Sappho," Old Slick touched upon this:

> 'Twas still thy fateful part
> To feel all we have known of fruitless strife,
> The weight of incommunicable pain,
> And passionate longings of the poet-heart
> For some far good, some life beyond all life.

The college he served is a wholly different place now. Wake Forest is a vortex of driving energy, surging up toward such a college as Old Slick hardly dreamed of, with a brand-new, fifteen-million-dollar plant, and an endowment to match it. It is splendid, it is superb, and no Wake Forest man can fail to rejoice in the wider horizon and the shining destiny that beckon his Alma Mater. Nevertheless, it will not mean much unless she can contrive, in her new opulence, somehow to salvage the "passionate longings of the poet-heart / For some far good, some life beyond all life" that the broken men working among the rubble with broken tools felt. For it is just this imponderable that makes a man or an institution great.

It is ten years now since Old Slick quit the Wake Forest campus for the *Campi Elysii*, where in meads of asphodel by Oceanus' stream he strolls among his compeers. His hearing is perfect there, and his sight so keen that he mistakes none of the Illustrious Ones, but he says little, for who would give tongue when he might listen while Dante and Vergil and strong John Milton debate the art of song? But it is impossible to believe that he is always silent, for sometimes the talk must drift to lighter things; and then, without doubt, the giants in their turn listen with chuckling appreciation to his tart, unflattering comments on the way the place is run.